Praise for *The Out-of-Sync Child*

P9-DGY-256

"Having fun isn't something that just happens for most children with severe sensory issues. Everyday activities can be a struggle and can cause much frustration and sadness for both the child and his/her family. Like *The Out-of-Sync Child*—my Sensory Bible—*The Out-of-Sync Child Has Fun* is a 'must-have' for parents and teachers. They will start changing lives with these simple ideas that work with ALL children—and many adults, too!"

—**Laurie Renke, mother, DSI Parent Connections National Coordinator**

"Carol opened the eyes and hearts of caregivers with *The Out-of-Sync Child*, allowing children who were once afraid of movement, who are overly sensitive to noise and touch, to grow and emerge from their cocoons of sensory dysfunction. Now, in *The Out-of-Sync Child Has Fun*, she gives parents and teachers a cookbook of activities to orchestrate a new hum, a new rhythm, and a common vibration to those who once were adrift. This book is like having a therapist whispering in your ear, '*try this now, and this, and now this . . .*'"

—**Rondalyn V. Whitney, M.O.T., O.T.R., author of *Bridging the Gap: Raising a Child with Nonverbal Learning Disorder***

"Oh, the pleasures your children will gleefully enjoy with any one of the activities in this marvelous book! OTs, parents, and teachers get ready to have fun, too, as you get in sync with your out-of-sync child through these important and clinically credible methods of attaining and retaining new life skills."

—**Audrey Lande, M.S., O.T.R., vice president, Occupational Therapy Association of Colorado**

Praise for the *The Out-of-Sync Child*

"This book is a wonderful contribution that raises awareness of DSI among parents and educators. I recommend it to all the families who come to see us at the STAR Center."

—**Lucy Jane Miller, Ph.D., O.T.R., associate professor, University of Colorado Health Sciences Center, and director of <u>S</u>ensory Integration Dysfunction <u>T</u>reatment <u>A</u>nd <u>R</u>esearch (STAR) Center at The Children's Hospital in Denver**

"This book is great. It is a real contribution to the parents of many children who are so hard to understand. It will let parents off the hook of blaming themselves . . . and will help them get on to the job of addressing the child's underlying difficulties."

—**T. Berry Brazelton, M.D., president and chairman of the Brazelton Foundation**

"This book will bring both hope and practical help to parents who wonder why their kid doesn't 'fit in.' "

—**Jane M. Healy, educational psychologist and author of *Your Child's Growing Mind***

continue . . .

"*The Out-of-Sync Child* does a masterful job of providing detailed, practical help for children with sensory integration problems."

—**Stanley I. Greenspan, M.D., child psychiatrist and coauthor of *The Child with Special Needs***

"This is a great book and a must-read for any parent who thinks their child might have unusual behavior difficulties. Its calming tone and no-nonsense approach give parents the power to positively address their child's sensory integration dysfunction."

—*Exceptional Parent Magazine*

"*The Out-of-Sync Child* opened the door for thousands of parents and teachers to uncover 'mysterious' behaviors and struggles with sensory integration dysfunction (DSI)."

—**Diana A. Henry, M.S., O.T.R./L.,** *Tools for Parents* **handbook and** *Tools for Teachers* **videos**

The
Out-of-Sync Child Has Fun

Activities for
Kids with Sensory
Integration
Dysfunction

CAROL STOCK KRANOWITZ, M.A.

Illustrations by T. J. Wylie

A Perigee Book

A Perigee Book
Published by The Berkley Publishing Group
A division of Penguin Putnam Inc.
375 Hudson Street
New York, New York 10014

Copyright © 2003 by Carol Stock Kranowitz, M.A.
Text design by Tiffany Kukec
Cover design by Ben Gibson
Cover photo by Brian Smith

First edition: January 2003

Visit our website at www.penguinputnam.com

Library of Congress Cataloging-in-Publication Data

Kranowitz, Carol Stock.
    The out-of-sync child has fun : activities for kids with sensory integration dysfunction / Carol Stock Kranowitz ; illustrations by T.J. Wylie.
        p.   cm.
    Includes bibliographical references and index.
    ISBN 0-399-52843-1
    1. Sensory integration dysfunction.   2. Sensorimotor integration.
3. Perceptual-motor learning.   4. Games.   I. Title.

RJ496.B7 K7197   2003
618.92'8—dc21

                                                                    2002025232

Printed in the United States of America

10   9   8   7   6   5   4

For every child who wants to have fun

CONTENTS

3. Balance and Movement (The Vestibular Sense)

Conclusion

Appendix

ACKNOWLEDGMENTS

The greatest pleasure in creating *The Out-of-Sync Child Has Fun* was working with people who understood my intent, celebrated the concept and supported the project from start to finish. Their generous spirits infuse this book.

Originally, my plan was to delineate my own favorite activities. After 25 years of teaching at St. Columba's Nursery School in Washington, DC, I had plenty. As the book grew, I began to add sensory-motor experiences that teachers and parents, especially "SI Moms," were glad to share. Then, to fill in the gaps, I sought successful home and school ideas from several brilliant therapists—my mentors and idols—whose inspiring work has revolutionized my teaching style.

New activities and new facets to old activities poured in. Some came in the form of a few sentences in casual conversations. Others came typed and structured, in formal, clinical language. My joyful job was to shape these gems to fit the setting here.

In addition to the contributors whose names are listed on the following pages, I am deeply indebted to the following friends:

Trude Turnquist, Ph.D., O.T.R./L., Rondalyn V. Whitney, M.O.T., O.T.R., and *Kimberly A. Geary, M.S., O.T.R./L.* These extraordinary occupational therapists, working in the field of sensory integration, played a substantial role in editing my presentation of the activities. They polished my work nearly word-by-word with their incisive critiques. They suggested how to refine the drawings to illustrate correct positioning. They gently advised "mindfulness," without shattering my enthusiastic belief that sensory integrative activities will work for nearly all children all the time.

Julia Berry, Laura D. Glaser, Diana Henry, Aubrey C. Lande, Lucy Jane Miller, Kathleen Morris, Joye Newman, Jill D. Spokojny, and Janet Stafford. These splendid therapists and teachers reviewed the manuscript, offered continuous guidance, and shared their sparkling sense of fun.

Donna Becker, Laurie Renke, and Angela Gilbert. Three amazing and seemingly tireless SI Moms somehow found the time to study the manuscript and to suggest wonderful ways to make it better.

T. J. Wylie! When it comes to picturing out-of-sync kids in action, this marvelous illustrator "gets it." Collaborating with him has been pure delight.

Lynn Sonberg and Meg Schneider of Skylight Press. Their steadfast support of my work began back in the days when dysfunction in sensory integration was a subject "no one had ever heard of."

Sheila Curry Oakes, Executive Editor at Perigee Books. We share the same vision of a shelf of "friendly" books to guide parents and teachers of challenging children. She has my everlasting gratitude and affection.

Alan Kranowitz. During our 35 years together, my beloved late husband was my most significant advisor and teacher.

Jeremy Kranowitz, Jenny Pleasure, Eden Pleasure-Kranowitz, David and Melissa Kranowitz, Ellen Stern, Dena Mann, Nomi Simonoff, and Barbara Harris. My closest, dearest family members are always there for me.

The children. Over the years, my chief collaborators and primary sources have supplied the raw material for this book. They have taught me what works, what doesn't, and what adaptations can be made so that everybody feels successful. For these special children, I am full to the brim with love, appreciation, and awe.

Indeed, I shall be forever thankful to all the bighearted individuals who have shared their work and play, actions and thoughts with me so I could share them with you. Naturally, any flaws in this book are due to my misinterpretation of their contributions and suggestions. Whatever errors you may find are mine alone.

Finally, I thank you for picking up this book and getting ready to have fun!

CONTRIBUTORS

CHILDREN

BEN, p. 122

CHASE, p. 43

CHRISTIAN, p. 105

CYRUS, p. 14, 244

ERIC, p. 137

GARY, p. 91, 196

HAYLEY, p. 141

JACKSON, p. 54

JAKE, p. 105, 256

JESSE, p. 145

KATIE, p. 2, 31

KYLE, p. 19

LIZZIE, p. 137

MATTHEW, p. 65

MAX T., p. 54

MAX R., p. 194

PRYCE, p. 155

ROBIN, p. 141, 145

SAM, p. 50

SANDY, p. 109

SCHYLER, p. 109

ZAC, p. 9

PARENTS

BARBARA, p. 7, 14, 244
Lexington, Kentucky

DEBBIE, p. 16 Indiana

LISA, p. 210 Texas

RAENA, p. 260 Oklahoma

SARA, p. 260 Connecticut

SONYA, p. 54 Cleveland,
Alabama

MARTA ANDERS, p. 137
Cornwall-on-Hudson, New York

DONNA BECKER, p. 71, 74,
114, 116 Rockaway Township,
New Jersey

STEPHANIE BECKER, p. 43
Traverse City, Michigan

ANGELA GILBERT, p. 91,
196 Spring Branch, Texas

DIXIE HENDRIX, p. 50
Oklahoma City, Oklahoma

RACHEL HOWELL, p. 114
Baton Rouge, Louisiana

JODY JARVIS, p. 109
Gardnerville, Nevada

SUSAN KEELEY, p. 262
Chicago, Illinois

PENNY KELLY, p. 2, 31
Bristol, Connecticut

RENEE MESH, p. 105

LAURIE RENKE, p. 105, 194,
256 Londonderry, New
Hampshire

BONNE SANDARS, p. 19
Round Rock, Texas

RACHEL VIVACE, p. 33
Indianapolis, Indiana

RONDALYN WHITNEY, p. 9,
145 Santa Clara, California

KATHY WINTERS, p. 137
Warminster, Pennsylvania

WHAT THE INITIALS AFTER A SPECIALIST'S NAME MEAN:

B.C.P.: Board Certified in Pediatrics

C.O.T.A./L.: Certified Occupational Therapy Assistant/Licensed

D.S.I.: Dysfunction in Sensory Integration (formerly known as "SID")

F.A.O.T.A.: Fellow of the American Occupational Therapy Association

F.C.O.V.D.: Fellow of the College of Optometrists in Vision Development

M.A.: Master of Arts

M.Ed.: Master of Education

M.O.T.: Master of Occupational Therapy

M.P.H.: Master of Public Health

M.S.: Master of Science

O.D.: Doctor of Optometry

O.T.: Occupational Therapist

O.T.R./L.: Occupational Therapist, Registered/Licensed

P.T.: Physical Therapist

P.T.A.: Physical Therapy Assistant

S.L.P.-C.C.C.: Speech/Language Pathologist—Certification of Clinical Competence

ABILITIES CENTER, INC., STAFF
Commerce Place
2075 West Maple Road, Suite B-204,
    Commerce Township, Michigan 48323
(248) 855-0030
Fax: (248) 737-9620
www.abilitiescenter.com

ANNE BARBER, O.D.
Director of Program Services,
    Optometric Extension Program
    Foundation, Inc.
Ed., *Behavioral Aspects of Vision Care*
oep@oep.org

BARBARA BASSIN, O.T.R./L., B.C.P.
Sensory Integration & Vision Therapy
    Specialists
6509 Democracy Blvd., Bethesda,
    Maryland 20817
(301) 897-8484
drstrab@erols.com
www.earthmed.com/vision and
    www.visionhelp.com

JULIA H. BERRY, M.A.
St. Patrick's Nursery School
Washington, DC

DON CAMPBELL
P.O. Box 4179, Boulder, Colorado 80306
(303) 440-8046
Fax: (303) 440-3353
Mozartef@aol.com
www.mozarteffect.com

SANFORD R. COHEN, O.D., F.C.O.V.D.
Wheaton, Maryland
reidcohen@aol.com

KIMBERLY GEARY, M.S., O.T.R./L.
Rockville, Maryland
(301) 251-2849
bgeary@erols.com

LAURA D. GLASER, M.A., S.L.P.-C.C.C.
The Kids' Communication Center
Washington, DC
(202) 237-7079
dlglaser@msn.com

ELIZABETH HABER, M.S., O.T.R./L.
Bakersfield, California
eahaber@aol.com

JOANNE HANSON, M.S., S.L.P.-C.C.C.
Building Blocks Therapy
Falls Church, Virginia
(703) 533-8819
buildingblocks@erols.com

ADRIENNE B. HAUSMAN
Magic Art & More
Olney, Maryland
Phone and Fax: (301) 570-9665
adrienne17301@yahoo.com

MELANIE HAWKE, O.T.R.
South Australia
melsie@granite.net

DEBRA WILSON HEIBERGER, M.A.
Redding, California
(530) 247-6993
www.snowcrest.net/debihi

MARGOT C. HEINIGER-WHITE, M.A., O.T.R.
California
margot@oregontrail.net

LYNNE ISRAEL, O.T.R./L.
Lynne Israel and Associates
Washington, DC, and Santa Barbara,
   California
lciotassoc@aol.com

ANNEMARIE KAMMANN, PT
Michigan

TERI KOZLOWSKI, O.T.R.
Integrated Therapy Services (ITS) for
   Children and Families, Inc.
Kensington, Maryland
(301) 962-0800

AUBREY C. LANDE, M.S., O.T.R./L.
Boulder, Colorado
aubreylande@aol.com

NOEL S. LEVAN, M.A., O.T.R./L.
noel_levan@hotmail.com

BARBARA H. LINDNER, M.ED., O.T.R./L.
Therapeutic Integration Services
10911 Bonita Beach Road, #1071
Bonita Springs, Florida 34135
(941) 495-5536
Fax: (941) 495-5465
www.therapeuticintegration.com

CRISLER LOVENDAHL, M.A., C.C.C.-S.L.P.
SpeechKids * Play Partners * Classroom
   Connection
Chicago * Highland Park * Libertyville,
   Illinois
(847) 681-0324
Fax: (847) 681-0484
cris@speechkids.net

MARY F. MARCOUX, PH.D.
Beauvoir, The National Cathedral
   Elementary School
Washington, DC
inlandekal@aol.com

BARB MCCRORY, M.A., O.T.R./L.
Integrated Therapy Services (ITS) for
   Children and Families, Inc.
Kensington, Maryland
(301) 962-0800

LORI L. MERKEL, C.O.T.A./L.,
   of Slatington, Pennsylvania
Pediatric Therapy Associates of the
   Lehigh Valley, P.C.
Allentown, Pennsylvania
(610) 821-0123
Fax: (610) 821-4366

LUCY JANE MILLER, PH.D., O.T.R.
Executive Director, KID Foundation
Departments of Pediatrics and
   Rehabilitation Medicine and
   Pediatrics
University of Colorado Health Sciences
   Center, Denver, Colorado
(303) 794-1182
lucy.miller@frii.com
www.SInetwork.org

HEATHER MILLER-KUHANECK, M.S.,
O.T.R./L., B.C.P.
Clinical Supervisor, Connecticut Center
for Pediatric Therapy
Wallingford, Connecticut
(203) 949-9337
hmillerot@yahoo.com

MARSHA MITNICK
Director, The Village Educational Center
Birmingham, Michigan

KATHLEEN MORRIS, M.S., C.C.C./S.L.P.
Director, Lakewood Pediatric Therapy,
Inc., and Sensory Integration Center
of Dallas
Dallas, Texas 75214
(214) 821-9083
lpt@airmail.net
www.lakewoodpediatric.com

JIM MULHOLLAND
Raleigh, North Carolina

JOYE NEWMAN, M.A.
Founder and Director, Kids' Moving
Company
Bethesda, Maryland
(301) 656-1543
www.kidsmovingco.com

BERT RICHARDS, P.T.A.
Abilities Center, Inc.
West Bloomfield, Michigan

DEANNA IRIS SAVA, M.S., O.T.R./L.
Buffalo Grove, Illinois
deannasava11@msn.com

NANCY C. SCHEINER, M.S., O.T.R.
Chevy Chase, Maryland
theScheiners@msn.com

JANET STAFFORD, O.T.R./L.
President/Owner
Kidz Play Pediatric Therapy/Wellness
Center
Londonderry, New Hampshire
www.kidzplay.org

TRUDE TURNQUIST, PH.D, O.T.R./L.
Minneapolis, Minnesota
(952) 449-9323
Fax: (952) 449-0735

RONDALYN V. WHITNEY, M.O.T., O.T.R.
Santa Clara, California
Rondalyn@aol.com

OTHER INSPIRING PEOPLE

A. JEAN AYRES, O.T.R.,
PH.D.

JOHANN SEBASTIAN BACH

MARY D. BENBOW, M.S.,
O.T.R./L.

T. BERRY BRAZELTON, M.D.

JEAN KEATING CARTON

JEFF CIRILLO

RHETA DE VRIES

MARSHALL P. DUKE, PH.D.

AUGUST DVORAK

EDWARD I, KING OF
ENGLAND

HARRISON FORD

SHEILA M. FRICK, O.T.R.,
& RON FRICK

STANLEY I. GREENSPAN,
M.D.

MEGAN GUNNAR, PH.D.

WOODY GUTHRIE

BARBARA E. HANFT, M.A.,
O.T.R., F.A.O.T.A.

FRANZ JOSEPH HAYDN
JANE M. HEALY, PH.D.

DIANA A. HENRY, M.S.,
O.T.R./L.

PEG HOENACK

CONSTANCE KAMII

SHELLY J. LANE, PH.D.,
O.T.R.

LISA D. LEWIS, PH.D.

Hugh Lofting

Wolfgang Amadeus
   Mozart

Stephen Nowicki, Jr.,
   Ph.D.

Patricia Oetter, M.A.,
   O.T.R., F.A.O.T.A.

Hap Palmer

Roger Tory Peterson

Maurice Joseph Ravel

Eileen Richter, M.P.H.,
   O.T.R., F.A.O.T.A.

Gioacchino Antonio
   Rossini

Camille Saint-Saëns

Karyn Seroussi

Igor Stravinsky

Julia Leigh Wilbarger,
   M.S., O.T.R.

Patricia Wilbarger,
   ME.d., O.T.R.,
   F.A.O.T.A.

Wizaublo

William Wordsworth

FOREWORD

In our post–September 11 consciousness, families seek new opportunities for deepening their bonds. Nothing is more natural than wanting to play together. Through play, parents and their children develop reciprocal, interactive connections: the medium for love and attachment. But not all children are easy to play with.

Carol Stock Kranowitz's first book, *The Out-of-Sync Child*, describes many types of children whose sensory processing problems make them difficult playmates. These children have underdeveloped and inefficient means of organizing sensory input. For some of these children, hypersensitivity to touch, sound, visual stimuli, balance, and certain body movements severely distracts them. They may be preoccupied with the lights being too bright or their clothes being too tight. For other children, sensory modulating problems mean that they have no internalized sense of how much swinging is *too much* to avoid getting sick.

The Out-of-Sync Child has become a life-saver to parents, day care providers, teachers, and professionals who often puzzle over the confusing behaviors characteristic of *sensory integration dysfunction (DSI)*. By demystifying and describing these invisible, bewildering conditions and their causes in plain English, the author has earned universal praise.

Now in this companion volume, *The Out-of-Sync-Child Has Fun*, Carol invites us *into the action* by delivering tried-and-true pretested activities designed just for this special group of young children. Her contagious enthusiasm, heartfelt sensitivity, and expert wordsmithing make this book a joy to read.

She suggests practical techniques such as *following* the child's lead and *adapting* the activity to the child's response. This approach serves to build trust and reciprocity with these hard-to-reach children. She instructs the adult in ways to further diminish the child's fear, such as lowering your voice as well as your body in space.

Most importantly, the author describes how these 115 activities work to strengthen a child's sensory development. Her Coping Tips explain how an activity can be creatively adapted. Interspersed throughout are highlighted sections, called A Mother Says, that present further ideas from parents and therapists. These serve to actively connect the reader to others and give encouragement. Parents and teachers of children with these sensitivities can feel confident that they are not alone; others share their journey.

I appreciate Carol's work both for professional and personal reasons. As an occupational therapist, I feel that she has successfully translated the field of sensory integration and our work as therapists into the mainstream, making the language, theory and intent accessible to the general public. She has helped bring the work of Dr. A. Jean Ayres to a wide population. Many of us have long despaired that the pioneering work of Dr. Ayres has remained "in house" within our own profession for thirty years and has not reached a broader, more accepting audience.

In retrospect, I have witnessed the enormous difficulty that the average parent or teacher has had trying to follow the clinical, neurologically-based terminology, acronyms, and jargon we often use. It has also been confusing for outsiders to observe our treatment sessions and, without knowing the theory and intent that drives them, distinguish them from pricey playdates. For years I lugged heavy copies of anatomy books with Dr. Frank Netter's beautiful anatomical drawings, xeroxed glossaries, and multisensory props to parent and school conferences, making every effort to educate others about sensory integration. Now I bring a single copy of *The Out-of-Sync Child*, a short report, and a few photographs of the child in action.

As a licensed marriage and family therapist, I also admire this book for providing discouraged parents a new paradigm for play. Carol synthesizes a nursery school teacher's awareness with the best advice of many experts by providing some new rules for cooperative play. I know from my practice that children with sensory processing problems often exasperate and exhaust their parents and are barely tolerated by siblings. They are *too much work* and besides, *why can't they just have fun!*? But "having fun" is an elusive goal to many out-of-sync children.

Overly sensitive children fear and dread the rough and tumble of body contact or of losing their center of gravity. These sensitivities help place them on the sidelines of life. By gradually introducing them to active, whole body activities, we can show them that they need not become further isolated from peers and siblings nor relegated to passive computer and video games. It is *so much better* that they learn to join in the action. This book tells the reader how to include them.

For sensory seekers or children labeled "hyper" and "out of control" who need help knowing *when and how to stop*, the whole family could participate on a Saturday morning by building a crash pad, obstacle course, or inner-tube game. These are familiar and well-used staples of OT clinics around the country, and they can be simply built with ingenuity and very few materials. Used with the recommended guidelines and cautions, these activities can provide months of fun for the whole family.

Lastly, I have the added advantage of seeing Carol, herself, *in action*. My daughter, Casmir, was a nursery school student of hers in 1991–92. I am a first-hand witness to her undaunted spirit, creativity, and acute sensitivity to children. While visiting her music and movement class at St. Columba's Nursery School in Washington, DC, I watched Carol cleverly adapt "The Gingerbread Man" (on page 72) to include two children who sat wistfully on the sidelines. Tentative and fearful of joining in the fun, these children were not among the others begging her for more turns. Carol used many of the techniques described here to gently coax these two outsiders into the game. Now a decade later, she has compiled an entire book to help parents and other teachers succeed as well.

Bravo and thank you, Carol, for writing this wonderful, timely book!

Trude Turnquist, Ph.D., O.T.R./L.
Minneapolis, Minnesota
September 2002

1

~~~~~~

Kids Gotta Move—Safely!

Are you a parent, teacher, or daycare provider of a child who is sometimes—or frequently—"out of sync"? Is your child receiving occupational therapy or another treatment that helps him or her function better at home, at school, and in the community? With or without a therapist's guidance, have you found that activities like swinging, jumping, and pulling or pushing heavy loads get the child in gear? Do you sense that, just as birds gotta fly and fish gotta swim, kids gotta move and touch? And do you yearn to learn more activities to do with your child?

Then, *The Out-of-Sync Child Has Fun* is for you. A sequel to *The Out-of-Sync Child: Recognizing and Coping with Sensory Integration Dysfunction* (1998), this book includes some of my all-time favorite activities. Many are activities that I invented or adapted while teaching preschool, leading Cub Scouts, conducting birthday parties, parenting, and now, with utmost joy, grandparenting. Others are variations of "sensory diet" activities that occupational therapists design for a child to do at home. Still others have come from people who thoughtfully observed their child and discovered what worked. And a few of the ideas came from the children themselves, who showed us what felt "just right."

While children with Dysfunction in Sensory Integration (DSI) are the book's focus, many young children—out of sync or not—will have fun with these activities!

Envisioning the Out-of-Sync Child

Most children are out of sync some of the time. Most children know how it feels occasionally to be out of tune, out of place, out of order, out of control, or out of it altogether.

Some children, however, are out of sync *most of the time*. Because of a neurodevelopmental problem, they may have trouble functioning in daily life and interacting successfully with the world around them. Envision a child who . . .

- Is over-sensitive to sensations of touch, movement, sight, or sound.
- Is underresponsive to sensations of touch, movement, sight, or sound.
- Has an unusually high or unusually low activity level.
- Is impulsive, fidgety, inattentive, and easily distracted.
- Has a poor sense of body awareness.
- Has immature gross motor skills (running, climbing) and fine motor skills (drawing, cutting), and is uncoordinated and clumsy, often falling and tripping.
- Has poor bilateral coordination (using both body sides together) and difficulty crossing the midline (using an eye, hand, or foot in the space of the other).
- Has poor motor planning (organizing one's body to do a complex action).
- Fatigues easily, slouches, and sprawls.
- Has poor oral-motor skills (chewing, speaking).
- Frequently misjudges distances between herself and other people and objects.
- Has a poor sense of rhythm and timing.
- Responds slowly to verbal instructions or questions, or is flustered by them.
- Becomes very emotional and quickly frustrated when things aren't just right.
- Prefers the "same old, same old" and resists giving anything new a chance, such as foods, scenes, clothes, toys, games, story or song variations, rearranged furniture, babysitters, or substitute teachers.

A Mother Says . . .

Penny Kelly, in Connecticut, says about her 4-year-old, "I let my daughter do things to help her sensory system that other children might be told not to do. I let Katie jump on the beds. I let her play with beans in the living room, and sometimes they get all over the place. I let her bounce on cushions and pull cushions off to make 'sandwiches' with her. I let her do many other things other children may be told 'no' to. Of course, I do not let her do this in other people's houses—only her own. Since she has been getting the stimulation she needs at home, she behaves very well in others' places."

- Has a hard time with transitions, even when shifting between familiar activities.
- Has difficulty revving up or calming down, waking up in the morning, and falling and staying asleep at night.

What is the underlying reason for these confusing behaviors? The answer may be hard to pinpoint. Certainly, a variety of developmental delays, physical impairments, medical conditions, or emotional problems can affect a child's behavior. Dysfunction in Sensory Integration (DSI) may be a significant contributing factor—particularly if the child responds in atypical ways to sensations.

What Is Sensory Integration?

Sensory integration (SI) is the normal neurological process of organizing sensations for our use in everyday life. We use sensations to survive, to learn, and to function smoothly.

Typically, our brain receives sensory information from our bodies and surroundings, interprets these messages, and organizes our purposeful responses. As we climb the stairs, our brain senses that we're moving upward, forward, and from side to side. Usually without conscious effort, we make adaptive responses. We flex and extend our legs, alternate our feet, slide our hand along the banister, maintain our balance, keep upright, and watch where we are going. We are probably not even aware that our bodies are making these adjustments.

Most people could name five senses: vision, hearing, smell, taste, and touch. Actually, we have several other vital senses. According to the research of A. Jean Ayres, O.T.R., Ph.D., who formulated the theory of SI, the fundamental sensory systems include:

1. The *tactile* sense, which provides information primarily through the surface of our skin, from head to toe, about the texture, shape, and size of objects in the environment. It tells us whether we are actively touching something or are passively being touched. It helps us distinguish between threatening and nonthreatening touch sensations.
2. The *vestibular* sense, which provides information through the inner ear about gravity and space, about balance and movement, and about our head and body position in relation to the surface of the earth.
3. The *proprioceptive* sense, which provides information through our joints, muscles, and ligaments about where our body parts are and what they are doing.

These sensory systems, which are sometimes called the "hidden senses," develop very early in the womb. They interact with vision and hearing, smelling and tasting, which develop slightly later. As a result of typical sensory integration, self-control, self-esteem, motor skills, and higher level cognitive functions can develop as Mother Nature planned.

SENSORY INTEGRATION FUNTION IS IMPORTANT FOR:

Academic skills	Hand preference
Attention	Healthy relationships with others
Auditory perception	Kinesthesia
Balance	Muscle tone
Bilateral coordination	Postural stability
Body awareness	Praxis,[1] including motor planning
Body position	Self-comforting
Emotional security	Self-esteem
Eye-foot coordination	Self-protection
Eye-hand coordination	Self-regulation
Fine motor skills	Social skills
Flexibility	Speech and language skills
Force, or grading of movement	Tactile perception
Gravitational security	Visualization
Gross motor skills	Visual perception

Difficulty in these areas may be caused by Dysfunction in Sensory Integration.

What Is *Dysfunction* in Sensory Integration (DSI)?

Dysfunction in sensory integration (DSI), also called Sensory Integration Dysfunction, occurs when the brain inefficiently processes sensory messages coming from a person's own body and his or her environment. The person has difficulty responding in an adaptive way to everyday sensations that others hardly notice or simply take in stride.

Generally, the red flags of DSI are unusual responses to tactile, vestibular, and proprioceptive sensations—the sensations of touching and being touched, of moving and being moved. The senses of seeing, hearing, smelling, and tasting may be involved, too.

---

[1]Praxis: the ability to conceptualize (or "ideate"), to plan and organize, and to carry out a sequence of unfamiliar actions; to do what one needs and wants to do in order to interact successfully with the physical environment.

DSI plays out differently from person to person. DSI can also vary in the same person from day to day, depending on factors such as fatigue, emotional distress, or hunger. DSI may coexist with attention deficit disorder with or without hyperactivity (AD/HD), Asperger's syndrome, autism, cerebral palsy, Down syndrome, fetal alcohol syndrome (FAS), fragile X, spina bifida, pervasive developmental delay (PDD), nonverbal learning disorder (NLD), bipolar disorder, and other problems. Sometimes DSI is severe, sometimes mild. Sometimes it occurs continuously, sometimes occasionally. Inconsistency is one of its hallmarks.

The child who avoids ordinary sensations or seeks excessive stimulation, whose body is uncooperative, whose behavior is difficult, and who doesn't "fit in" is our out-of-sync child. The out-of-sync child receives sensory information just like everybody else. He, too, receives tactile sensations about the clothes touching his skin. He, too, gets movement sensations on a playground swing. He, too, hears a dog bark, smells a banana, chews toast, and sees people coming and going.

But, unlike most people, the child may misinterpret or be unable to use that information effectively. For instance, he may have a tantrum because the tag in his shirt scratches his skin—or, he may not notice that his pants are on backward. He may feel seasick swinging for a few seconds—or persist in swinging for a "million minutes."

> **An Occupational Therapist Says . . .**
>
> Janet Stafford, O.T.R./L., in New Hampshire, says, "There is no cookie cutter shaped like a child with DSI!"

He may panic when the dog barks a greeting—or ignore the dog's eagerness to knock him down. He may gag at food smells and textures—or cram all sorts of things, edible or not, into his mouth. He may shrink from visual stimulation such as flashing neon lights—or ignore the sight of rushing cars and run heedlessly into the street.

Why is this child out of sync? Dysfunctional patterns of sensory integration may be the root of the problem.[2] Among these patterns are: dysfunction with sensory modulation, dysfunction in sensory discrimination, and dyspraxia.

1. If the child has *Sensory Modulation Dysfunction* (SMD), he may fluctuate between over-reacting and under-reacting to sensory messages. His reactions are out of sync because, deep inside, his central nervous system organizes and

---

[2]Lucy Jane Miller, Ph.D., O.T.R.; Shelly J. Lane, Ph.D., O.T.R.; and Barbara E. Hanft, M.A., O.T.R., FAOTA. "Toward a Consensus in Terminology in Sensory Integration Theory and Practice, Parts 1–3." *Sensory Integration Special Interest Section Quarterly*, 23 (2000, March, June, September): No 1–3.

regulates them inaccurately. These physiological reactions are internal, unconscious, invisible—and out of the child's control.

What happens next? Often, the child who *reacts* atypically to sensations also *responds* atypically. While we cannot see his inward reactions, his outward responses may be intense, frequent, long-lasting, and very noticeable indeed!

The *overreactive* (hypersensitive) child may be overresponsive, or "sensory defensive," to certain sensory stimuli. For example, a door clicking shut may sound too loud, a shimmering Christmas tree may look too bright, a rising elevator may move too fast or an elastic waistband may feel too tight. Usually, the overreactive child is a sensory-avoider and tends to be either fearful and cautious, or negative and defiant.

The *underreactive* (hyposensitive) child is under-responsive to certain sensory stimuli. She may be a sensory-seeker and crave intense sensations, such as spinning, jumping, twirling—or, she may withdraw and be difficult to arouse.

Another child with SMD may be *both overreactive and underreactive*. The child may avoid some stimuli such as light or unexpected touch sensations, while craving other stimuli such as intense proprioceptive and vestibular experiences.

2. If the child has *dysfunction in sensory discrimination,* he has difficulty differentiating among and between stimuli. His central nervous system inaccurately processes sensations, with the result that he cannot use the information to make purposeful, adaptive responses and get on with the day.

The child misgauges the significance and value of things. He may not "get" sensory messages that other children use to protect themselves, to learn about their world, and to relate successfully to other people.

Is this an eraser—or a cookie? A snap—or a button?

How hot is this birthday candle? How high is the curb? How loud is his voice? How full is his mouth? How full is his cup? How hard should he pedal? How soon should he brake? How low should he duck? How much force is he using to hold a pencil, draw with a crayon, change a doll's outfit, add blocks to a structure, kick a ball, stroke a kitten, or lean on a friend? For the child with poor sensory discrimination, interpreting such ordinary demands and responding appropriately may require enormous effort.

3. If the child has *dyspraxia*—dysfunction in praxis—she has difficulty conceiving of, planning, organizing, and carrying out a sequence of unfamiliar actions. Dyspraxia interferes with doing what one needs and wants to do to interact successfully with the physical environment. (The dyspraxic child often has poor sensory modulation and poor sensory discrimination, too.)

Performing unfamiliar actions is difficult for the dyspraxic child, and successfully going through all the steps of a familiar action may be difficult as well. Getting dressed, pouring milk into the cereal bowl, climbing into the school bus, and opening her locker may be hard. Sharpening a pencil, putting papers in a three-ring binder, and organizing the steps to write a book report may be daunting. Tying shoes, kicking balls, and skipping . . . making a sandwich and setting the table . . . saying vocabulary words . . . going after school to a new friend's house . . . all these undertakings may be troublesome indeed. Struggling to keep up with other kids can be discouraging and not much fun.

Sensory Integration Therapy

DSI is a complex problem. It may affect children's development, behavior, learning, communication skills, friendships, and play. It may affect one or all of their sensory systems. It may impede sensory-related skills needed to function effectively throughout the day. It may make children overly self-protective or not self-protective enough. Their strongest sense may be a sense of uncertainty.

Children with DSI often do not feel safe. When they attempt to meet ordinary challenges, their responses may be ineffective and clumsy. Try as they might to be careful and to succeed, they frequently fall short. Unfortunately, children don't grow out of DSI; they grow into it, finding compensatory ways to cope with confusing, unpredictable, and threatening sensations. They do what they must to survive, playing it as safe as necessary.

More often than not, a child with DSI will need extra coping assistance. When DSI gets in a child's way, sensory integration–based occupational therapy is highly recommended. Occupational therapy (abbreviated as "OT") encompasses evaluation, assessment, treatment, and consultation.

Occupational therapy is the use of purposeful activity to maximize the independence and the maintenance of health of an individual who is limited by a physical injury or illness, cognitive impairment, a psychosocial dysfunction, a mental illness, a developmental or learning disability, or an adverse environmental condition. For a child, purposeful activities include swinging, climbing, jumping, buttoning, drawing, and writing. Such activities are the child's "occupation."

An occupational therapist (also "OT") is a health professional who has received a baccalaureate or master's degree after completing a course of study, plus internship experience, in the biological, physical, medical, and behavioral sciences. Coursework includes neurology, anatomy, orthopedics, psychology, and psychiatry.

The OT may work with your child individually or in a group at school or in a clinic, hospital, community mental health center, or your home. The ideal OT is one who specializes in pediatrics and who has received additional, postgraduate training in sensory integration theory and treatment. (To find an OT, contact Developmental Delay Resources or American Occupational Therapy Association, listed in the appendix.)

Another treatment that helps children with DSI is physical therapy ("PT"). Physical therapy is a health profession devoted to improving an individual's physical abilities. It involves activities that strengthen the child's motor coordination and muscular control, especially of his large muscles, to improve his voluntary movement. Increasing numbers of physical therapists ("PTs") receive added training in SI theory and treatment.

Under the guidance of an SI-trained therapist, the child actively takes in movement and touch information in playful, meaningful, and natural ways. The child responds favorably to SI treatment because it helps him learn to succeed—and he *loves* it!

SAFE Activities Help Kids Get in Sync

Meanwhile, what can parents, teachers, and others do to help a child get in sync?

Think about your childhood play. Chances are that your best fun times were sensory rich. Chances are you felt safe, successful, and happy while playing in traditional ways: swinging, climbing trees, roller-skating, riding bikes, jumping rope, shaping sand castles, throwing snowballs, stomping through mud puddles, running under the sprinkler, and slurping "chocolate soup."

Now, think about your children's play. Chances are they have fewer opportunities to touch things, move about, and concoct their own imaginative, open-ended, child-driven fun. Perhaps their "play" is soccer or gymnastics—highly structured activities that are driven by the coach. Perhaps their "play" is staring at a TV, computer, or hand-held gizmo—sedentary, solitary activities that are driven by electricity or batteries.

Numerous experts, including educators, physicians, psychologists, optometrists, occupational therapists, and brain researchers, say that spending more than an hour a day before a "glowing box" hinders a child's development.[3] Replacing active play with computer or video time does little to foster essential sensory-motor skills. Despite these ubiquitous reports, parents keep buying stuff of dubious educational value.

Here's one example of this worrisome trend: A zealous mother rushed up to me at a "Getting Kids in Sync" conference and eagerly described her preschooler's newest "educational" computer game. Just click the mouse, she told me, and presto—one, two, three oranges bound into a bucket. Click again, and they jump out, one, two, three. Isn't that a fabulous way to learn counting? And to develop eye-hand coordination? And to amuse her son, who is loose and floppy and doesn't move around very much or very well? What, she asked, is my opinion, as a teacher?

"How about giving him a bucket and three oranges?" I replied. "Then he can touch and squeeze them, put them in and take them out of the bucket himself, smell them, roll them, toss them, and enjoy a *real* experience. In a few more years, he'll be ready to juggle!"

"Those are things my sister and I did as kids," she says wistfully. "We used to squeeze our own orange juice, too. And I remember poking cloves into an orange to make a pomander with my grandmother. Nowadays, though, that kind of activity seems so, oh, I don't know, so old-fashioned."

Old-fashioned is right! And sometimes old-fashioned is better.

Times change, but children don't. Regardless of their abilities or developmental age, kids still need the good old experiences that children have always relished. Three-dimensional, hands-on, hard-work play builds better brains and bodies.

An out-of-sync child, however, may not have the know-how to get started with the most beneficial kinds of play. And you, as a significant adult in the child's life, may be unsure about what activities are best, and the when, where, and how of offering them.

---

[3]Rondalyn Whitney, M.O.T., O.T.R., and her son Zac made up this term. She says, "Zac would go to the TV, and I'd say, 'No TV.' He'd go to the computer, and I'd say, 'No computer.' He'd go to the video games, 'No video games,' and to the Game Boy, 'No Game Boy.' So then I just would say, 'No glowing box,' and that was that. Then he'd find something better to do."

The suggestions in this book will give your young child hours of pleasure as well as tools for life. The activities are just a start. Let them encourage you to try other games and experiences, perhaps ones that you loved once upon a time, to help your child get in sync. The games in this book have been held to a strict criteria. They are all SAFE.

"SAFE": Sensory-motor, Appropriate, Fun, and Easy

Keeping out-of-sync children safe is critical. As Jane M. Healy, Ph.D., author and educator, says, "The brain needs safety and involvement for positive learning experiences. If little children are not motivated to learn, check how safe they feel!"

S = SENSORY-MOTOR

Each activity in this book is a Sensory-motor activity. "Sensory-motor" refers to the relationship between sensation and movement. Sensory messages come in from our bodies and the world around us. Our central nervous system (CNS) integrates and processes the messages. Then we use the sensory information for meaningful motor responses (i.e., movement), thoughts, or feelings.

Kids who are out of sync may have difficulty making the sensory-motor connection. Because their best attempts are often inadequate and unsatisfying, these children may give up trying or just lose interest. They may opt for sensory activities that require negligible motor response, such as watching television, listening to music, or reading. The gap between sensory input and motor output widens, because the less they do, the less they may be able to do.

A child with DSI may walk into a spider web (the sensory part) and not know what to do in response (the motor part). You and I would brush the web away, but she would be unable to "get it together" to respond efficiently. She may become very anxious and upset.

Before she has a meltdown, how about an on-the-spot game of *Go Away, Glue* (chapter 2) or, adapting it to the situation, *Go Away, Cobweb*? Rub your cheeks, rake your fingers through your hair, and swipe cobwebs—imaginary or real—off your arms, hands, fingers, torso, and legs.

Silly? Maybe.

Effective? Absolutely, especially if it is a familiar game.

The more sensory-motor experiences young children have, the more easily they learn to function in daily life. To smooth out their sensory processing—to "grease the skids"—they need lots and lots of practice with sensory-motor experiences that engage the whole body.

A = APPROPRIATE

The activities in this book are **A**ppropriate for most young children. (Whenever you are in doubt, please discuss the activity with the therapist.)

Just as sensory avoiders may shun the very experiences that could be helpful, sensory seekers may go for intense, daredevil experiences that could be harmful. Other children may actually be sensory-seekers but appear to be sensory-avoiders; their low arousal means they lack "get up and go." Our task is to keep children safe and healthy *and* help them satisfy their sensory needs.

So, when a sensory-seeker clambers to the diving board although he can't swim, we must rechannel his out-of-sync behavior. Alternatives could be *Tra La Trampoline* or *Barrel of Fun* (chapter 3) to give him a vigorous movement experience.

When a sensory-avoider watches her friends play and doesn't join in, her behavior may be saying that she would participate if she could. She may welcome a game with *Stretchy Bands* (chapter 4), giving her a key to enter the group and also get her body in gear.

When the child with low arousal has trouble getting started, but once started has trouble stopping, an activity like *Hands on Toes* (chapter 9) may help with rhythm and timing, body awareness, and motor planning.

Behavior means something! When a child's behavior is unsafe or inappropriate, we need to stop and interpret it before jumping in with our own inappropriate response. Then we can guide the child into more suitable activities. You will find plenty here.

F = FUN (FUNCTIONAL AND FAMILY BUILDERS, AS WELL!)

These activities are **F**un. Fun is elusive to many out-of-sync children. They would like to have fun in socially acceptable ways but often can't function well enough to do so.

In *Sensory Integration and the Child*, Dr. A. Jean Ayres says, "When the child experiences challenges to which he can respond effectively, he 'has fun.' To some extent, 'fun' is the child's word for sensory integration." It is our obligation to provide activities that the child can choose, direct, and enjoy, while making increasingly mature and complex adaptive responses. Dr. Ayres writes, "This is what growing up is all about."

SAFE activities promote integration, as they engage the whole **F**un-loving child. Furthermore, as they improve the child's skills, they are **F**unctional; and, as they draw parents and siblings into the play, they are **F**amily builders. You will see when you try *Blow Away Blues* (chapter 8), *Beanbag Jai Alai* (chapter 5), or *Obstacle Course* (chapter 9)!

E = EASY (ECONOMICAL, ENVIRONMENTALLY FRIENDLY, AND EMOTIONALLY SATISFYING, TOO)

The activities are Easy to set up, once you have gathered the necessary equipment. Basic cooking, sewing, and carpentry skills are necessary to prepare some of the equipment. If the instructions for making *Playdough* (chapter 2), a *T-Stool* (chapter 3), or a *Crash Pad* (chapter 4) seem daunting, turn to *Recommended Materials* in the appendix.

The activities should be easy enough for your child to taste success. When they are too challenging, your child may resist doing them. Think how frustrating it is to be a child who wants to have fun, wants to please you—and can't! Therefore, go back to an easier level of difficulty and let your child play while working up to a new level of mastery. When you are certain that your child has mastered basic skills, such as mirroring your simple motions in *Beanbag Mania* (chapter 11), then you can introduce increasingly complex demands. The "just-right challenge" is key.

There are three other "E" benefits. One is that the activities are Economical. They will not break your budget. Supplies for activities like *Billions of Boxes* (chapter 5) and *Squeeze a Breeze* (chapter 9) are what teachers call "beautiful junk." Many materials are items you already have around the house; now you will find new, valuable uses for them.

Another "E" bonus is that the activities are Environmentally friendly. Also, they are Emotionally satisfying for your child—and for you, too, when you are present, participating, and witnessing the joy and success of the moment!

Setting Up SAFE Activities

Each chapter of this book focuses either on a sensory system, like touch or hearing, or on a by-product of sensory integration, like bilateral coordination or fine motor skills.

Many **SAFE** activities could be placed in more than one chapter. A game to strengthen vision, for instance, almost always involves touch, body position, and motor planning as well. I have opted to sort the activities by the primary sensory system and sensory-related skill they address. (The *Activity Cross-Reference Chart* at the end of the book indicates the various senses and skills that each activity benefits.)

This book suggests **what** to do, **where** and **how** to do it, and frequently **why** it works. The book does not always suggest **when** to offer an activity, however, because the same experience may calm one child, arouse another, and overwhelm a third. You must use your judgment to find what fits your child at the particular moment. Every child's needs differ, and you know your child best.

Please keep in mind:

1. Your supervision, compassion, and playfulness are essential in all activities.
2. Always allow your child to do the activities in his or her own way—as long as that way is safe. Given the opportunity, children will usually teach you what they need.

EACH ACTIVITY INCLUDES THE FOLLOWING INFORMATION

- **Developmental Age Range**. The level(s) at which most typically developing children are able to succeed at the activity. Developmental age is not the same as chronological age. Ability, not birth date, determines a child's developmental age level. In most ways, a child is as old as he or she acts. Some activities will appeal primarily to "young" children, and many will be fun for children of all ages and stages. For example, the suggested age range for *Dramatic Dress-Ups* (chapter 2) is "2 and up" meaning that 2-year-olds, 7-year-olds, and preteens will all benefit from getting in and out of differently textured clothes.
- **What You Will Need**. A list of supplies. See *Recommended Materials* in the appendix if supplies and equipment are unfamiliar.
- **Preparation**. What will need to be done before the activity to prepare materials or your play space.
- **What You Can Do**. "You" is an adult or older sibling.
- **What Your Child Can Do**. Suggestions, not rules.
- **Variations**. Because everyone is different, because your time and space will vary, and because your child's interests and needs will change.
- **Benefits of the Activity**. How **SAFE** activities encourage the development of the child's sensory systems and physical, cognitive, language, social, and emotional skills.
- **Coping Tips**. Suggestions for what to do when a child is having trouble with the activity and needs a grown-up's help.
- **A Mother Says** . . . Words of wisdom from "SI Moms" and other experts.

DO'S AND DON'TS
Do begin where the child is, developmentally.
A child's abilities depend on how developed his skills are. If his body awareness is immature, for instance, at first he may be tentative playing *Positions,*

Everybody! (chapter 4). He needs to start "where he's at"—even if his skill level is lower than you wish—and build from there.

Do the activities outdoors whenever possible.

Americans spend about 90 percent of their time indoors. Children need to be moving and playing outdoors where they can inhale fresh air. Dry, stale, reused indoor air can cause breathing problems, while fresh air encourages healing and "happy" chemicals (endorphins) to stave off viruses and other bugs. Especially in the winter, going outside is just what the doctor should be ordering. Also, many activities that work well in a room are even better on the sidewalk or grass. So go out and play!

Do note the child's "self-therapy."

Watch what your child likes to do. Sensory seekers often make it quite clear what their sensory systems need. For example, does your child love to spin in circles? Offer *Sally Go Round the Sun* (chapter 3). Does your child love hands-on, body-on tactile experiences? Lay out the supplies for *Paw Prints* (chapter 2).

At the other end of the spectrum, sensory avoiders' needs may be harder to determine. Is your child most comfortable stroking certain soft, dry textures? Spread out items for *No-Mess Messy Play* (chapter 2), or for *Tactile Road* (chapter 2). Gently, draw the child into the play, one finger or toe at a time. Another approach is to lay out the materials, without discussion, and wait, as in *Peanut Butter Jar* (chapter 11). Sometimes a hypersensitive child needs to evaluate a new experience for a while before feeling ready to partake in it.

> **A Mother Says . . .**
>
> Barbara says, "In my son's mind there has only ever been one thing for sensory organization—hand drumming. The weight of the heavy drum, the hand proprioception from playing it, and the careful listening to the beat calms and organizes Cyrus in a way nothing else does."

Do build on the child's particular interest.

"Value passion wherever you find it," says T. Berry Brazelton, M.D. If planets are your child's passion, give *Voyage to Mars* (chapter 3) a whirl. If dinosaurs are the child's delight, try a taste of *Dinosaur Morning*[4] (chapter 8).

Indeed, to make any ordinary activity more exciting—dressing, bathing,

---

[4]If the child has an intense interest in one subject and persists in following a narrow line of play, you may need a therapist's guidance to help you take a different approach.

preparing for bed, or practicing handwriting—make it thematic, focusing on the subject that sparks your child's imagination. This thematic concept can be successful everywhere. At home, at school, and abroad, interspersing words, actions and ideas inspired by the child's interest can make even humdrum activities productive and fun.

Do offer SAFE Activities that will instill a sense of control.

Children with DSI have great ideas about what they want to do—and then feel frustrated when their bodies refuse to cooperate. Give them the fun and responsibility of being in charge, whenever possible. Activities such as *Flashlight Tag* (chapter 5) or *Slide Whistle Stretch* (chapter 6), which allow them to be the leader, will strengthen their internal self-control and build self-esteem.

Breaking steps down into small, manageable bits can be very helpful, especially when the activities are challenging. You can also reduce steps to reduce stress. Practicing two or three motions rather than the 15 or so suggested in *Going on a Bear Hunt* (chapter 11) is just fine. The objective is for your child to say, "Hey, I did it!" and "Can we do it again?"

> ## An Occupational Therapist Says . . .
>
> Aubrey Lande, M.S., O.T.R./L., says, "Fit the activity into a larger narrative about something that interests the child so that the activity becomes more motivating, pulling in more attention, persistence, meaning, and memory. For example, the child who is really into football may need an afternoon routine to get through classes at school without a meltdown. This child may benefit from 'running offense' into a pile of pillows, followed by a few squirts of semi-frozen lemonade from a team logo bottle. The activity routine might be given a name like 'The Pillow Pounce,' and be included in his overall sensory diet, which might be named his 'NFL training program.' "

Do take immediate advantage of a successful SAFE Activity.

A **SAFE** activity will organize the child's functioning and help her focus and pay attention. Seize the moment! Kathleen Morris, CCC-SLP, Director of the Sensory Integration Center of Dallas, reminds us to help the child reap the benefits. After several minutes of balancing on *Matthew's Teeter-Totter* (chapter 3), for example, he may be able to read a story, or do 10 math problems, or write a paragraph, or come to the table for a peaceful family dinner.

Do try again.

If you try an activity like *Scale Songs* (chapter 6) and it's a dud, don't write it off. Maybe now is the wrong time. Wait, and then try again next month, or try part of it during another activity. Sometimes it takes several attempts until the child's brain and body are ready. To learn a new skill, repetition is a necessity.

Do use SAFE Activities as complements to a sensory diet.

A balanced sensory diet, which must be designed by a certified OT or PT, is a program individualized for a specific child's needs. The activities in this book are "over-the-counter," a term used by Diana A. Henry, M.S., O.T.R./L., to describe occupational therapy strategies that parents and teachers can use at home and school.[5] The **SAFE** activities here are meant to be used as "sensory side dishes" or "snacks" to accompany an official sensory diet.

Playdough (chapter 2), for example, is an old stand-by that improves a child's tactile processing, proprioception, fine motor skills, tool use, and eye-hand coordination. You need not wait for a therapist to suggest playdough; you can make it and play with it right away. Here, you'll find elaborations on this sensory diet staple, as well as many other "nutritious" ideas.

By all means, check out these activities with your child's OT or PT. Maybe you will learn to restructure, intensify, or avoid certain activities. Maybe you and the therapist will become more consistent in how you work and play with your child. Maybe the therapist will learn something new.

Do let your child do.

The only way children can learn sensory-motor skills is by practicing them. They can't learn when they don't have the chance to try. They can't learn when everything is done for them. Children learn by doing.

---

[5]Diana Henry's *Tools for Parents: A Handbook to Bring Sensory Integration and into the Home* (2001), and *Tool Chest for Teachers, Parents and Students* (1998), are wonderful resources. Youngtown, AZ: Henry Occupational Therapy Services.

Don't continue an activity if your child becomes distressed.

Loving grown-ups may have an intuitive understanding of what activities will work best. Most of us, however, lack the therapist's skill and experience of knowing *how frequently, how intensely,* or *how long* the child should engage in an activity. Overdoing very physical activities such as *Gentle Roughhousing* (chapter 3), *Barrel of Fun* (chapter 3), or *Push-Me-Pull-You* (chapter 9) can cause a meltdown or other negative response. Thus, we must always use caution and commonsense. When in doubt, cut it out.

Don't think that these activities will "fix" children with DSI.

When used with common sense and good judgment, these activities are **SAFE** for many children with DSI, with the exception of those who are medically fragile. While developmentally appropriate and beneficial in many ways, *the activities are not a substitute for treatment under a qualified therapist's supervision.*

> ## Signs of Distress That Mean "Stop!"
>
> Consult with a therapist if the child exhibits any of these signs.
>
> - Adamant avoidance behaviors
> - Dramatic change in heart rate
> - Crying or great unhappiness
> - Gaze aversion
> - Excessive sweating
> - Hyperventilation (excessive respiration), unusually prolonged, rapid, and deep
> - Loss of balance and unusually disorganized movements
> - Nausea or vomiting
> - Nervous laughing
> - Saying, "Stop, stop!"
> - Variation in skin color

DISCLAIMER: The activities in this book have all been used with considerable success by certified occupational therapists, other SI-trained specialists, and many parents and teachers as well. However, some of these activities can be too challenging for some children. In all cases, consideration should be given to the individual child's capabilities and needs. The reader is urged to discuss these activities with the child's therapist before engaging in them and whenever questions or concerns arise. Supervision by an adult is important at all times.

THE SEVEN DROPS

Parenting and teaching children with DSI requires understanding and patience, together with ingenuity and love. When your child is having a bad day, consider these "Seven Drops."

1. DROP YOUR VOICE.

When your child is explosive, demanding, and loud and needs immediate emotional first-aid, lower the volume of your voice. When you whisper, people will listen.

2. DROP YOUR BODY.

Research about stress and early brain development shows that children relax when caregivers are physically on their level. Megan R. Gunnar, Ph.D., at the University of Minnesota's Institute of Child Development, shows that children's cortisol level goes down when caregivers are responsive and close. (We need cortisol to survive because it readies us to protect ourselves. Too much cortisol, however, makes us anxious, aggressive, and unable to calm.) Grown-ups standing over a child, arms akimbo, or sitting in a chair, reading, can potentially raise the child's stress. Grown-ups on the floor can reduce the child's stress.

Another proponent of being on the floor with a child is child psychiatrist Stanley I. Greenspan, M.D. FloorTime, based on his work, is a systematic technique that fosters children's healthy emotional development through intensive, one-on-one interactions with adults who are literally on the child's level.

Drop your body, and you will see your child relax and relate.

3. DROP YOUR TV REMOTE.

Certainly, you cherish your precious few moments to watch television, read the newspaper, or concentrate on a task without interruption. Still, when your child approaches you in an undemanding way and makes an observation or asks a question, seize the moment. This is your chance to relate in a positive and meaningful way. You will never have another opportunity just like it again.

4. DROP YOUR GUARD.

Let your child take risks. Risks, that is, that are **SAFE**. Taking calculated risks is how we learn new skills. Every now and then, let your child fall down on a padded surface. You cannot protect him forever from the ups and downs of life. He most certainly will stumble, and he must learn all by himself, in his own way, how to cope and recover.

5. DROP YOUR DEFENSES.

So your mother-in-law says you're too lenient, the teacher says your child must learn how to get along, and the next-door neighbor shakes her head when you're dealing with your child's meltdown in the front yard. People like order; your child is disorderly.

What should you do about the blaming, misunderstanding, and head shaking? Don't ignore it; meet it.

A Mother Says . . .

To explain DSI to others, Bonne Sandars, M.S., says, "Kyle has a neurological condition in which his nervous system doesn't work like yours and mine. (Sort of like people who have diabetes have an endocrine system that doesn't work like ours). We really have eight senses: the five we learn about in school, plus one that controls our balance, one that controls the touch of things against us, and one that controls the amount of pressure input we feel. Like when we sit on a chair, we know where our bottom needs to go, we know how far to squat to get there, and we know to sit in the middle of the chair so we won't fall . . . all without thinking too hard about it. Kids with DSI have inputs that are not 'read' correctly by their brain.

"How this affects Kyle . . . You know that feeling you get when a bee almost lands on you? Your heart races or jumps? That's a fear response. Kids with DSI get the fear response from things we don't. And they react . . . just like we do to a bee. We jump, brush the bee away, run, hit at it, or, if we have been taught to do so, do nothing til the bee flies away, just like a beekeeper does. Or we get used to the bee stings just like a beekeeper. Or, we have allergic reactions, and never want to be near a bee. Certain kinds of things are 'bees' for Kyle . . . very loud noises, echoes, people sitting too close, visually busy walls, etc. Therapy helps him overcome this as it 'teaches' his nervous system, just like a beekeeper learns.

"Because his nervous system processes things differently, the feelings and textures of things matter greatly to him . . . it's like everything on him is magnified in terms of how he feels things. And, he has figured out how to overcome that with his needs. Kyle needs his blanket, spinning, and thumb sucking to regulate his outside world. These are like his 'insulin,' just like kids with diabetes need insulin need to help their inner body regulate its system with regard to food.

"I encourage people to think of a child who needs glasses. If he doesn't wear his glasses, he squints, squirms, tries to get closer to what he needs to see, or quits trying. All of these are *behaviors* caused by a physical thing (lack of correct vision). People don't yell at him, 'Quit squinting!' They tell him to put his glasses on. Well, the blanket is my child's glasses. And if he can't find them, adjust them properly, or get them to work, then I help, just as I would with a child who couldn't see.

"Then I ask if they have any questions. Most people do; then we talk."

6. DROP YOUR BATTERIES.

Batteries are required to turn on a flashlight, but to turn on a child they can't hold a candle to hands-on experiences. Battery-operated toys, which often serve as electronic babysitters, can dim a child's appetite to gain new physical and mental skills. Active bodies and brain cells are a child's primary energy source. Give "kid power" a chance.

7. DROP YOUR MISCONCEPTION THAT FUN IS FRIVOLOUS.

We are all born to be pleasure-seekers. We gotta have fun—or else we rust. Good sensations are neither an "extra" nor a reward; they are a necessity. Let's put our best resources together to help out-of-sync kids savor pleasurable experiences—**SAFE**, of course!

SAFE Activities for Sensory Systems

2

Touch (The Tactile Sense)

The whole family has gathered at a restaurant to celebrate Grandma and Grandpa's 50th anniversary. Three of the grandchildren have tactile dysfunction.

Aimee, 4, is oversensitive to touch stimuli and has tactile defensiveness. When Grandpa reaches for a hug, she shrinks back to the wall. Wringing her little hands, she anxiously watches family members bustling around the room. A cousin walks past, lightly brushing Aimee's skirt. Aimee shrieks, "Ouch! She touched me! She's trying to hurt me!" Her father looks up from a conversation and moves quickly to comfort Aimee. Having learned to be prepared for potentially stressful situations, he pulls out a "squeezy" ball. She takes it gratefully. Fidgeting with the toy calms her, for now.

Teddy, 6, is underresponsive to touch sensations. Like a bull in the china shop, he tears around the restaurant, bumping and crashing into everything and everybody. Although his mother attempts to capture him, he breaks away and collides with a waiter. They both lose their balance, and the tray of piggies-in-the-blanket falls on Teddy's head. Teddy guffaws, scrambles to his feet, and lurches toward a large fish tank. He clambers onto a chair, shoves the cover off the tank, plunges his arms in, and swishes his hands in the water. Grandma finally reins him in and corrals him securely on her lap. He presses his head against her and begins to calm down.

Ethan, 10, has poor tactile discrimination. He and an older cousin slip away from all the relatives and go to an arcade next door. The cousin asks to borrow a quarter to play a video game. Eagerly, Ethan gropes in his pocket for a coin and offers it. His cousin laughs, "This is a measly dime! Can't you feel the difference between a quarter and a dime?" Ethan blushes. Of course, he can see the difference when he looks at the coins, but feeling the difference is another matter. He hopes he'll get it right the next time.

The tactile system plays a major part in determining physical, mental, and emotional human behavior. Every one of us, from infancy onward, needs steady tactile stimulation to keep us organized, functioning, and healthy.

We get tactile information through sensory receiving cells, called receptors, in our skin, from head to toe. Touch sensations of pressure, vibration, movement, temperature, itch, and pain activate tactile receptors. We are always actively touching or passively being touched by something—other people, furniture, clothes, spoons, the ground under our feet, and the air on our skin. The ability to process tactile sensations effectively is very important, not only for visual perception, motor planning, and body awareness, but also for academic learning, emotional security, and social skills.

In the big family picture, Aimee, Teddy, and Ethan are out of sync. Understanding their underlying problems with sensory integration is not easy. Sometimes other people sense when and how to help, and sometimes they don't.

The children's tactile systems do not function smoothly, making it difficult for them to modulate, discriminate, coordinate, or organize touch sensations adaptively. Many characteristics of tactile dysfunction, listed below, are getting in their way.

CHARACTERISTICS OF TACTILE DYSFUNCTION

The child who is oversensitive to touch stimuli may:

☐ Have *tactile defensiveness* (oversensitivity to unexpected, light touch), rubbing off kisses or casual touches and pushing others away to avoid closeness.

☐ Instantly and intensely exhibit a "fight or fright" response or a "flight or freeze" response to harmless touch sensations.

☐ Dislike messy activities (cooking, painting, using chalk or tape).

☐ Be bothered by certain types of clothing, and be particularly sensitive to sock seams, shoes, and tags in shirts.

☐ Prefer wearing long sleeves and pants, even in summer, or dress lightly, even in winter.

☐ Become anxious or aggressive on windy, "hair-raising" days.

☐ Be a picky eater, avoiding some foods (rice, chunky peanut butter, lumpy mashed potatoes, vegetables) because of texture, or preferring food to be the same temperature, hot or cold.

☐ Dislike swimming, bathing, brushing teeth or having hair cut.

☐ Have poor peer relationships.

The child who is underresponsive to touch sensations may:

☐ Touch people and objects constantly.

☐ Seem unaware of touch unless it is intense, showing little reaction to pain, and getting hurt without realizing it.

☐ Not realize he has dropped something.

☐ Have poor body awareness, requiring firm pressure to know where his body was touched.

☐ Not notice how his clothes feel or whether they are on straight.

☐ Be insensitive to room temperature.

☐ Be a sloppy eater and be unaware of messiness on his face, mouth, and nose.

☐ Chew on inedible objects (fingernails, hair, shirt cuffs, collars, toys, and pencils).

☐ Physically hurt other people or pets, not comprehending the pain that others feel.

☐ Inappropriately "invade" others' space.

The child with poor tactile discrimination may:

☐ Seem out of touch with his hands, as if they are unfamiliar appendages.

☐ Have trouble holding and using tools (pencils, scissors, forks).

☐ Avoid initiating tactile experiences, such as picking up items that appeal to others.

☐ Have trouble perceiving objects' physical properties (texture, shape, size, density).

☐ Without the aid of visual cues:

  ☐ Be unable to identify what body parts have been touched.

  ☐ Be unable to identify familiar objects solely through touch.

  ☐ Be clumsy performing tasks such as zipping, buttoning, unbuttoning, tying shoes, and adjusting clothes.

  ☐ Prefer standing to sitting, to ensure visual control of his surroundings.

  ☐ Squirm or sit on edge of chair.

When processing tactile sensations is the problem, sensory integration-based occupational therapy usually benefits the child. The **SAFE** activities here are meant to complement the child's sensory diet.

Activities for the Tactile Sense

◆ Messing Around with Un-Paint

For all children, touch sensations are imperative. A child with tactile defensiveness, however, may avoid messy play, while a child with hyposensitivity to tactile stimulation may seek it in inappropriate ways. Here are several **SAFE** variations on a theme of messing around in mushy, slimy, gooey "un-paint."

DEVELOPMENTAL AGE RANGE 2 to 7

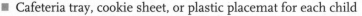

WHAT YOU WILL NEED
- "Un-Paint" (choose one):
  - Shaving cream (unscented, if possible) or bath foam
  - Hand lotion
  - Damp sand
  - Luscious mud
- Cafeteria tray, cookie sheet, or plastic placemat for each child
- Towels and wash-up bucket of water
- Oilcloth or newspaper to protect table and floor (unless your child is enjoying the activity outdoors where nobody cares about a mess)

PREPARATION
Squirt, pour, or spoon a blob of un-paint on the tray.

WHAT YOUR CHILD CAN DO:
- Press both palms into the un-paint and smoosh it around on the tray.
- "Polish" fingernails and toenails with the un-paint, or rub it on arms and legs.
- Draw or write letters, numbers, or shapes with a finger or several fingers.
- Make "lazy 8s," a Brain Gym®[1] idea:

---

[1]The Brain Gym® system, a set of 26 specific movements, readies the body to learn by integrating visual, auditory, and kinesthetic functioning. Stimulating the nervous system equally in all brain parts and strengthening neural pathways between the two hemispheres, the activities effect rapid and often dramatic improvements in concentration, memory, reading, writing, organizing, listening, physical coordination, and more. See *Helpful Organizations*.

- With his body centered in front of the tray, slowly trace a horizontal figure 8 with his left hand. He starts at the mid-point and moves his hand up and to the left, in a counterclockwise arc. He comes back to center and moves his finger up and toward the right, this time going clockwise.
- Trace a figure 8 with his right hand, moving up and to the right, in a clockwise arc.
- Trace a figure 8 with a few fingers of both hands, side by side.

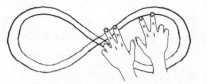

BELOW ARE DIRECTIONS FOR FOUR MORE *MESSING AROUND IN UN-PAINT* ACTIVITIES
- *Shaving Cream Car Wash*
- *Slimy Shapes*
- *Sand Dunes*
- *Feely Shapes*

Shaving Cream Car Wash

This variation was suggested by Abilities Center, Inc., in Commerce Township, Michigan.

WHAT YOU WILL NEED (IN ADDITION TO TRAYS, TABLE COVER, AND CLEAN-UP GEAR)
- Small toy cars in a plastic bin
- Popsicle sticks, plastic construction blocks, and small balls

WHAT YOUR CHILD CAN DO
- Squirt shaving cream on the tray.
- "Drive" a toy car through the shaving cream "car wash."
- Drive the car in vertical or diagonal patterns, or "write" with it.

- Build a car-wash maze with blocks, sticks, and balls. Take a car over, under, and around the obstacles in the course.
- Drive two cars at once:
  - Crash the cars together in straight or diagonal patterns.
  - Make a figure 8 "highway." (It's fine for the "lanes" to cross.)
  - Make highway "exit ramps," like Mickey Mouse ears, by pushing cars in circles, in the same direction, and then in opposite directions.
- Rinse, dry, and put the cars away.

⭐ Slimy Shapes

This variation, suggested by Melanie Hawke, O.T.R., from South Australia, is a finger-lickin'-good activity, ideal for the child who still tends to put everything into her mouth. Before you start, make sure the children's hands and the placemats are clean!

WHAT YOU WILL NEED (IN ADDITION TO PLACEMATS, TABLE COVER, AND CLEAN-UP GEAR)

Melanie Hawke's Pouring Custard

- 2 tablespoons of custard powder or cornflour
- 1 tablespoon of sugar
- Dash of vanilla essence for flavoring
- 2 cups of milk, or soy milk, or other milk substitute
- Optional: chocolate bits or mashed banana

PREPARATION

Whisk the ingredients together. Microwave for two minutes. Whisk again. Microwave for two minutes more, or until thick.

WHAT YOU CAN DO

- Pour a small amount of custard onto each child's placemat.
- Allow the child to experiment, or, if he has difficulty getting started, make suggestions, such as "Please draw a circle."
- Ask an older child to draw spelling words in the custard.

- If he cannot draw or write from memory, assist with:
  - Verbal cues (say, "To finish that nice 'H' that you've begun, draw a flat line between the two tall lines").
  - Auditory cues (thread elastic tape through several small bells and put it around his wrist or the finger he draws with, so he can hear how his movements are progressing).
  - Visual cues (draw a figure for him to imitate).
  - Kinesthetic cues (guide his motions, your hand over his hand).

WHAT YOUR CHILD CAN DO

- Dip the index finger of his preferred hand into the custard and draw squiggles or pictures on the placemat to make *Slimy Shapes*.
- Make shapes, numbers, letters, or words for *Slimy Spelling*.
- After completing a figure, "erase" it, lick his fingers, and begin anew.

VARIATIONS

Instead of pouring custard, try:

- Chocolate, banana, butterscotch, vanilla, or tapioca pudding
- Gelatin dessert, partially gelled
- Sweetened, condensed milk, perhaps with food coloring
- Grains (farina, cornmeal, grits, wheat germ, and so on), uncooked, or cooked and cooled

⭐ Sand Dunes

This variation was suggested by Abilities Center, Inc., in Commerce Township, Michigan.

WHAT YOU WILL NEED (IN ADDITION TO TRAYS, TABLE PROTECTION, AND CLEAN-UP APPARATUS)

- Clean, dry sand
- Spray bottle filled with water
- Little dinosaurs or beach critters (fish, birds, shells, starfish, people) and objects (boats, paper umbrellas meant for cocktails, beach blankets cut from paper towels, plastic palm trees)
- Cookie cutters

- Spread sand on the tray.
- Spray water on the sand until it is thoroughly damp.
- Mold sand into dunes and lagoons and play "Beach" with the toys.
- Put toys away, smooth out the sand, and write and draw with fingers.
- After the sand dries on the tray, use cookie cutters to cut out shapes.

⬛ Feely Shapes

This variation was suggested by Melanie Hawke, O.T.R., from South Australia. Certainly, you want your children to be expressive with words and motions. Have you ever considered encouraging them to be expressive with spaghetti? Today's the day!

WHAT YOU WILL NEED (IN ADDITION TO TRAYS OR PLASTIC PLACEMATS, TABLE COVER, AND CLEAN-UP GEAR)

- Package of spaghetti
- Cooking pot, half-filled with water

PREPARATION

- Together, cook the spaghetti.
- Rinse the spaghetti with cold water until it is cool enough to touch and manipulate. (You can refrigerate it to speed up the process.)

WHAT YOU AND YOUR CHILDREN CAN DO

- Starting with one or two strands of spaghetti at a time, "draw" shapes and designs on the placemat. Bend whole strands or separate them into smaller pieces.
- For children who need a jump-start, you can make designs on your placemat for them to observe and copy.

VARIATIONS

- Depending on the children's ages, guide them to make geometric shapes (circle, square, triangle, and so on), numerals, or alphabet letters.
- Include different kinds of pasta for more *Feely Shape* experiments.
- Let shapes dry on a cookie sheet; glue them to paper or cardboard; and paint them.

- Hands-on "painting" and playing with different textures increases tactile perception, body awareness, and creative exploration.
- The concrete experience of forming lines, shapes, letters, and numbers improves recognition and visualization of these abstract concepts.
- Squirting shaving cream and water and handling cookie cutters improves tool use, hand strength, and eye-hand coordination.
- Drawing with fingers and pushing toys through the un-paint improve kinesthetic awareness, fine motor skills, visual-motor integration, and the skills necessary to move the eyes, hands, and body together.
- Using two hands or driving two cars simultaneously improves bilateral coordination, symmetrically and asymmetrically.
- Making a figure 8 highway helps the child orient his body to the midline, and then to cross the midline. Crossing the midline is important for establishing hand dominance, for reading and writing, and for many other physical and academic skills.
- Playing in clean messes informs the sense of smell.
- Eating cold spaghetti and licking custard and other messy food off the fingers strengthens gustatory awareness.

> ## A Mother Says . . .
>
> Penny Kelly: "At bath time, I use funny foam with my daughter. It is spray foam that comes in different colors and is a shampoo and body wash together. I have found it at Kmart in the soap aisle. Katie loves the feeling of it. Great tactile experience! She has learned to use one finger to push down the handle to get the foam to come out. Great fine–motor skill development! We write the alphabet on the wall in the tub for another learning experience. She can write on herself and me, too! It floats in the water, too, which she also finds fun. It is not only fun— it also gets her clean at the same time."

COPING TIPS

- If your child refuses to touch the un-paint, offer a stick, spoon, swizzle stick, straw, or pretzel rod (for edible materials). Alternatively, try finger cots, available at drugstores.
- If your child is still too uncomfortable to get into the play—and really wants to—try *No-Mess Messy Play* (p. 44).

◆ Playdough

Handling homemade playdough is a mildly messy—and usually pleasant—tactile experience. For children with or without DSI, playdough is also an antidote to minor ailments such as Bad Weather Blues, The Hissy Fits, The Blahs, and Nothing-to-Do-itis. Some children can use a playdough experience every day.

DEVELOPMENTAL AGE RANGE 3 and up

WHAT YOU WILL NEED
- 2 cups flour
- 1 cup salt
- 4 teaspoons cream of tartar
- 2 cups water
- 4 tablespoons vegetable oil
- Large cooking pot and wooden spoon(s)
- Optional: sand, plastic "ice cubes," food coloring, or vanilla, peppermint, or other extract (not the oil, which burns sensitive fingers)
- Air-tight plastic container, to keep playdough for weeks. (Refrigeration is not necessary but will help it last longer.)

PREPARATION (PARENT AND CHILD WORKING SIDE-BY-SIDE, IF POSSIBLE)
- In a large pot, stir flour, salt, cream of tartar, water, and oil over very low heat until the dough comes away from the edge of the pot and makes a soft ball. Let the playdough cool.
- To heighten tactile sensation, stir in some sand or add plastic "ice cubes."
- To engage the visual sense, add food coloring. Barbara Lindner, M.Ed., O.T.R./L., suggests dividing the playdough into two portions. Add blue food coloring to one portion, yellow to the other. Have the child squeeze each portion until the color is smoothly mixed in. Then blend the two portions together to make green. (Blue + red = purple; red + yellow = orange; and blue + red + orange = brown.)
- To arouse the olfactory sense, blend in a few drops of vanilla, peppermint, or other extract. (Do not use cinnamon, which, like oil flavorings, may burn sensitive fingers.)

WHAT YOUR CHILD WILL NEED TO PLAY WITH PLAYDOUGH

- Rolling pin (or cylindrical wooden block, or short piece of a wooden dowel)
- Dull children's scissors
- Butter knife, fork, and spoon
- Kitchen gadgets, such as a garlic press, egg slicer, potato masher, and meat tenderizer
- Cookie cutters and molds, including letters and numbers
- Coins, keys, paper clips, buttons, plastic hair curlers, hairpins, shells, marbles, pebbles, and other small objects

WHAT YOUR CHILD CAN DO

- Roll the playdough in fat sausages and skinny snakes.
- Pinch (with fingers) or cut (with scissors) the snakes from left to right to reinforce directionality of reading and writing.
- Make a bird's nest and little eggs.
- Make big eggs and squeeze them through the egg slicer.
- Make spaghetti or hair by squeezing playdough through a garlic press.
- Make people and animals.
- Make patterns and interesting shapes with a potato masher and meat tenderizer.
- Press cookie cutters and other objects into the dough.
- Imitate shapes that another person makes.

BENEFITS OF THE ACTIVITY

- Molding, kneading, pounding, rolling, squeezing, and poking playdough develop tactile perception, proprioception, upper-body strength, fine motor skills, and motor planning.
- Squeezing the garlic press and manipulating other utensils, tools, and gadgets build hand dexterity, visual-motor skills, and the ability to follow directions.
- Working with playdough is a resistive activity that provides proprioceptive input and is extremely organizing and calming. Perfect *Playdough* moments are before an outing or in the middle of an activity that may be overstimulating for the child.

> **A Mother Says . . .**
>
> Rachel Vivace, in Indiana, has a great idea:"Have you tried using playdough as a pencil grip?"

- Blending color into playdough is hard work! Mixing it in thoroughly is unnecessary; a marbleized effect is beautiful, too.
- Dust your child's fingers with flour to prevent fresh playdough from sticking.
- If your child is extremely tactile-defensive, offer vinyl gloves as a buffer. (Avoid latex, as some children are allergic to this synthetic.) Or try finger cots (individual finger "mittens"). Get them at the drugstore, or make them by snipping the fingers off the gloves.
- When some kids work with their hands, they often work their mouths simultaneously. They do this because the mouth is a great organizer. Thrusting out their tongues, biting their lips, and chewing their collars are oral-motor behaviors that help them focus on a task. If your child needs something to mouth while using playdough, offer a piece of vinyl tubing or a piece of gum.
- Children with an intolerance to gluten can still enjoy *Playdough* if it is made without wheat. See *Recommended Materials* for books by Lisa Lewis and Karyn Seroussi that suggest recipes you can live with.

◆ Heavy Hands

Theraputty™ is exercise putty that is more resistant and less sticky than playdough. It lasts a long time, it is extremely beneficial for developing sensory-motor skills, and—best of all for the kid with a supersensitive nose—it has no odor! (Its disadvantages are that it stains clothes and is difficult to remove from clothing and carpeting, so be careful.) Teri Kozlowski, a pediatric OT in Maryland, suggests these structured activities to help kids get in sync.

DEVELOPMENTAL AGE RANGE About 2 to 8

WHAT YOU WILL NEED

- One pound of Theraputty (see *Recommended Materials*):
  - Soft resistance (yellow) for small children
  - Medium-soft resistance (red) for school-age children
- Smocks and floor protection

WHAT YOU CAN DO

- Help the child "hide" his hand (or foot) in the Theraputty. Pack it on well.
- Lift the child's hand up, in five gradual stages. At each level, say the word "Heavy" with rising inflection, or sing up a musical scale.
- When his hand is at the top, let it drop, at the same time cascading your voice on the word, "H-a-n-d." Like this:

heavy . . .   H

heavy,   a

heavy,   n

"Heavy,   d!"

- After you lift and drop his hand or foot several times, ask, "Where's your hand? Hiding? Let's see you get it out."

WHAT YOUR CHILD CAN DO

Push, pull, and pry the putty to get it off.

BENEFITS OF THE ACTIVITY

- "Hiding" hands and feet inside Theraputty helps to diminish tactile defensiveness.
- Feeling added weight on hands and feet alerts the hyporesponsive child and improves body awareness.
- Removing the resistant putty strengthens proprioception and improves motor planning.
- Using both hands to pry putty off a foot helps bilateral coordination.

◆ Hide-and-Seek with Little Toys

Teri Kozlowski, O.T.R., says that playing *Hide-and-Seek with Little Toys* is a "great before-dinner game when things are hectic, children may be grumpy, and Mom or Dad needs to get supper on the table."

DEVELOPMENTAL AGE RANGE 3½ and up

WHAT YOU WILL NEED

- One pound of Theraputty
- Small rubber characters, 3 or 4 inches in size
- Little "treasures," such as buttons, beads, pretty pebbles, and coins
- Little containers for sorting: film canisters, egg cartons, jewelry boxes, plastic cups, or a piggy bank

Playing Hide-and-Seek with Little Toys
(In Order of Difficulty)

WHAT YOU CAN DO	WHAT YOUR CHILD CAN DO
1. Lightly pack Theraputty around several small (3 or 4 inches) rubber characters. Ask, "Now, where did that purple dinosaur go?"	1. Pull off the Theraputty to reveal the characters.
2. Hide the characters again, now packing the putty on thicker. Leave a little opening in the putty, so the child can use vision to see the toy inside.	2. Peek inside the mound of Theraputty to see the character, and uncover it.
3. Pack the characters in putty again, now covering them thoroughly, allowing no holes for peeking. To increase the challenge, offer a few "empty" mounds.	3. Squeeze the mounds to discover through tactile discrimination alone which are "red herrings" and which encase toys. Uncover the toys.
4. Hide buttons, beads, coins, and other small objects inside putty for a treasure hunt. Provide small containers for sorting.	4. Hunt for little treasures, pick them out, and sort them into the containers.

BENEFITS OF THE ACTIVITY

- Squeezing the putty strengthens tactile discrimination and proprioception.
- Pulling the putty off improves motor planning, fine motor skills, and bilateral coordination.
- Seeking desirable objects improves attention.

◆ Simon Says, "Make My Supper!"

Simon (of "Simon Says" fame) is extremely demanding, especially when he's hungry. For some reason, children usually try to oblige this imaginary friend. Perhaps they tolerate his insistent and absurd behavior because it feels familiar.

This is another wonderful suggestion from Teri Kozlowski, O.T.R. The active ingredient in Simon's supper? Whimsy!

DEVELOPMENTAL AGE RANGE 3 to 8

WHAT YOU WILL NEED
Theraputty

WHAT YOU CAN DO
Be there, and play!

How to Play *Simon Says, "Make My Supper!"*

WHAT YOU CAN SAY	HOW YOUR CHILD CAN FIX SIMON'S SUPPER
Simon says, "I'm hungry! Make my supper!"	Sit at the table and get ready to "cook."
Simon says, "Squeeze me some lemon juice! Squeeze me some meatballs! Squeeze me some cookie frosting!"	Squeeze putty to make "lemonade," form "meatballs," and decorate "cookies."
Simon says, "Push!"	Knead "bread" or "cookie."
Simon says, "Pull!"	Pull "string cheese," or "cornhusks," or "drumsticks" off a "chicken."
Simon says, "Pinch!"	Pinch a "pie crust," "ketchup packet," or dash of "oregano."

WHAT YOU CAN SAY	HOW YOUR CHILD CAN FIX SIMON'S SUPPER
Simon says, "Roll!"	Roll "hot dogs" or "sausages."
Simon says, "Twist!"	Twist "breadsticks" and "pretzels."

BENEFITS OF THE ACTIVITY

◾ Manipulating the putty in different ways improves motor planning, fine motor skills, tactile discrimination, and bilateral coordination.

◾ Attending to verbal directions improves auditory awareness and communication skills.

◾ Using the motions to "cook," the child learns skills that he may generalize later when he handles kitchen toys, plays "Let's pretend" with friends, and helps prepare real meals.

COPING TIPS

◾ To help the child understand the verbal instructions, give a visual cue by demonstrating how to squeeze, push, and so on.

◾ To help with motor planning, give a physical cue with hand-over-hand assistance.

◆ Touch Pantry

Sifting fingers and wiggling toes in different foodstuffs usually feels wonderful. This activity may appeal to the child with tactile defensiveness more than a really messy activity. Of course, this activity makes a mess too, but it is a dry mess and worth the trouble to sweep up. (For a sensational mess, add water to the ingredients, or turn to *Dinosaur Morning*, p. 224.)

DEVELOPMENTAL AGE RANGE 2 and up

WHAT YOU WILL NEED

- Coffee cans
- Turkey roasting pans or cookie sheets
- Dry foods, such as beans, lentils, split peas, rice, oatmeal, cornmeal, pasta, popcorn, nuts
- Foam letters and numbers and soft, small toys such as tiny koosh balls, plastic bears, felt finger puppets, or foam jigsaw puzzle pieces (at least two of each kind)
- Tarp or shower curtain
- Carton for storage

PREPARATION

- Fill cans about half full with one of the dry foods.
- Bury little toys and foam letters in the food.
- Spread the tarp on the kitchen floor under the cans, or take the cans outdoors where making a mess is no problem.
- When your child has finished playing, put the lids on the cans and store them and the tarp in a carton for another day.

WHAT YOUR CHILD CAN DO

- Sift his fingers through the dry food, or stir it with a spoon.
- Grope around with his fingers to find the toys and letters and try to identify them by feel alone (no peeking).
- Pretend that the animal or people toys are diving, swimming, eating, seeking, and finding one another, and so on.
- Pour the food and objects into roasting pans and stir.
- Walk barefoot in the material and pick up objects with his toes.
- Sort objects into piles of letters, numbers, balls, and so on.

BENEFITS OF THE ACTIVITY

- Playing with dry food promotes tactile perception and feels good.
- Playing with dry food provides mild smell sensations for the hypersensitive child.
- Stirring with a spoon provides auditory and proprioceptive feedback.
- Feeling, identifying, and sorting toys and letters promote integration of forms.
- Pretending that little toys are engaged in various activities strengthens visualization, social awareness, imagination, and playfulness.

This feel-good, look-cute activity is fun at any time when you are in a place where you can make a mess. The idea comes from Crisler Lovendahl, M.A., C.C.C.-S.L.P., of Highland Park, Illinois—although she says she can't claim credit.

DEVELOPMENTAL AGE RANGE 2 and up

WHAT YOU WILL NEED
- Cornstarch
- Two mats (one of which is a dark color)

PREPARATION
Sprinkle a generous amount of cornstarch on a mat.

WHAT YOUR CHILD CAN DO
- Remove shoes and socks.
- Cover palms and soles in cornstarch.
- Move to the second, dark-colored mat and make "paw prints."

VARIATIONS
- Rather than cornstarch, use flour, fingerpaints, or pudding. (Do not use talcum powder, which should not be inhaled in large quantities.)
- Spread cornstarch on a tray and write or draw in it.
- Sift the cornstarch.

BENEFITS OF THE ACTIVITY
- May improve tactile perception and help with tactile desensitization.
- Positioning the body in different ways improves proprioception, body awareness, motor planning, and eye-hand/eye-foot coordination.
- Messing around with cornstarch is usually calming and soothing.

✦ Pretzel People

When our boys were small and out-of-sorts, making *Pretzel People* was a sure way to get them back in sync. We experimented successfully with different recipes. It didn't seem to matter which recipe we used; what did matter were the sensory pleasures of kneading the dough, forming the *Pretzel People*, inhaling the aroma as they baked, and breaking bread together.

DEVELOPMENTAL AGE RANGE 2 and up

WHAT YOU WILL NEED
- Your favorite soft pretzel recipe, or a gluten-free, casein-free mix for those with allergies or intolerances to wheat, dairy, eggs, and other ingredients (see *Recommended Materials*)
- Fresh ingredients
- Bowls, baking sheets, racks, spatulas, and so on.
- Utensils such as rolling pins, meat tenderizers, dull knives, and other playdough tools

PREPARATION
- Together, prepare the pretzel dough as directed and let it rise. This process takes a long time, so plan to do it earlier rather than later in the day.
- When the dough is ready, call the kids back to the table to make a happy, productive, and creative mess.

WHAT YOUR CHILDREN CAN DO
- Press wads of dough between their palms to make patties. Use these for the *Pretzel People's* torsos and heads.
- Roll dough between their hands to form "snakes." Divide the snakes into small sections for arms and legs, hands and feet, fingers and toes.
- Make self-portraits, family members, pets, zoo animals, and monsters.
- Help you bake and eat the finished products.
- Help you clean up.

BENEFITS OF THE ACTIVITY
- Kneading, rolling, and shaping the dough promotes tactile perception, strengthens proprioception, and provides a calming experience.

- Forming *Pretzel People* improves body awareness, visualization, and fine motor skills.
- Smelling the dough during its preparation and baking provides olfactory input.
- Chewing and eating provide gustatory and oral-motor input.
- The process of making *Pretzel People* nourishes social interactions, language skills, and much giggly merriment.

◆ Holiday Ornaments

This activity entices children who love messy play as well as those who usually avoid it. The recipe is delightfully simple, and the aroma is wonderful.

DEVELOPMENTAL AGE RANGE 2½ and up

WHAT YOU WILL NEED
- ½ cup cinnamon
- ½ cup applesauce
- Optional: 1 teaspoon white school glue, to prevent crumbling (do not use glue if you are overly concerned about your child eating it)
- Bowl or large zippable baggie
- Cookie sheet or waxed paper
- Rolling pin, cookie cutters, spatula, and rack
- Toothpick and pretty ribbon
- Ornament hangers (for the Christmas tree) or suction hooks

WHAT YOUR CHILD CAN DO
- Use his hands to mix the cinnamon, applesauce, and glue in a bowl, or, if he refuses to touch the mixture, in the plastic baggie.
- Roll the mixture out on a cookie sheet or waxed paper, about ½ inch thick.
- Press cookie cutters into the thick and fragrant dough.
- With the toothpick, poke a generous hole near the top of each ornament.
- Place the ornaments on a cookie rack and let them dry for 12 hours.

- Thread pretty ribbon through the holes and hang the ornaments on the Christmas tree or from suction hooks on the kitchen window.

- Blending the ingredients with the hands is beneficial "messy play" for the tactile system.
- Using both hands on a rolling pin develops bilateral coordination.
- Pushing and pulling the rolling pin over the dough improves proprioception and grading of movement.
- Poking holes in the ornaments and threading ribbon through them promotes eye-hand coordination and fine motor skills.
- Smelling the fragrant mixture informs the olfactory sense.

> **A Mother Says . . .**
>
> Stephanie Becker, in Traverse City, Michigan, says, "Oh, this is a great sensory ornament recipe! We just made some, and, to my surprise, Chase, my tactilely defensive child, touched it. They're fun to make and they smell great!!"

◆ Magic Tissue Transfers

This lovely activity comes from the staff of Abilities Center, Inc., in Michigan. It is fun for one, and more fun for a group.

DEVELOPMENTAL AGE RANGE 3 to 10

WHAT YOU WILL NEED

- Mixture of one part glue and two parts water, in a small bowl
- Tissue paper (dark colors work best)
- Paper
- Paintbrush (optional)
- Scissors

PREPARATION
Cover the child with a smock and the table with newspaper.

WHAT YOUR CHILD CAN DO

- Cut or tear tissue paper into strips or shapes.

- With fingers or paintbrush, spread glue mixture onto one side of the tissue paper pieces.
- Place tissue paper pieces, glue side down, onto the paper. Press firmly.
- Immediately peel tissue paper off and throw it away. The paper goes in the trash can, and the color stays behind!
- Repeat process with different colors of tissue paper torn in different shapes to make a creative, colorful work of art.

BENEFITS OF THE ACTIVITY

- Spreading glue and working with wet, gooey, and sticky textures provides strong tactile input.
- Cutting or tearing tissue paper improves fine-motor skills, and peeling the tissue paper away strengthens the pincer grasp.
- Using a paintbrush and scissors develops tool use.

◆ No-Mess Messy Play

This activity is fun for every child, especially the one with tactile defensiveness. The child who can't tolerate touching paint may still be longing to experiment with it.

DEVELOPMENTAL AGE RANGE 2 and up

WHAT YOU WILL NEED

- Red, yellow, and blue fingerpaint or colored hair gel
- Zippable plastic bags
- Optional: duct tape

PREPARATION

- Put one blob each of red and yellow paint into one bag and zip it up. To prevent leaking, insert the bag, seam down, into a second bag, or seal the seam with duct tape.
- Prepare a bag with yellow and blue paint, and another bag with blue and red paint.

WHAT YOUR CHILD CAN DO

- Squish the blobs together to see that red and yellow make orange, yellow and blue make green, and blue and red make purple.
- Practice "writing" letters, numbers, and shapes through the plastic.

VARIATIONS

- Put three or four colors together in one bag, and learn about brown!
- Experiment with different gelatinous materials, such as hair gel, cornstarch in water, or ketchup.
- Puncture a small hole in the bottom of the plastic bag and squeeze it like a pastry bag to write and draw on paper or a tray.

BENEFITS OF THE ACTIVITY

- This hands-on activity brings the tactilely defensive child closer to the fun. Maybe your child will be so entranced that he or she will soon "graduate" to putting those reluctant fingers directly into the paint.
- Opening and closing the fingers and squeezing the bag improve fine motor skills and proprioception.
- Making letters and figures in the un-paint is good practice for developing writing and phonics skills.

Go Away, Glue!

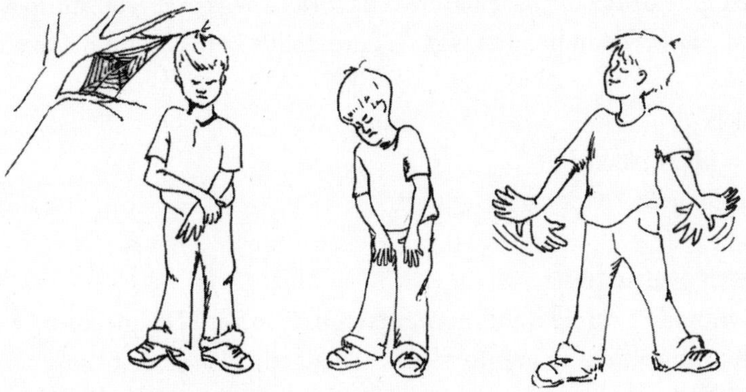

Getting unstuck is what this activity is all about. Here are a handful of situations when it may come in handy:

1. The child is about to have a meltdown because she has just touched something messy or uncomfortable, such as a dab of fingerpaint, a wet leaf, a cobweb, or sand in her shoe.

2. The child is about to have a meltdown because she is threatened by the possibility of touching something unpleasant (to her).
3. The child is underresponsive or unresponsive to the activity around him and needs to be jump-started.
4. The child is out of focus, and it is necessary for him to settle down now and pay attention.
5. The child needs help to make a transition between activities, such as eating lunch and listening to a story.
6. The child needs help to "step away" from a distressing or overwhelming experience that may have nothing to do with messiness.

DEVELOPMENTAL AGE RANGE 3½ and up

WHAT YOU AND YOUR CHILD CAN DO

- Say, "Ooo, icky-sticky! Go away, glue! Get off!" Depending on the milieu, shout if you can, whisper if you must.
- To comb out the imaginary glue, run your fingers roughly through your hair (roughly, in order to increase deep pressure). Rub your hands over your face and around your neck. Rub the glue off your shoulders and torso, arms and hands. "Pull" it off your fingers, one at a time, as if removing tight rubber gloves. Continue rubbing the glue off your legs and feet.
- Stand tall. Hold your arms out to the sides and shake, shake, shake the last glue drops off your hands. Shake your legs and feet. Jump around.
- Take a few deep breaths, say, "There, that's better," and move along.

VARIATIONS

- *Get Off, Cobweb!*
- *Be Off with You, Scary Monster!*

BENEFITS OF THE ACTIVITY

To cope with life's unpleasant moments, the child with DSI needs to learn new strategies, rather than falling to pieces. This activity is one of those strategies. It diffuses distress or fear because it gives the child something positive to do in response to a demand from the environment. It connects him to his body, increases his self-awareness, and helps him become more in control of the situation. Also, the premise of the activity—being covered with glue or cobwebs—is ridiculous. A sense of humor is as worthy to develop as the sense of touch.

◆ Tactile Road

Too wet or cold to go outside to play? Lay out an indoor *Tactile Road* to keep children focused and moving in this totally **SAFE** activity.

DEVELOPMENTAL AGE RANGE 3 to 10

WHAT YOU WILL NEED
- Tactilely pleasing "step-upons," such as:
  - Carpet squares
  - Large swatches of velvet, corduroy, satin, chiffon
  - Sheepskin or fake fur
  - Foam packaging (the kind used to protect a shipment of grapefruit)
  - Down comforter, chenille bedspread, terrycloth towels
  - Pillowcases filled with large beads or beans
  - Foam "egg crate" bedding
  - Large sheets of bubble wrap
  - Corrugated cardboard, sandpaper
  - Cabdriver's wooden-ball seat cover
- Carton in which to store step-upons, until the next rainy day

PREPARATION
- Lay out the step-upons in a large circle. At first, place the step-upons close together. As the child gains confidence, move them apart to encourage stretching and jumping.
- Have your children remove their shoes and socks.

WHAT YOUR CHILD(REN) CAN DO
- Walk, leap, or jump—forward, backward, and sideways—from one textured item to another.

- Get down on the floor and roll or crawl over the path.
- Try to walk very quietly, even over bubble wrap.

BENEFITS OF THE ACTIVITY
- Pressing the feet, hands, and body on different textured materials develops tactile awareness and discrimination.
- Judging the distances between one step-upon and the next improves attention, oculomotor skills, and visual-spatial perception.
- Traveling from one material to another involves balance and movement, proprioception, kinesthesia, and motor planning.

COPING TIP

Gravitational insecurity ("G.I.") may be the reason that your child is fearful when moving across unstable surfaces. To reduce her anxiety, hold her hand, or have her proceed through the *Tactile Road* on hands and knees.

◆ Dramatic Dress-Ups

For children with poor tactile function, dry items may be a more acceptable beginning activity than messy play. A permanent dress-up box, filled with cast-off clothes from thrift shops or the back of your closet, promises hours of multisensory fun.

DEVELOPMENTAL AGE RANGE 2 and up

WHAT YOU WILL NEED
- Large, sturdy cardboard or plastic storage boxes
- Fancy clothes, such as old bridesmaid dresses cut down to size, and new "bridal veils," made from a yard of white tulle stitched to a stretchy athletic sweatband
- Uniforms and professional outfits: Nurse, doctor, mail delivery person, police officer, firefighter, soldier, sailor, astronaut, airline pilot, bus driver, railroad engineer, construction worker, cowboy/cowgirl, chef, magician, clown, ballerina, angel, princess, king, and so on

- Scarves, neckties, ribbons, aprons, silky slips, camisoles, and peignoirs
- Feathery boas, old fur jackets, woolen shawls, and capes
- Fabric remnants, such as gold and silver lamé, velvet, fleece, and faux fur
- Hats, caps, and headbands; belts and sashes; goggles and glasses
- Shoes, including high heels, slippers, sandals, clogs, and boots
- Briefcases, handbags, tote bags, and backpacks
- Chunky costume jewelry such as Mardi Gras beads, rings, necklaces, bracelets, and clip-on earrings
- Props such as sections of garden hose, bells, cymbals, drums, and magnifying glasses
- Full-length mirror

PREPARATION

- Store all dress-up items in labeled, accessible, and easy-to-open boxes.
- Periodically, wash, repair, and replace the dress-ups so they are always fresh and appealing. You may wish to toss scented sachets into the boxes as well.

WHAT YOUR CHILDREN CAN DO

Dress up, check out how they look in front of the mirror, change into other outfits, and play make-believe.

BENEFITS OF THE ACTIVITY

- Handling and wearing differently textured clothes and accessories provide many touch experiences that promote tactile perception.
- Orienting the body to get in and out of clothes and accessories strengthens grading of movement, motor planning, and awareness of body position.
- Zipping, snapping, tying, and buttoning improve fine motor skills.
- Trying on different clothes encourages imaginative play and frees up the child to "try on" different roles and personalities.
- Play-acting with others promotes socially appropriate behaviors, language, and gestures.

◆ Mummy Wrap

The purpose of *Mummy Wrap* is to provide uniform, deep pressure, which can calm an oversensitive nervous system. Lynne Israel, O.T.R., has used this at home and in her clinic with great success.

DEVELOPMENTAL AGE RANGE 5 and up

WHAT YOU WILL NEED
Medium weight, 50-yard length of latex-free, stretchy exercise band (see *Recommended Materials*)

An Occupational Therapist and Mother Says . . .

Lynne Israel says, "I used *Mummy Wrap* with my own daughter when she was really wound up. She had an incredible sense of her body in space related to movement and balance (she did flips on the balance beam in gymnastics). However, regulation has always been a struggle. When she was a gymnast working out four hours a day she would have difficulty settling down for bed after practice (which ended about 8:30 at night). *Mummy Wrap* was the one thing that really helped her. Usually she would jump on a trampoline while wrapped (and while I stood by, of course) for about 15 minutes. Then she would say, 'OK, Mommy, I'm ready.' After that she was able to get ready for bed and go easily to sleep."

Another Mother Says . . .

Dixie Hendrix says, "My sensory seeking yet tactile defensive 9-year-old son has loved to do 'mummy wrapping' with crepe paper. It has been fun to see Sam 'use' this activity in different ways over the past years since being diagnosed at 4 with DSI. We now use this at all of our kids' parties (birthday, Halloween, Christmas), because it truly is organizing and calming. One person (kid or adult) wraps the other with a large roll of crepe paper from feet to neck—even head, if they keep the nose free. Then the child 'busts' out of the wrappings. (My son likes to hop around in his tight mummy cocoon for awhile making mummy noises.) Then the kids are so in sync that they pick up the busted wrappings and put it all in a trash bag!

PREPARATION

Wrap resistive band around the child like a mummy, from shoulders to ankles. As you wrap, be careful that the band is taut but not too tight. The more evenly you apply the pressure, the better.

WHAT YOUR CHILD CAN DO

Walk and roll around.

BENEFITS OF THE ACTIVITY

Taut pressure from the resistive band organizes the tactile system and is both calming and regulating.

◆ Hot Dog Roll

The deep touch pressure of this activity feels fabulous, all over. (Remember, children with tactile defensiveness are often fine with deep pressure and may seek it out.) Because it is so relaxing and calming, this is a great activity to do right before and/or just after a more stimulating tactile experience.

DEVELOPMENTAL AGE RANGE All ages

WHAT YOU WILL NEED

- Sleeping bag, foam mat, or flexible gym mat
- Large beach ball or therapy ball (see *Recommended Materials*)
- Optional:
  - Variously textured household items such as a washcloth, sponge, pot scrubber, vegetable brush, basting brush or large paintbrush, wooden foot massager, and fabric swatches
  - Vibrating massager (see *Recommended Materials*)

- Spread the mat or sleeping bag on the floor or bed.
- Have the child lie tummy down on the mat, near one end. The child's head should be off the mat.

WHAT YOU CAN DO
- With consistent, firm pressure, roll and press the ball up and down all over the child's body. (No ball? Press with your flattened hands.) Say, "I'm making sure this hot dog is really well packed."
- Ask, "Want me to press harder? Not so hard? More? Tell me when you want me to stop." (Give the child the chance to be in control and to guide the activity.)
- Say, "It's time to make you extra delicious. Here's some ketchup." Rub your child's arms, legs, and back with the optional washcloth, sponge, or vibrating massager—or just use your hands. Continue, "Here's some mustard. Chopped onions would be tasty, too. And how about some marshmallow fluff?" As you talk, spread or firmly apply the imaginary condiments, using downward motions (in the direction that the child's hair grows).
- Now, crouch next to your child and roll him gently and tightly in the mat, toward the other end. Put one hand on his shoulder and the other hand on his hip. Rock him to and fro for a moment.
- Say, "Guess what? There's too much ketchup in this hot dog! I'll have to squish some out." Press down firmly on the child's arms, legs, and back, until you have squished out the excess mustard and mayonnaise.
- When you and your child agree that he's "done," grasp the edge of the mat firmly while he unrolls.

WHAT YOUR CHILD CAN DO
- Soak it all in!
- Suggest other delicious condiments—such as strawberry jam, peanut butter, pickles, tomatoes, sauerkraut, and so on.
- After being thoroughly cooked himself, make a hot dog out of you.

VARIATIONS
- Prepare a "burrito" or "taco," with plenty of salsa, guacamole, cheese, lettuce, sour cream, onions, and so on.
- Make a "jelly omelet."

- Deep touch pressure from the mat, textured materials, and your hands provides input to your child's somatosensory (tactile/proprioceptive) system. The optional vibrating massager also provides a vibrotactile effect that calms and regulates the senses.
- Feeling strokes and textures, as you apply the make-believe garnishes, promotes tactile discrimination.
- The rotary action of rolling organizes his vestibular system. (Also see *Become a Butterfly*, p. 112, a similar activity with more emphasis on the vestibular system.)

COPING TIP

If the sensation of rolling on the floor like a hot dog overwhelms your child's vestibular system, he can be wrapped and unwrapped on his feet. While he stands, you hold the mat or sleeping bag and circle around him.

◆ Splendor in the Grass

Some children who crave tactile experiences are eager to grab hold of everything—mud, wet leaves, and bugs included. Other children may shun tactile experiences, keeping their hands in their pockets and feigning disinterest in the natural world. Given the "just-right" tools, both the sensory seeker and the sensory avoider may glory in this opportunity to examine a microcosm at their feet.

The title of this activity comes from William Wordsworth's ode, *Intimations of Immortality from Recollections of Early Childhood*. Remember these lines?

> *Though nothing can bring back the hour*
> *Of splendour in the grass, of glory in the flower;*
> *We will grieve not, rather find*
> *Strength in what remains behind . . .*

DEVELOPMENTAL AGE RANGE 4 and up

WHAT YOU WILL NEED

- 12-inch plastic hoop, or a stick to scratch a circle in the ground
- Tweezers

- Paper plate or metal pie tin
- A large-mouth jar
- Magnifying glass
- Optional: vinyl gloves or finger cots (to protect hands) and towel to lie on

WHAT YOUR CHILD CAN DO

- Choose a spot on the ground to place the circle. This is your sample area, or "transect," a specifically designated area (usually in the form of a grid) for gathering data about plants and other things living in the vicinity.
- Lie down and look carefully into the circle.
- With fingers or tweezers, carefully pick up things that are inside the circle and place them onto the plate or in the jar. Items may include:
  - Plants or vegetables, such as acorns, dandelions, violets, petals, grass, leaves, twigs, bark, mulch, seeds, and pine cones
  - Animals, such as ants, caterpillars, cicadas, centipedes, earthworms, grubs, sowbugs, and spiders
  - Minerals, such as gravel, quartz, mica, pebbles, and grains of sand
  - Miscellany, such as bottle caps, popsicle sticks, and remains of old sandbox toys
- Watch to see if the critters make adaptive responses to a new environment. Some bugs will scurry for cover, some will curl up and play dead, and some will wander around not knowing what to do—just like people!
- Examine the findings carefully. A magnifying glass adds a new dimension to looking closely at the research samples.
- Depending on his age and interest, categorize the items:
  - Animal, vegetable, or mineral
  - Living or nonliving
- Tip the containers over and return everything to its home.

A Mother Says . . .

In response to a friend whose daughter "dislikes being outside, doesn't like it when the wind is blowing, and refuses to get dirty," Sonya, who lives in Locust Fork, Alabama, says, "Have you thought of bringing in some of the 'outside' and letting her deal with it on her 'own turf'? You could get some twigs, leaves, and pebbles and put them in an easy-to-clean area. You could help her build a house with the twigs, make walls with the leaves, and put the pebbles in the yard area. Also, many kids, like my Jackson and Max, benefit a *lot* from just running their hands through the pebbles, sand, or other textured stuff. Once she feels safe playing with it indoors, she may be more willing to go outside and play with it."

BENEFITS OF THE ACTIVITY
- Handling natural materials increases tactile discrimination.
- Manipulating small objects with the tweezers or fingers very carefully improves fine motor skills and eye-hand coordination.
- Lying prone strengthens gross motor control and resistance to the pull of gravity.
- Spending time observing a whole, new, busy world improves the ability to focus and attend, and sorting categories strengthens perceptual skills.

COPING TIP

Kids with limited fine motor control may inadvertently crush bugs when handling them. An option is to entice the insects to crawl onto a leaf or twig, like a tiny stretcher.

◆ Nature Bracelet

"Going for a walk together is an eye-opening experience for both you and your child, because there is so much in the world to discover," says Lori L. Merkel, COTA/L. "Making a *Nature Bracelet* is like bringing home a souvenir of your journey. You might want to take along the roll of tape, as your child will most likely ask to make more! I can recall many walks with my two children and how proud they were of their beautiful creations."

DEVELOPMENTAL AGE RANGE 2 and up

WHAT YOU WILL NEED
Masking tape (wide width works the best)

PREPARATION
- Tear off a piece of tape just long enough to go around your child's wrist, with about ½ inch overlapping
- Place the tape, loosely or snug, on your child's nondominant wrist, sticky side out.

WHAT YOUR CHILD CAN DO
- As you walk, pick up small items such as flowers, leaves, feathers, herbs, and grasses.

- Place these items on the sticky part of the tape, and add items until tape is covered.
- Back home, remove the bracelet and hang it on the refrigerator, or glue it to paper.

VARIATIONS
- Place nature bracelets on both wrists.
- Staple or tape rows of masking tape, sticky side out, on cardboard. Place items on the tape to make a nature collage or picture.

BENEFITS OF THE ACTIVITY
- Wearing the bracelet, touching items found, and touching the sticky part of the tape increase tactile perception.
- Walking and talking together, naming items found, and retelling the story of the walk with the help of the items on the bracelet all develop vocabulary and language skills.
- Sighting interesting natural items improves visual figure-ground perception.
- Picking flowers strengthens eye-hand coordination and pincer grasp, and pressing them to the tape improves fine motor skills.
- Smelling items like freshly picked flowers and herbs provides olfactory information.
- Bringing two hands together to decorate the bracelet improves bilateral coordination.
- Bending, stretching, and reaching improve gross motor skills, force, and motor planning.

COPING TIPS
- The bracelet can be placed on the adult's arm if wearing it bothers the child.
- Depending on the child's tolerance, pick stronger-smelling or milder flowers and herbs.
- A nonambulatory child can direct the adult to pick items, and then he can stick them on.

◆ Slurp Party

When the food is desirable and the company is fine, having a *Slurp Party* can nourish body, mind, and spirit. Aubrey Lande, M.S., O.T.R./L., credits her mother, Jean Keating Carton, for inventing this luscious idea. Aubrey says, "Always invite one or two children who will absolutely love this activity, as they will establish the proper mood!"

DEVELOPMENTAL AGE RANGE All ages

WHAT YOU WILL NEED
- Favorite, messy foods, such as:
  - Spaghetti
  - Beans and franks
  - Potato salad
  - Pudding
  - Cake
  - Ice cream
  - Applesauce
  - Gelatin dessert
  (served with a straw)
- Paper or plastic plates
- Washable picnic blanket
- Buckets of warm water or finger bowls
- Sponges, towels, and change of clothes for each participant

PREPARATION
- Spread the blanket on the grass and have the kids situate themselves comfortably.
- Put the dog and cat inside the house.
- Serve the food—*without* utensils.

WHAT YOUR CHILDREN CAN DO:
- Eat the food with straws or their hands—or no hands!
- Take a sponge or fingerbowl break every five minutes or whenever necessary.
- When the festive slurp-a-thon is over, wash off and change clothes.

BENEFITS OF THE ACTIVITY
- Handling messy food is especially helpful for the child with mild tactile/oral defensiveness.
- Any eating experience integrates smell and taste sensations.
- Slurping along with a bunch of friends builds good social skills.

COPING TIPS

- If your child is extremely sensory defensive, before the party give her deep pressure (e.g., *Hot Dog Roll,* p. 51) or use a brushing technique called the Wilbarger Protocol (a treatment approach designed by Patricia Wilbarger, M.Ed., O.T.R., F.A.O.T.A., and Julia Leigh Wilbarger, M.S., O.T.R.), which a trained OT can teach you to use.
- If the kids seem reluctant, bring out the camera; it may motivate them to dive in.
- You dive in, too! When adults participate, kids know they are not going to be in trouble for making a mess or having deplorable table manners.
- Keep a merry, kind, compassionate attitude. If the activity doesn't appeal to the kids this time, maybe you can schedule another *Slurp Party* next season.

3

$\sim\!\sim\!\sim$

Balance and Movement (The Vestibular Sense)

Martin, 6, is overresponsive to movement and avoids it. Running, sliding, and swinging are so scary. His babysitter, however, insists on going to the playground. She says that the walk and the fresh air every day are important. She's very patient, and he really likes her. Yesterday he agreed to let her help him get on the low swing. She stood close by and didn't push, thank goodness—he hates being pushed! Sitting there and swaying slowly was not too bad, because his feet were grazing the ground. Today he's willing to try it again.

Krystyna, 5, is underresponsive to movement experience and craves extra stimulation. She loves to swing upside down on the playground. She swings for 20 minutes or more, sometimes lying on her stomach, sometimes on her back, sometimes whirling on the tire swing, never getting dizzy. Back home, Krystyna jiggles and rocks in the chair while she and her babysitter have a snack. Then her babysitter reads a story while Krystyna stands on her head in the corner. Being in that position really helps her to pay attention and remember every detail of the story.

LaVerne, 10, does not have a modulation problem. Her problem is making use of vestibular sensations to move smoothly, because her nervous system does not process them well. She's loose and floppy, her rhythm and timing are faulty, and her muscles don't have much "oomph." Although her clumsiness is embarrassing, she has to play soccer because the graduate student who takes care of her after school is the neighborhood girls' soccer coach. Besides, playing soccer is what every kid does in her community, and LaVerne desperately wants to fit in. Her babysitter/coach wants LaVerne to improve too, so at home they practice starting *and stopping, running, turning, aiming, and kicking really slow balls. Practice doesn't exactly make perfect, but it certainly helps her balance and movement through space.*

The vestibular system is the unifying system, giving us a sense of where we stand in the world. Movement and gravity stimulate special receptors in the little "vestibule" of the inner ear. The vestibular system takes in messages about balance and movement from the neck, eyes, and body; sends the messages to the central nervous system for processing; and then helps generate muscle tone that allows us to move smoothly and efficiently.

The vestibular system tells us where our heads and bodies are in relation to the surface of the earth. It tells us whether we are upright, upside-down, or at a tilt; whether we are moving or standing still; and whether objects are moving or motionless in relation to our body. It also informs us where we are going and how fast, and if we are in danger or in a relaxing place.

At the playground and on the playing field, Martin, Krystyna, and LaVerne are out of sync. Fortunately, their babysitters sense what kinds of movement experiences help their charges function better.

The children's vestibular systems do not function smoothly, making it difficult for them to modulate, discriminate, coordinate, or organize balance and movement sensations adaptively. Many characteristics of vestibular dysfunction, listed here, affect their active play.

CHARACTERISTICS OF VESTIBULAR DYSFUNCTION

The child who is oversensitive to balance and movement stimuli may:
- ☐ Be intolerant to movement, and therefore avoid it.
- ☐ Overreact, negatively and emotionally, to ordinary movement sensations.
- ☐ Dislike physical activities such as running, biking, sledding, or dancing.
- ☐ Dislike using playground equipment, such as swings, slides, jungle gyms, and merry-go-rounds.
- ☐ Be cautious, slow-moving, and sedentary, hesitating to take risks.
- ☐ Not like the head to be inverted, as when being shampooed over the sink.

- ☐ Be very tense and rigid to avoid changes in head position.
- ☐ Be uncomfortable on stairs, clinging to walls or banisters.
- ☐ Feel seasick when riding in a car, boat, train, airplane, escalator, or elevator.
- ☐ Appear to be willful, manipulative, uncooperative, or a sissy.
- ☐ Demand continual physical support from a trusted peer or adult.
- ☐ Have the additional problem of *gravitational insecurity*, a great fear of falling experienced as primal terror.

The child who is underresponsive to balance and movement sensations may:
- ☐ Crave intense, fast, and spinning movement (rocking/swiveling in chairs, jumping on a trampoline, riding roller coasters, racing around corners) and not get dizzy.
- ☐ Be a thrill seeker and daredevil—enjoying riding over speed bumps and jumping from high places.
- ☐ Need to move constantly (rocking, swaying, spinning, jiggling, shaking her hands or head, fidgeting) in order to function. The child may have trouble staying seated.
- ☐ Enjoy being upside down, hanging over the bedside or swinging while lying on her tummy.
- ☐ Have poor balance, falling easily and often.
- ☐ Bump into objects and furniture, apparently on purpose.

The child with poor discrimination of balance and movement sensations may:
- ☐ Easily lose her balance when climbing stairs, riding a bike, stretching on tiptoes, jumping, or standing on one foot.
- ☐ Move in an uncoordinated, awkward way.
- ☐ Be fidgety.
- ☐ Have low muscle tone and be "loose and floppy."
- ☐ Tire easily during physical activities.
- ☐ Have poor posture and difficulty remaining upright when seated.
- ☐ Be confused about whether she or something else (a train, a tennis ball, or another person) is moving.
- ☐ Have problems with directionality, often moving in the wrong direction.

When a child has vestibular dysfunction, sensory integration therapy is suggested. Parents and teachers can provide **SAFE** activities, too, bearing in mind that the vestibular sense is our most primal and powerful sense and therefore the one we must address with the highest caution. We must never impose vestibular experiences under any circumstances.

That said, all children require vestibular input for proper development. While some are eager for the input, others may feel easily overwhelmed and even fear it. Still others, who register vestibular sensations poorly, may not realize when they have had enough and may depend on your observations to help them learn to feel their own bodies. The following reminders from Rondalyn Whitney, M.O.T., O.T.R., will guide your observations as your child plays:

> **An OT Says . . .**
>
> Melanie Hawke, O.T.R., says, "I usually remind parents that any vestibular activity should be undertaken carefully, and only for short periods of time at first, until the child builds a greater tolerance for the sensation. Parents must keep a close eye on any overreactions by the child (nausea, change in pallor, excessive sweating), which are indications to cease the activity and take it easier next time. Slow and steady wins the race."

- Most vestibular input is during the start/stop phase of the movement.
- Fast start/stops are alerting.
- Slow rocking is soothing and calming.

The wisest approach may be to start slowly, take frequent breaks to check in with the child's response, ask if he wants more or feels all done with the activity, add some proprioception (next chapter), and then, if the child is ready, go back for more.

Activities for the Vestibular Sense

◆ T-Stool

Most kids love sitting on a *T-Stool*, which you can make or buy (see *Recommended Materials*). It compels them to find their balance and stay in the center, which is Mother Nature's intent. While balancing on a one-legged stool may sound improbable, just give it a try. You will be happily surprised at its amazing effect.

DEVELOPMENTAL AGE RANGE 3 and up

WHAT YOU WILL NEED
- Two sections of a wooden two-by-four:
    - For the seat of the stool, a piece about 12 inches long
    - For the leg, a piece that will allow the child to sit with her feet square on the floor and her knees at a right angle (about 10 inches long for a 3-year-old, 11 inches long for a 4- to-5-year-old, 12 inches long for an elementary school age child)
- Two long wood screws

PREPARATION
- Measure twice, cut once!
- Screw the pieces of wood together to form a T shape.

WHAT YOUR CHILD CAN DO WHILE BALANCING ON A T-STOOL
- Listen to a story—with keen attention!
- Play rhythmic and musical games, such as:
    - *Going on a Bear Hunt*, p. 269
    - *Metronome Workout*, p. 245
    - *Scale Songs*, p. 164
    - *Slide Whistle Stretch*, p. 155
- Sing up-and-down and body parts songs (see *Recommended Materials*), such as:
    - "Clap, Clap, Clap Your Hands"
    - "Dry Bones"

- "Eensy Weensy Spider"
- "Father Abraham Had Many Sons (or Kids)"
- "Head and Shoulders, Knees and Toes"
- "Johnny Hammers with One Hammer"
- "Noble Duke of York"
- "Put Your Finger in the Air" (by Woody Guthrie)
- "This Old Man, He Played One"

▪ Sit at a play table to eat snacks and to enjoy tabletop activities, such as:
  - *Magic Tissue Transfers*, p. 43
  - *Shaving Cream Car Wash*, p. 27
▪ Toss a beanbag back and forth with other T-stool sitters.
▪ Play "Categories: Names of . . ."

BENEFITS OF THE ACTIVITY

▪ Sitting on a T-stool improves the child's sense of balance. Balancing may be hard at first. Then, when the child discovers the tripod formula for positioning his body (two feet in front + the stool leg directly underneath), balancing becomes a triumph.

▪ T-stool sitting improves body awareness and postural stability. Sitting tall and upright increases the ability to watch, to listen, to focus and attend.

▪ Figuring out how to prop up a T-stool and to orient his body to sit on it improves motor planning.

▪ Sitting in a circle with other T-stool sitters motivates children to "Stay on the Stool and Be Cool."

COPING TIPS

▪ If your child is "tippy" on the T-stool, have him sit on it with his back against a wall. With the wall to support him, he must balance only from side-to-side. Once he masters that skill, he can work on balancing from front-to-back at the same time.

▪ If your child has a very hard time balancing on a T-stool, offer a therapy ball or "peanut" ball instead (see *Recommended Materials*). Even a beach ball or playground ball is a suitable substitute. Balancing, bouncing, and jiggling on a ball are all ways to benefit the vestibular system.

◆ Matthew's Teeter-Totter

Matthew began preschool when he was three. Developmental delays caused his low muscle tone and uncoordinated movements. Nonetheless, he had true grit, creative ideas, and a fondness for heavy work.

The teacher was glad to let him "help" set up the daily *Obstacle Course* (see p. 239). Hard work, she knew, was an important part of his sensory diet.

One morning, with great effort, Matthew hauled a long board across the grass and positioned it over a railroad timber. One end of the board rested on the grass; the other end was about a foot off the ground. While the teacher hovered nearby, Matthew crouched and crept up the inclined board toward the center. Cautiously, he stood and straddled the fulcrum of his little seesaw. Then he tipped from side to side—tall, straight, balanced, and gloriously pleased with himself.

The other children ran over to investigate his invention. They loved it! Many years later, everybody still agrees that *Matthew's Teeter-Totter* is the special ingredient that makes an obstacle course so much fun.

DEVELOPMENTAL AGE RANGE 3 and up

WHAT YOU WILL NEED
- For the base: railroad timber, or a 4 × 4 that is about 1 yard long
- For the top: 1 × 3 foot board, or 3 × 4 foot sheet of plywood

PREPARATION
- Place the railroad timber on the grass or on a gym mat.
- Place the midpoint of the board over the midpoint of the timber so the two pieces are perpendicular. The "midpoint" does not need to be exact.

WHAT YOUR CHILD CAN DO
- Walk, jump, or crawl from one end to another.
- Sit or stand over the fulcrum and tip from side to side.
- Pull, push, shove, lift, and otherwise carry out a plan to get the board back onto the timber after it slips off.

- Finding the balancing point on the board improves the sense of where the child's own body center is.
- Balancing improves body awareness, motor control, postural stability, force, and self-esteem.
- Because back and forth motion stirs up the language centers of the brain, the child's speech and language output may increase after teetering and tottering for a few minutes.

◆ Tra La Trampoline

Jumping improves rhythm and helps to regulate the nervous system. Always be nearby while your child enjoys this activity.

DEVELOPMENTAL AGE RANGE 3 and up

WHAT YOU WILL NEED (see *Recommended Materials*)
- Mini trampoline (the kind used for exercise)
- Pillows and beanbag cushions
- Chalkboard and chalk, or big paper and marker
- Books of favorite songs, jump-rope chants, and poems
- Optional: Recordings of rhythms, rhymes, songs, and music with a steady beat

PREPARATION
- Place the pillows around the edges of the trampoline and on the floor.
- Together, make a list of songs and rhymes to jump to.
- To add visual cues, draw a representative symbol after each title, such as a star for "Twinkle, Twinkle," or a watermelon for "Down by the Bay."

WHAT YOU CAN DO
Stand near the trampoline and recite or sing the chosen ditty while your child jumps.

- Read the title aloud or point to the picture representing the song or rhyme of his choice.
- Jump to the rhythmic beat and chant or sing the words along with you.

BENEFITS OF THE ACTIVITY
- Vigorous jumping (a form of oscillation) on the resistive trampoline provides strong vestibular input as the child moves up and down.
- Jumping provides deep pressure to the joints and muscles to strengthen proprioception and gross motor skills.
- Thinking up songs and rhymes promotes auditory memory.
- Choosing a title from the chart encourages visual discrimination and early reading skills.
- Jumping to the beat promotes auditory discrimination and ear–body coordination.
- Jumping on a trampoline stimulates the speech and language centers of the brain. Your child may be more articulate than usual when the jumping is done.

COPING TIPS

A child with low tone or gravitational insecurity may be uncomfortable jumping. Other calming experiences are standing on the trampoline and just bending and straightening his knees, or sitting on it and rocking.

◆ Barrel of Fun

A carpeted barrel appeals to almost every child, even the child with a vestibular problem. Working to raise that child's tolerance to vestibular stimulation can be very helpful. Start slowly, monitor the child's tolerance, and increase the movement as the child's tolerance develops. Barbara H. Lindner, M.Ed., O.T.R./L., and Noel S. Levan, M.A., O.T.R./L., contributed their ideas for this "must" piece of equipment.

DEVELOPMENTAL AGE RANGE
- 2 to 4—with close supervision
- 5 and up—when crawling through or resting inside, initially with close supervision, then with general supervision
- All ages—when rolling or tumbling, with constant and close supervision

PREPARATION

See *Instructions* below, or go to *Recommended Materials*.

Before you roll out the barrel, please read this message.

An Occupational Therapist Says . . .

Noel Levan says, "A cautionary note is important regarding potential overstimulation of vestibular channels. Vestibular stimulation has a powerful potential to overwhelm anyone (just think about your last roller-coaster experience), particularly people who evidence great need and/or appreciation of it.

"If your child has the tendency to 'overdo it' out of ignorance or enjoyment of the new experience, and if you—the parent or supervisor—are not well-schooled in how the central nervous system (CNS) responds to cumulative stimulation, you MUST BE AWARE:

OVERSTIMULATION CAN BE HAZARDOUS TO YOUR CHILD.

"Do not think that 'if a little stimulation is good, then more should be better.' Instead, consult with a knowledgeable professional, such as an occupational therapist or other sensory integration-trained expert, to ensure that the child enjoys the barrel in safe, appropriate ways."

(Please see Signs of Distress, p. 17.)

WHAT YOU NEED TO DO

■ Consult with a professional regarding the most beneficial ways to use the barrel.

■ Be present at all times while your child plays with this moving piece of equipment!

■ Be careful that your child's fingers do not get run over by the barrel rim. Always remember to remind children to "keep your hands inside."

WHAT YOUR CHILD CAN DO

■ Rock or roll inside, while you guide the barrel.

■ Crawl through the barrel and a tunnel made by stretching the mouth of fabric tubing over one end of the barrel. (See *Obstacle Course*, p. 239, and *Fabric Tube Tricks*, p. 113.)

■ Straddle and "ride" the barrel. (*Caution:* This is not recommended for "big" children, such as developmentally delayed teenagers or adults, whose weight may collapse the cardboard cylinder.)

■ Stand on a stool and climb feet first into the barrel while you hold it steady and upright. Then, with you still holding on, press his hands against the inside of the barrel to tip it gently onto a *Crash Pad* or mat, and crawl out.

■ Stretch out or curl up inside the barrel, away from distracting sights and sounds, to read, do homework, and have some restful quiet time.

■ Later, stand the barrel up in a corner and load it with toys and other equipment.

BENEFITS OF THE ACTIVITY

- Rocking and rolling provides vestibular, kinesthetic, and proprioceptive input.
- Crawling and climbing improves motor planning, postural control, and bilateral coordination.
- Straddling increases postural muscle strength and improves righting
and equilibrium reactions.
- Resting inside allows the child to take a break and get away from it all.

Instructions for Making a *Barrel of Fun*

WHAT YOU WILL NEED

- Pasteboard packaging barrel, like one used to ship soap powder to a
laundromat or to collect recycled plastic bags at a grocery store
- Saber saw (a portable electric jigsaw)
- Carpet remnants, available from carpet installers
- Flooring adhesive and trowel

PREPARATION

- If the barrel is lined with protective plastic, strip off the plastic to reveal
the clean, brown, heavy-duty cardboard.
- Use the saber saw to remove the barrel's bottom (and the top, if there is
one). To maintain the round barrel shape, be careful to keep the metal
rims intact.
- Cut carpet pieces to fit inside and outside the barrel. If the carpet remnants are large enough, you can use one single piece, or one for the
inside and another for the outside. If the remnants are smaller, a patchwork arrangement will be fine.
- Using a flooring adhesive trowel, smear flooring adhesive on the cardboard and press the carpet piece(s) to the barrel surfaces. Push the cut-
out bottom inside to help keep interior carpet pieces in place until the
adhesive dries. Pay particular attention to ensure that carpeting completely covers the metal rims as well.
- Be sure to allow several days for the adhesive to "cure" to eliminate any
noxious odors. Trim off any fibers that have not been secured. Now
you're ready to rock and roll!

◆ Gentle Roughhousing

Just like kittens and puppies, children need to tumble around with one another. All mammals—including us—must learn how to touch and be touched, to move and be moved, and to "roll with the punches." All children—including dainty little girls—benefit from whole-body horseplay. Safe and appropriate physical fun strengthens our muscles and teaches us what our bodies can and can't do, how to protect ourselves, how to anticipate what's coming at us, how to make smart choices, how to make and keep friends, etcetera, etcetera.

Many modern kids, with or without DSI, do not have enough appropriate physical contact with other people. Excessive television and other screen time, unavailable parents, boring playgrounds, vanishing recess, "no heavy lifting," and the fallacy that physical fun is "not educational" all contribute to this flabby thinking.

We must and can do something to get our children moving again, by playing together, hand to hand, foot to foot, body to body. Here, to jog your memory of the fun you used to have as a kid, are some ideas for **SAFE** and *Gentle Roughhousing*.

DEVELOPMENTAL AGE RANGE Infancy to 6

WHAT YOU WILL NEED
Soft ground surface, such as grass, sand, gym mat, carpet, or *Crash Pad* (p. 90)

Gentle Roughhousing Activities

A. ROWBOAT
Sit facing each other, legs in a "V." Take each other's hands. Press your toes or soles of your feet against your child's. (Your knees may need to bend a little.) Sing, "Row, Row, Row Your Boat" while pushing and pulling the "oars" (each other's hands). "Row" forward and back as far as you can go—until your backs touch the floor, if safe, appropriate—and possible!

B. FISHING BOAT

Lie on your back, knees to your chest, ankles together. Have your child lie on your shins, straddling your ankles, with his knees bent and toes in the air. For a secure "mooring," you can hook your toes outward and anchor them around the back of his thighs. Hold his hands or shoulders. Then rock back and forth, from head to toe, as if riding the waves.

Then, for a nice proprioceptive finish, lie on your back and hug your child in your arms. Use your legs to power a nice, wide rock, simultaneously giving "squeezy hugs."

C. AIRPLANE

Lie on your back, knees bent, toes pointing outward. Take your child's hands in yours, place your feet on his lower abdomen, and lift him up for a smooth "takeoff." When he is suspended over your head, encourage him to straighten his legs horizontally.

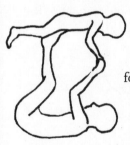

How high can the little airplane fly? It all depends on your child's delight, comfort, and gravitational security. Keep your knees bent and place your hands under his chest, if he feels more secure flying low. Stiffen your arms and legs, if he's ready to soar.

> ## A Mother Says . . .
>
> Donna Becker says, "My four-year-old calls it 'parachutes' when he does his crash landing on my body from the airplane position. Crash landings are good for the child who is gravitationally insecure. Falling on Mommy is always less scary, and so we practice falling this way a lot."

D. HORSEY

Kneel and have the child come behind you and put his arms around your neck. Hold his hands with one hand to help him orient his body *and* to protect yourself from being strangled. Gradually lower your other hand to the ground, until your back is horizontal. Have your child straddle your back and sit up in the "saddle." He can place his hands on your shoulders or hold on to "reins" (the ends of a long scarf, looped under your armpits and across your chest). Hee haw! Take your cowboy for a ride.

E. THIS IS THE WAY THE LADY RIDES

Take your child on your lap. Holding his waist, take him for three little rides while chanting or singing "This Is the Way the Lady Rides," to the tune of "Here We Go Round the Mulberry Bush."

■ Bounce your child lightly on your knees while quietly singing the first verse:

> *This is the way the lady rides, the lady rides, the lady rides,*
> *This is the way the lady rides, so early in the morning.*

■ Bounce more vigorously, up and down, while singing Verse 2, somewhat louder:

> *This is the way the gentleman rides . . .*

■ Alternately raise and lower your knees so that your child tips rather dramatically from right to left. Belt out verse 3, loudly and cheerfully:

> *This is the way the cowboy rides . . .*

F. FOX AND GINGERBREAD MAN

Remember the Gingerbread Man, who is almost impossible to catch? "Run, run, as fast as you can! You can't catch me; I'm the Gingerbread Man!" he chants. Ah, but the crafty Fox outwits that saucy cookie, saying, "Get on my back, and I shall carry you to safety."

Kneel on a soft surface (grass, sand, carpet, or gym mat) and have your child climb aboard your back, as in the *Horsey* activity above. Creep forward a bit. Then tip the child gently off your back. Pretend to take a big bite. "Yum! You are so delicious! I love you SO much!" Hug each other tightly.

G. WHEELBARROW WALK

This one is great for proprioception, too. Have your child lie tummy-down, with her palms resting on the ground near her shoulders. If your child is little (age 3 or 4), place your hands under her thighs, just above her knees, and lift her legs—the "wheelbarrow handles." Kneel or crouch to lower the wheelbarrow handles and keep her body almost horizontal.

Increase the challenge for a kindergartener or older child by inching your hands closer to her ankles. As her muscle sense matures, she will be able to support more of her own weight.

Hold her securely as she "walks" on her hands. To stretch her imagination, ask her what is in her wheelbarrow. Ask her where she's going—"over to the garden" or "in a circle"—to help her feel in charge. After resting, she may enjoy holding up the wheelbarrow handles of a not-too-heavy friend or sibling.

H. PIGGY-BACK RIDE

To "upload" your child for a piggyback ride, one approach is to kneel as for *Horsey* and then stand up. Another way is to stand with your back toward your child, and he can reach for you from a step, couch, ledge, or van.

Whee, whee, whee, whee! All the way home!

(Do you know that pigs have nothing to do with "piggyback"? The word is a distortion of "pick-a-back," which may originally have been "pick me up and carry me on your back.")

I. DOUBLE DANCER

Stand facing your child. Take his hands (or, if he needs more support, let him hug you). Have him place his feet on top of yours. Take a rhythmic sashay around the room, while you count, sing, hum, recite a poem, or listen to music. Vary your:

- Tempos: slow (lento), medium (andante), and fast (presto).
- Directions: forward, backward, sideways, and diagonally.
- Rhythms:
  - ONE-TWO, ONE-TWO (i.e., LEFT-RIGHT, LEFT-RIGHT) for the rhythm of a two-step

- ONE-two-three, ONE-two-three (i.e., LEFT-right-left, RIGHT-left-right) for a waltz
- ONE-two-three-four, ONE-two-three-four (i.e., LEFT-right-left-right, LEFT-right-left-right) for a fox-trot

J. UPSY-DAISY COTTONTAIL

Stand facing your child. Holding hands, have him "walk" up your legs. When his feet reach your waist, have him tip his head way back and flip his feet and "tail" through your arms and over his head. Loosen your grip on his hands so that they can rotate in yours, as he turns up and over. Deposit him safely on the ground or *Crash Pad*.

A Mother Says . . .

Donna says, "Isn't it amazing how old-fashioned experiences are so loaded with sensory input? Piggyback rides, for instance, are great for vestibular input and also for proprioceptive and tactile input. I think the proprioceptive input of my son holding on to me, all by himself, really helped him get over his gravitational insecurity and improve his postural stability. I would put one hand under his bottom for a just-in-case situation, but mostly I made him do all the work, and then I had my hands free. I would let him slide down my back, and slowly he got used to the sensation of controlled falling, while receiving lots of proprioceptive and touch input by pressing against my body. We even did spinning like this. Of course, I held him, then!"

BENEFITS OF THESE ACTIVITIES:

- Changing head position, defying gravity, maintaining balance, rocking rhythmically, moving in different directions, and flexing and extending muscles are some of the moves that provide input to the vestibular system.
- Deep touch pressure and joint pressure organize and calm the tactile and proprioceptive systems.
- Assuming and holding different positions strengthen body awareness, muscular control, and postural security.
- Playful roughhousing with a trusted adult or buddy builds trust, self-esteem, emotional security, social skills, and a foundation for all kinds of learning.

COPING TIPS

As in any activity, when your child says "Stop" or "I don't like this" do not continue. These energetic activities may overload a child, so please be careful.

◆ The Laundromat Game

In this game, getting clean is the make-believe part; providing intense sensory input is for real. Kimberly Geary, M.S., O.T.R., almost guarantees that this activity will help regulate your child. If he is a sensory-seeker, wanting to touch, push, kick, and whirl through space, this game is **SAFE**. It begins by stimulating the child's senses through movement and tactile input, and then moves on to calming and soothing his body through deep pressure, resistive stretching, and long, sustained proprioceptive input.

DEVELOPMENTAL AGE RANGE 3 and up

WHAT YOU WILL NEED
- "Washing machine"—made from 3 yards of stretchy swimsuit material (from a fabric store), or a Body Sox™ (see *Recommended Materials*)
- "Detergent"—plastic balls used in ball pits, available from catalogs
- "Paper" to wrap "laundry bundles"—a bed sheet
- Gym mat or carpeted/padded floor
- Optional: "Clothesline"—a chinning or trapeze bar from the Rainy Day Indoor Playground™ (see *Recommended Materials*)
- Optional: Therapy ball

PREPARATION
If sewing is easy for you, hem the ends of the material and sew up the sides, like a pillowcase. If sewing is not easy, please buy a Body Sox.

WHAT TO DO
- Ask your child, "Are you clean or dirty laundry today?" Once he knows how this game goes, he'll probably answer, "Dirty!"
- Say, "Okay, Dirty Laundry, load yourself into the washing machine." Encourage him to wriggle his body into the material without your help.
- Say, "Here's some detergent." Pour the plastic balls on top of the child.
- With one hand, close the material lightly at the top.
- Ask, "Do you want a slow or fast washing speed?" Honoring the child's request, toss him around and rock him back and forth. If possible, lift

him slightly off the floor to intensify the sensations. You may need to enlist the help of another adult to swing and rock the "washing machine."

- After a few minutes of washing, say, "Now it's time to rinse." If the child can tolerate rotary movement, spin him around.
- Say, "Now it's time to wring you dry." Have the child stretch out his arms and legs inside the material. With your free hand, gently and firmly apply deep pressure by massaging his limbs until he is "damp dry." You can also use a large ball to roll over him. Take lots of time with this "drying" step to calm, relax, and soothe your child after his invigorating "wash."
- Say, "You're all clean, now! You can get out." The child will wriggle out, calm, collected, and "clean"!
- Now have the child lie down on the sheet at one edge. Roll up the "clean laundry" in the "paper" and pat it dry. The tightly rolled laundry load also provides calming, deep pressure. (Just remember not to restrict the child if he wants out.)
- If you have a bar in a doorway, say, "Now you need to hang on the clothesline to dry completely." Encourage the child to hang for as long as possible.

VARIATIONS

See *Hot Dog Roll* p. 51; *Fabric Tube Tricks* p. 113; and *Become a Butterfly* p. 112.

BENEFITS OF THE ACTIVITY

- Wriggling into the washing machine helps body awareness, motor planning, and kinesthesia.
- Getting washed, rinsed, and wrung out provides vestibular input.
- The stretchy, resistive material and the big ball provide deep pressure and proprioceptive input to skin and muscle receptors. Very calming!
- Hanging from a bar increases proprioception, strength, and muscle extension.

COPING TIPS

- Always respect your child's fears and wishes. Do not force this activity on a child who is reluctant to partake in it in any way.
- If your child has vestibular sensitivities, lift, swing, or move him only as little or as much as he requests.

- If your child does not like being in an enclosed sack—and still wants to play the game, let him sit in a large plastic laundry tub or beach bucket.
- Add or subtract balls, based on his tolerance.

◆ Swing, Bat, and Pitch

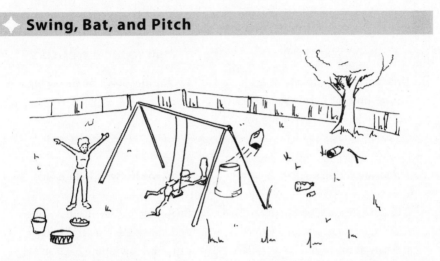

Swinging is usually pleasurable, as the forward and backward motion nourishes the vestibular system. Slow swinging promotes calming, and faster swinging increases alertness. Add batting and pitching to make this complex activity a tripleheader!

DEVELOPMENTAL AGE RANGE 4 and up. Whatever the child's age, she will enjoy this game most if she has good extension (the ability to stretch out and hold up arms, legs, and head against the pull of gravity), as well as the ability to stabilize her eye movements while she moves in the swing.

WHAT YOU WILL NEED
- Playground or backyard swing, set low to the ground
- Plastic trash can
- For batting:
  - Large, lightweight, plastic baseball bat, or a sturdy cardboard cylinder
  - Plastic water jugs—some empty, some filled halfway with sand
- For pitching:
  - Basketful of "baseballs"—beanbags, balls, squeeze toys, sponges
  - To add an auditory component, which will aid the child with poor vision *and* make the game even more interesting:
    - Bucket of water

- A drum
- Pennies, bottle caps, spoons, or aluminum pans to jingle in the trash can

How to Play *Swing, Bat, and Pitch*

WHAT YOU CAN DO	WHAT YOUR CHILD CAN DO
1. Turn a trash can upside down just beyond your child's reach as she swings. Put a plastic jug on the can.	1. Lie tummy-down on the swing.
2. Hand your child the bat.	2. Hold the bat with both hands.
3. Call out "Nice try!" or "Homer!" or other encouraging words while she bats at the jug.	3. Swing the bat from side to side and knock the jug off the trash can, while swinging back and forth.
4. Mark where the jug lands, and continue to put other jugs on the trash can for more whacks "into the bleachers" and "out of the park!"	4. Try to bat harder and send the next jugs farther. Continue batting practice until ready to switch to pitching.
5. Turn the trash can upright. Add auditory options: • several inches of water in the trash can, or a bucket of water beside it • a drum beside the trash can • pennies, bottle caps, spoons, or pans in the trash can	5. Toss the bat aside. Now sit on the swing and get ready to pitch.

WHAT YOU CAN DO	WHAT YOUR CHILD CAN DO
6. Hold out a "baseball," keeping your arm steady to make the object easier to grab. If your child is right-handed, stand on her left side, and vice versa, so she must cross the midline to take the ball.	6. Cross the midline to reach for the "baseball." Grab it and pitch it to make a pleasantly noisy splash in the water, thump on the drum, or rattle in the pennies.
7. Move the trash can and other targets closer or farther away to make the pitching easier or harder.	7. Count how many successful pitches she makes.

VARIATIONS

Batter for Batter

For a taste sensation, OT Aubrey Lande suggests a different and delectable target—a bowl of cake batter. Next time you prepare a cake with your child, make more batter than necessary. (Do not use raw eggs, which may cause food-borne illness. A banana or quarter cup of tofu can substitute nicely for each egg.) Pour what you need into the baking pan and leave the rest in the bowl. Then, while the cake bakes, the child can get on the swing and scoop batter with her finger. Yum! What could taste better than *Batter for Batter*?

Swing and Kick

Have the child sit on the swing. Line up cans, plastic jugs, *Bottle Babies* (p. 94), and sand buckets in front of the swing for the child to kick.

Earthquake

For children who are not ready to get on the swing, OT Rondalyn Whitney suggests a preparatory activity. Use fabric to make a hammock. With another adult, swing the child fast, at first, and then decrease the motion to slow rocking. The deep pressure helps many children tolerate this activity as a precursor to using the swings.

BENEFITS OF THE ACTIVITY

- Linear (to and fro) movement is usually calming input for the vestibular system.
- Lying tummy-down on the swing and holding up her head against the pull of gravity improves extension and strengthens muscle tone, which is an important function of the vestibular system.

- Holding the bat with both hands improves bilateral coordination.
- Swinging the bat from side to side and reaching out to grab the object to throw strengthen the ability to cross the midline.
- Grading her movements (flexing and extending muscles as needed) to swing the bat and applying force to hit the jug improve proprioception.
- Keeping an eye on fixed objects—the jug to hit and the object to grab—while moving strengthens the visual-motor skill of focusing.

COPING TIPS

- If your child becomes frustrated or dizzy, the reason may be that she lacks adequate extensor tone to resist gravity, or she may have difficulty stabilizing her eye movements while her body moves. Consult with an SI-trained optometrist or therapist about how to adapt this activity for your child. In the meantime, offer a less complex activity, such as *My Backyard's Clean* p. 102 or *Beanbag Jai Alai* p. 136.
- If your child resists passive movement, don't push her in the swing! Let your child propel herself. Then she will feel safer and in control.
- Don't let beanbags drop into the bucket of water. They'll get soaked and ruined.
- If your child craves swinging but you can't get to a playground, set up a Rainy Day Indoor Playground in a doorway in your home. (Save the "bat and pitch" parts of this activity for another day when you can go outside and have more space.)

◆ Voyage to Mars

Is the solar system your child's passion of the moment? Then use it as the scaffold for an out-of-this-world activity, suggests Nancy C. Scheiner, an OT specializing in neurodevelopmental treatment and sensory integration.

DEVELOPMENTAL AGE RANGE 4 to 8

WHAT YOU WILL NEED

- Swing (or suspended platform swing, if you have one)
- *Crash Pad* (see p. 90)
- Optional: Tarpaulin on the ground to protect the *Crash Pad* cover, if you're enjoying the activity outdoors
- Several large beach balls (or therapy balls) of different sizes

PREPARATION

■ Place the *Crash Pad* ("Mars") in front of the swing (the "rocket ship").
■ Together, discuss which ball is the Moon, which is Pluto, and so on.

How to Play *Voyage to Mars*

WHAT YOU CAN DO	WHAT YOUR CHILD CAN DO
1. Push or guide the swing in rotary or linear movement, with the child's permission. Make sure the child is tolerating this passive vestibular stimulation. If not, stop at once.	1. Pretend to be an astronaut taking a voyage into space. Pretend that the swing is the "rocket ship," and get "on board."
2. Together, count down to blastoff.	2. Count down to blastoff with you, while swinging back and forth or in circles: "Ten! Nine! . . . One! Blast-off!"
3. Hold the swing to prevent it from bonking the astronaut on the head as he makes a safe crash landing on Mars.	3. Press an imaginary "eject" button and vault onto Mars.
4. Roll a large ball toward Mars. Say, "Here is the Moon. Get ready to visit the Moon."	4. Depart from lumpy Mars to go to the "Moon." Sit and bounce on the Moon, or lie prone (tummy-down) or supine (tummy-up) over the ball.

WHAT YOU CAN DO	WHAT YOUR CHILD CAN DO
5. Say, "Bounce high on the Moon," to encourage a good sensory workout.	5. Sit and bounce vigorously on the Moon ball.
6. Say, "It's time to return to your ship," to help the child cool off and calm down.	6. Return to the rocket ship for a leisurely voyage back to Earth.
7. Say, "Prepare for reentry," and help slow the swing to a stop. "Come back to Earth for a big hug." Open your arms.	7. Get off the rocket and go to (Mother) Earth for a warm welcome home.

BENEFITS OF THE ACTIVITY

- Linear or rotary movement stimulates the vestibular system.
- Throwing himself on the *Crash Pad* provides vestibular and proprioceptive feedback.
- Getting from rocket ship to Mars to Moon improves motor planning, gross motor skills, kinesthesia, and visual-spatial skills.
- Bouncing on ball "planets" improves balancing.
- Discussing planets, the solar system, rocketry, and so on nourishes the child's interest and strengthens his vocabulary and language skills.
- Listening to and following directions improves attention and auditory skills.

COPING TIP

As in all vestibular activities, it is important to monitor the child's tolerance to movement. Stop if he shows any signs of overstimulation (listed on p. 17).

◆ Old Lady Sally

Whoever that old Sally is, she certainly likes to move! Here is a musical game from the classic repertoire of children's activity songs.

DEVELOPMENTAL AGE RANGE 3 to 6

PREPARATION

Clear an open space, or go outside.

WHAT YOU CAN DO:

- Say, "Here's a song about an old lady named Sally who loves to move in lots of different ways. She also likes to STOP. It's so much fun!"
- Sing the "Old Lady Sally" song, more or less to the tune of "Here We Go Round the Mulberry Bush." If you are reluctant to sing, you can chant. If you don't have a keyboard, xylophone, guitar, or autoharp, you can clap to mark the beat.
- Jumpity-jump and marchity-march along with the children to double the fun.
- After a few verses, ask, "What's your idea for another way to move?"
  - If the child can't tell you her idea, say, "Show me."
  - If she can tell you (e.g., "Like a cat!") but has difficulty showing you, help her orient her body for creeping like a cat, and get her started.
  - If she is stuck, to get her into the game, say, "I see you blinking (shaking your head, wriggling your fingers). Is that your idea? Let's do it!"

Old Lady Sally

Strum this note: G	B	D	G
Sing these words: Old Lady	Sally likes to	jumpity-	jump,
Strum this note: A	D	B	G
Sing these words: Jumpity-	jump,	jumpity-	jump.
Strum this note: G	B	D	G
Sing these words: Old Lady	Sally likes to	jumpity-	jump, and
Strum this note: A	B	G	
Sing these words: Old Lady	Sally likes to	STOP!	*(Rest.)*

Verse 2: Old Lady Sally likes to stretchity-strech . . . *(Reach wide and tall while standing or moving around.)*

Verse 3: Old Lady Sally likes to hoppity-hop . . . *(Hop on one foot and then on the other.)*

Verse 4: Old Lady Sally likes to rollity-roll . . . *(Lie down and roll like a hotdog across the floor, or down a grassy hill.)*

Next Verses: Tippity-toe, marchity-march, leapity-leap, crawlity-crawl, clappity-clap, shruggity-shrug, crunchity-crunch ... *(Tiptoe, march, leap, crawl, clap, shrug, make chewing motions, etc.)*

Last Verse: Old Lady Sally likes to sleepity-sleep ... *(Curl up and "sleep.")*

WHAT YOUR CHILD CAN DO

- All of the above!
- Suggest more ideas for moving around.

BENEFITS OF THE ACTIVITY

- Changing head position, moving rhythmically to a beat, flexing and extending, shifting balance, and using both sides of the body are all motions that help develop a good vestibular system.
- Practicing different forms of locomotion improves motor planning, gross motor skills, and kinesthesia.
- Moving through space promotes visual-spatial perception.
- Using both sides of the body together improves bilateral coordination.
- Following directions improves listening, body awareness, and attention.
- Stopping an action on command improves impulse control.
- Participating in a group activity strengthens social interactions.

◆ Sally Go Round the Sun

Here comes that old Sally, again! She must need as much vestibular activity as most children do. Some kids turn in circles just for the fun of getting dizzy. Others spin as a form of self-therapy. Still others prefer not to turn at all—and in this activity, they can simply walk in a linear path. If they love to fall down on purpose, they can do that, too.

DEVELOPMENTAL AGE RANGE 3 and up

WHAT YOU WILL NEED

- Crepe paper streamers, ribbons, scarves, or exercise bands (see *Recommended Materials*)
- "Chimney pots"—small traffic cones or large paper cups
- Xylophone (optional)

PREPARATION

Give every child a streamer, and spread "chimney pots" around the floor.

WHAT YOU CAN DO

Chant, or play the xylophone, while singing:

Sally Go Round the Sun

Play this note:	C	C	C	C	E	E	E	E
Sing these words:	Sally go	round the	sun		Sally go	round the	moon	
Play this note:	G	G	G E	C	E	D	C	High C
Sing these words:	Sally go	round the	chim-ney	pots,	Every	after-	noon.	BOOM!

WHAT YOUR CHILD CAN DO

■ Move around the room in big circles or spin in small circles, twirling the streamer in circles overhead, from side to side, and up and down, while trying to avoid bonking into chimney pots.

■ Collapse in a heap on the word "BOOM!"

BENEFITS OF THE ACTIVITY

■ Turning in circles provides vestibular input.

■ Moving along with the song improves auditory perception and rhythm, both of which foster receptive language development and the rhythm of writing.

■ Moving among the chimney pots improves balance, force, and kinesthesia.

- Avoiding the chimney pots involves the visual skills of focusing, depth perception, and figure-ground.
- Swishing the streamer improves the ability to cross the midline.
- Falling down on purpose provides a satisfactory proprioceptive jolt.

COPING TIPS

The child who is uncomfortable moving in circles can enjoy this activity by walking in straight lines.

◆ Looby Loo

In the olden days, many families took baths in the "loo," all on a Saturday night. (*Loo* is a mispronunciation of *l'eau,* French for "the water.") Without indoor plumbing, hauling and heating water to fill the big portable tub was an ordeal, so some families filled their tub once and everybody took turns. By the time the youngest child got a turn, the water was cold.

This song describes how the child would quickly thrust arms and legs in, yank them out, and shake off the water drops:

Chorus   Here we go looby-loo, Here we go looby-light,
Here we go looby-loo, all on a Saturday night.

Verses   1 You put your right hand in, you take your right hand out,
You give your hand a shake, shake, shake, and turn yourself about.
2 You put your left hand in . . .
3 . . . right leg . . .   4 . . . left leg . . .
5 . . . right hip . . .   6 . . . left hip . . .
7 . . . bottom . . .   8 . . . belly button . . .
9 . . . head . . .   10 . . . whole self . . .

DEVELOPMENTAL AGE RANGE $2\frac{1}{2}$ to 7

WHAT YOU WILL NEED
About 20 feet of rope

PREPARATION

- Lay the rope on the ground in a big circle to represent the bathtub, or "loo."
- Say, "Let's pretend that the rope is the bathtub, and inside the tub is very, very cold water!"

WHAT YOUR CHILDREN CAN DO

- Stand in a circle outside the "bathtub" and pretend to shiver.
- Join hands and circle right, while singing the chorus.
- Stand still, drop hands, and stick their right hands far into the circle, maybe bending forward to touch the cold "water" (the ground).
- Snatch their right hands up, out, overhead, and behind; give their hands a "shake, shake, shake"; and pivot in a circle.
- Join hands for the chorus, this time circling left.
- Proceed through some or all of the verses of the song until "all clean!"

BENEFITS OF THE ACTIVITY

- Circling with the group and pivoting in place are rotary movements that provide input to the vestibular system.
- Changing the position of the head while bending forward and backward also provides vestibular input.
- Putting individual body parts into the "water" improves proprioception, body awareness, and motor planning.
- Stretching body parts into and out of the water strengthens force, kinesthesia, and crossing the midline.
- Responding to sung directions improves auditory/language skills.
- Alternately circling right and left strengthens the visual-spatial processing skill of directionality.
- Participating in any circle game builds social skills.

COPING TIPS

Some children with tactile defensiveness will resist holding another person's hand. That's all right. They may be able to tolerate having you or someone else hold their sleeve or shirt hem. The important thing is for everybody to travel in the same direction and try to maintain the shape of the circle.

4

~~~~~~~~

Body Position
(The Proprioceptive Sense)

Paula, 7, is an uncoordinated little girl. She has a jerky way of moving, struggles to get her arms into sleeves and fingers into gloves, and needs to watch her feet when she goes up and down stairs. Whenever and wherever possible, Paula seeks deep pressure on her body. When she goes through a doorway, she bumps her shoulders against the doorjambs, ricocheting from side to side. When she goes down a hallway, she bangs her heels on the floor, or presses her back against the wall and drags her body along.

Having observed her "self-therapy," her parents made several simple accommodations at home. In the backyard, they installed sturdy play equipment. In the basement, they rigged up a chinning bar and laid out mattresses on the floor so that Paula can hang and jump. She uses the equipment regularly, because the additional proprioceptive input makes her feel more "together."

Proprioception refers to sensory information telling us about the position, force, direction, and movement of our own body parts. It helps integrate tactile and vestibular sensations. Receptors for the proprioceptive sense are in the muscles, joints, ligaments, tendons, and connective tissue.

Proprioception, the "position sense," sends messages about whether the muscles are stretching or contracting, and how the joints are bending and straightening. Even when we are motionless, gravity stimulates the receptors to create proprioceptive messages without our being consciously aware of them.

The functions of proprioception are to increase body awareness and to contribute to motor control and motor planning. Proprioception helps us with body expression, the ability to move our body parts efficiently and economically. It lets us walk smoothly, run quickly, climb stairs, carry a suitcase, sit, stand, stretch, and lie down. It gives us emotional security, for when we can trust our bodies, we feel safe and secure.

Paula is frequently out of sync because poor proprioception affects the way she positions and moves her body. Fortunately, her parents help her get some of the extra input to address the characteristics listed below.

CHARACTERISTICS OF PROPRIOCEPTIVE DYSFUNCTION

The child with inefficient integration of sensations coming from his muscles and joints may:

☐ Have problems with touch, or with balance and movement as well.

☐ Have a poor sense of body awareness.

☐ Be stiff, uncoordinated, and clumsy, falling and tripping frequently.

☐ Lean, bump, or crash against objects and people, and invade others' body space.

☐ Have difficulty carrying out unfamiliar and complex motions, such as putting on ice skates for the first time.

☐ Be unable to do ordinary, familiar things without looking, such as getting dressed.

☐ Manipulate hair clips, lamp switches, and classroom tools so hard that they break.

☐ Pull and twist clothing, stretch his tee shirt down, or chew sleeves or collars.

☐ Have difficulty ascending and descending stairs.

☐ Slap feet when walking, sit on his feet, stretch his limbs, poke his cheeks, pull on his fingers, and crack his knuckles (for additional feedback).

Proprioception is the great organizer of all sensations. A powerful form of input that can counter hypersensitivity in other systems, proprioception helps to increase alertness and decrease anxiety. It is the safest of all input, so, when in doubt, choose "prope"! The following **SAFE** activities may help get you started.

Activities for the Proprioceptive Sense

◆ Crash Pad

Does your child do self-therapy by bumping and crashing into people, furniture, walls, and doorjambs? If the answer is "yes," the child will greatly enjoy a *Crash Pad*. If the answer is "no," you may need to lead the child to it at first, and share the luxurious experience together.

DEVELOPMENTAL AGE RANGE 2 and up

WHAT YOU WILL NEED

- *Crash Pad* (see *Instructions* below), large dog bed, mattress, and down comforter, or a "Cloud Nine" (see *Recommended Materials*)
- Optional: carpeted scooter (see *Recommended Materials*)

PREPARATION

Clear some space in the living room, bedroom, or recreation room, and plop the *Crash Pad* on the floor.

WHAT YOUR CHILD CAN DO

- Leap from a couch or bed onto the *Crash Pad*.
- Sprawl and roll on it.
- Nap on it.
- Lie tummy-down on a carpeted scooter and fall off onto the *Crash Pad*.
- Use it in tandem with other **SAFE** activities, including:
  - *Fabric Tube Tricks* p. 113
  - *Gentle Roughhousing* p. 70
  - *Jack and Jill* p. 169
  - *Mrs. Midnight* p. 247
  - *Voyage to Mars* p. 80

BENEFITS OF THE ACTIVITY

- The jolt of landing on a *Crash Pad* provides deep pressure to muscles and joints, which is strong proprioceptive input.
- Leaping toward the *Crash Pad* and rolling around on it provide vestibular input.
- Rubbing against the fabric provides tactile input.

Instructions for Making a *Crash Pad*

WHAT YOU WILL NEED
- Four flat sheets
- Foam scraps from a reupholster or a surplus store, or old bed pillows
- For closure—zipper, Velcro, or button thread

PREPARATION
- To make the liner
  - Sew two sheets together on three sides, like a large cloth envelope.
  - Fill the liner with foam scraps or pillows.
  - Sew the fourth sides of the sheets together.
- To make the cover
  - Sew the other two sheets together on three sides.
  - If you can, sew in a zipper or Velcro strips for easy removal and washing.
- Stuff the foam-filled liner into the cover.
- If you have not installed a zipper, baste the fourth seam with strong thread. When the cover needs a wash, these big stitches are relatively easy to remove.

> ### A Mother Says . . .
>
> Angela Gilbert in San Antonio, Texas, says, "I filled an old duvet cover halfway with packing peanuts, tied it in a knot, and my 18-month-old son Gary *loves* it. It makes noise and gives a lot when he moves in it, plus it's *big*."

VARIATIONS
- Can't sew? At a department or furniture store, buy already-made duvets (covers for down comforters) or covers for futons (fold-up couches). Even better, call customer service at the store, and say that your child has special needs. Ask if they have floor samples of covers that they could give you for free.
- For a temporary *Crash Pad,* throw all the couch cushions, throw pillows, and down comforters on the floor. Or make a huge leaf pile in the back-yard.

◆ Inner Tube Sport

"Within every child," Dr. Ayres writes, "is a great inner drive to develop sensory integration." Give a child an inner tube and watch that inner drive get in gear! Many of these ideas come from Barb McCrory and Kimberly Geary, OTs in Maryland; from teachers and parents across the country; and, naturally, from the children.

DEVELOPMENTAL AGE RANGE 2 and up

WHAT YOU WILL NEED
- Used tractor/truck inner tube (look up "Tires" in the *Yellow Pages* to find free, used tubes, or to order new ones)
- To cover the valve, so it can't poke and scratch:
  - Rectangle of foam (about 10 × 8 × 29 inches)
  - Duct tape
- To lash inner tubes together:
  - 2-inch wide Velcro—about 3 yards for two tubes, and 6 yards for three tubes
  - Or about 6 to 8 yards of soft nylon rope
- To suspend the tube from a tree branch: More rope
- To provide a soft tumbling surface: A gym mat, thick carpet, or grass

PREPARATION
- Together, hose down and scrub the inner tube clean. (Remember, most children think that hard work is FUN.)
- At the gas station, fill the tube with air. You may need to ask the attendant for new needle valves and valve caps to prevent the air from escaping.
- Press foam over the valve and wrap duct tape over the foam.
- Place the tube on the grass or on a gym mat.
- If you wish to make a rubber barrel, cut the Velcro or rope into thirds and lash the tubes together in three different places.

Ways to Play with One Inner Tube

WHAT YOU CAN DO	WHAT YOUR CHILD CAN DO
Be there.	Climb in and out of the "doughnut hole."
	With feet together, inside or outside, sit on the edge and bounce.
	Sit with one foot in and one foot out, and scoot around the circle, bumping along on her bottom.
	Drape over it in different positions.
Offer your hand or finger for support.	Stand and walk on the rim.
Put the tube in a backyard pool.	Float.
Tie a long, strong rope around the tube and suspend it from a branch.	Swing.
Take the tube to a snowy hill.	Go "snow tubing."

Ways to Play with Two or Three Inner Tubes

WHAT YOU CAN DO	WHAT YOUR CHILD CAN DO
Spread the tubes out on the grass, or intersperse them in an *Obstacle Course* (p. 239).	Step in and out of the tubes.
Lash two or three tubes together with Velcro or rope to make a rubber barrel. Hold on to it while your child plays. (See *Barrel of Fun*, p. 67.)	Rock and roll, crawl through, and rest inside.

WHAT YOU CAN DO	WHAT YOUR CHILD CAN DO
Have the child lie on a mat. Roll the barrel toward her side and across her back (never over her head).	Lying on a mat, enjoy the barrel's deep pressure as it rolls over her back.

BENEFITS OF THE ACTIVITY

- Coordinating body parts to get into different positions promotes body awareness, motor planning, problem-solving skills, and self-esteem.
- Pressing body parts against the resistive rubber tube provides deep touch pressure and joint pressure.
- Standing and walking on the rim strengthens balance, eye-foot coordination, and kinesthesia.
- Bouncing and swinging on an inner tube provides vestibular input.
- Rocking and rolling in the tube barrel provides more vestibular input.

◆ Bottle Babies

These bottles prove how easily and inexpensively you can provide the most enjoyable, durable, and memorable toys.

DEVELOPMENTAL AGE RANGE 3 and up

WHAT YOU WILL NEED

- Several large (one liter), empty, soft-drink bottles, with labels removed
- For colorful bottles:
  - Liquid "non-stain" tempera paint
  - Food coloring

For visually interesting bottles:
- Mineral oil
- Sparkles and/or sequins
- Buttons, small shells, tiny pebbles

PREPARATION

- Fill bottles one-half or two-thirds full with water. Do not fill completely.
- Make some of the bottles colorful ones, by adding either a blob of "non-stain" tempera paint or several drops of food coloring.
- Make some of the bottles visually interesting by adding a few table-spoons of mineral oil, sequins, buttons, or other small objects.
- Screw caps on tightly.

WHAT YOUR CHILD CAN DO WITH BOTTLE BABIES

- Carry in hands.
- Cradle and rock, like a baby doll, in arms.
- Tip back and forth to watch the contents shift.
- Shake.
- Buy, sell, or trade at a pretend market.
- Stuff into jacket, like heavy cargo.
- Load into buckets and wagons.
- Push with a stick.
- Kick while running across the grass.
- Kick while swinging back and forth.
- Bury in sand.

BENEFITS OF THE ACTIVITY

- Proprioception improves as the child lifts, carries, kicks, and shoves the heavily weighted bottles.
- Body awareness improves as the child moves and exerts herself.
- Bilateral coordination improves when the child uses both hands to tip a bottle back and forth.
- Visual skills of focusing and tracking improve when she watches blobs of mineral oil or tiny objects swish around.
- Muscle control and grading of movement improve as she manipulates the bottles.
- Representational thinking improves as the child pretends that bottles are cargo, babies, pirate's treasures, dinosaur bones, magic potions, and so on.
- Communication and social skills improve when the child shares the bottles and plays games with others.

- Make enough bottles for everybody. (Sharing can be SO HARD—and making a few extra Bottle Babies is SO EASY.)
- Keep the bottles outdoors. While they are designed to last forever and will probably be difficult for little fingers to open but may crack after heavy use.

◆ Fun With a Rope

An ordinary object like a rope can be the best toy. Rondalyn V. Whitney, M.O.T., O.T.R., and Annemarie Kammann, P.T., contributed to the following list of ideas.

DEVELOPMENTAL AGE RANGE All ages

WHAT YOU WILL NEED

- About 8 yards of rope
- Optional: Drum or other rhythm instrument; bubbles; "tummy" scooter board

Ways to Have Fun with a Rope

ACTIVITY	WHAT YOU CAN DO	WHAT YOUR CHILD CAN DO
Pull	Hold tightly to your end and try to stand in one spot.	Pull himself toward you, hand over hand, while on his tummy or, if you have one, on a scooter board.
	Make knots for easier gripping. Try (gently) to tug the rope and child toward you.	Grab a knot and play tug-of-war.
	Help tie the rope, if necessary.	Tie it to a loaded wagon and pull.
	Park your car on top of the rope.	Pull the rope out.

ACTIVITY	WHAT YOU CAN DO	WHAT YOUR CHILD CAN DO
Walk	Lay it out in a linear, serpentine, circular, or figure 8 "path."	Straddle it (one foot on either side) and walk forward and backward.
	Drape a second rope over the first rope at several points.	Step over the intersections.
	Lay it out in a straight line or more complex path.	Walk on it sideways, toward the right and then the left. Or "tightrope walk," heel to toe, forward and backward. Wear shoes and socks, or go barefoot.
	Clap hands or beat the drum, keeping a steady beat.	Walk or march on the rope in time to the rhythmic beat.
	Blow bubbles toward the child.	Walk and poke at moving bubbles.

ACTIVITY	WHAT YOU CAN DO	WHAT YOUR CHILD CAN DO
Wriggle	Make a "spiderweb" by weaving the rope through a climber's rungs.	Wriggle through the web.

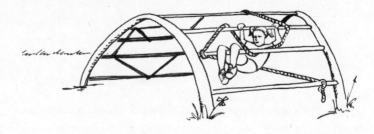

Jump	Lay the rope on the ground in a circle to make a pretend lake or bathtub.	Jump into the lake, and out onto dry land, into the lake, onto dry land. Or play *Looby Loo* (p. 86).
	Tie the rope to a post and swing it in circles, or back and forth, close to the ground. Establish a beat with jump rope chants and rhymes.	Jump rope to the beat.

BENEFITS OF THE ACTIVITY

■ Playing with a rope increases body awareness, motor control and motor planning, grading of movement, and postural stability, all functions of proprioception.

- Traveling in different directions on the rope improves movement and balance, muscle tone, bilateral coordination, crossing the midline, and gravitational security, all of which are important functions of the vestibular sense.
- Feeling the thickness, curve, and texture of the rope fosters tactile discrimination.
- Walking, marching, or jumping while attending to another person's steady beat improves the child's auditory perception, sequencing, timing, and rhythm.
- Watching where he places his feet builds visual attention, eye-foot coordination, and the basic skills of focusing and tracking.
- Thinking of new ways to use the rope promotes imagination and ideation.
- Cooperating with a friend sponsors social skills.

COPING TIP

Some children may get dizzy when changing direction while walking on the rope laid out in a circular or figure 8 design. To make the activity more enjoyable, lay out the rope in a straight path or one with gentle curves.

◆ Plastic Bag Kite

Here's a quickie activity for any breezy day. Try it in the summer on the beach or in the winter on a windy afternoon when your child may need a bit of encouragement to keep moving.

DEVELOPMENTAL AGE RANGE 3 and up

WHAT YOU WILL NEED
- Plastic grocery bag
- String
- Wide, colorful ribbon or crepe paper
- Scissors
- Stapler

PREPARATION
- Cut a length of string about 2 or 3 yards long.
- Attach one end of the string to one or both handles of the plastic bag.

- Cut ribbon or crepe paper into lengths about 1-yard long, for streamers.
- Staple streamers to bottom of the bag.

WHAT YOUR CHILD CAN DO

Hold the free end of the string and run into the wind. The air will fill the plastic bag and keep it aloft.

BENEFITS OF THE ACTIVITY

- Running into the wind is hard work and builds strong gross motor muscles, promotes kinesthesia, and improves bilateral coordination while keeping the runner warm.
- Sensing when the bag is full or empty promotes proprioceptive awareness.
- Stretching her arm to keep the bag up and tugging on it just right to keep it aloft improves grading of movement.

◆ Paper Bag Kick Ball

Overheard at the playground: "Son, how many times do I have to tell you? Don't push, don't kick! Now, sit on the bench and think about your bad behavior until I give you permission to go back to the sandbox."

What does Junior learn from this scolding? Nothing he can use—just that Mommy is mad at him, once again.

If Mom knew about sensory integration, she could be more effective. She could acknowledge his inner drive to get some active proprioceptive input into his muscles and joints. She could understand that he needs "time in," not "time out"!

Instead of punishing, Mom could discipline. To get his attention, she could calm him with a big hug, for deep joint pressure. She could say, "Son, you may not kick another person or animal, because kicking hurts them. But you may kick a thing that doesn't feel pain, like a ball. You may press down on a shovel, push bike pedals, or do jumping jacks. Let's think of a better idea to use your feet."

This better idea comes from Annemarie Kammann, a physical therapist formerly at Abilities Center in Michigan.

DEVELOPMENTAL AGE RANGE 2½ and up

WHAT YOU WILL NEED
Paper bags

PREPARATION
- Open up the bags.
- Optional: Remove shoes and socks.

WHAT YOUR CHILD CAN DO
- Kick the bag up into the air, and kick it again.
- Dribble the bag across the grass.
- Mark a start line, stand beside other kids, and have a kicking competition to see whose bag goes the farthest.
- Kick the bag back and forth with a partner.

BENEFITS OF THE ACTIVITY
- Flexing and extending his leg and foot promotes proprioception and kinesthesia.
- Connecting with the bag provides deep pressure to muscles and joints.
- Running and kicking improve balance, gross motor skills, bilateral coordination, crossing the midline, grading of movement, and motor planning.
- Aiming and kicking improve eye-foot coordination and visual-spatial perception.
- Finding a safe and appropriate way to channel his energy strengthens emotional development.
- Playing *Paper Bag Kick Ball* with others builds social skills.
- Being barefoot adds a tactile component to this multisensory game.

Two kids or a whole bunch of kids can play this multisensory, perceptual motor, environmentally correct game. The idea comes from Bert Richards, a physical therapy assistant consulting at Abilities Center in Michigan.

DEVELOPMENTAL AGE RANGE 4 to 12

WHAT YOU WILL NEED

- Old telephone books, magazines, catalogs, or newspapers
- Scissors
- Chalk, tape, or rope

PREPARATION

- Have your children:
  - Tear pages out of telephone books and magazines, or
  - Cut along the folds of newspaper pages to make single sheets, and
  - Place the papers in two tidy stacks.
- Use chalk, tape, or rope to designate a boundary between two "backyards."
- Place a stack of paper sheets in each backyard.
- Divide the players into two teams.

WHAT THE PLAYERS CAN DO

- Stay in their own "backyard" and work hard to keep it clean.
- Take individual pieces of paper from the stack and wad each paper into a ball.

- Throw the paper balls into the other team's backyard. (Aiming to hit another player is unacceptable, as it goes against the spirit of the game.)
- Return thrown paper balls or continue to wad up new sheets to throw.

VARIATIONS

- Toss paper balls into a wastebasket or laundry basket.
- Rip or shred the paper to use to line the guinea pig cage, or to pile into a huge mound. (Be prepared for a big paper mess!)
- Stand with their dominant hands down at one side, holding a paper by its corner. Using only their fingers, crumple the paper quickly, keeping their arms straight at their sides. (Devised by Debra Wilson Heiberger, M.A., and Margot Heiniger-White, M.A., O.T.R., authors of *S'cool Moves for Learning*, this "paper crumpling" activity strengthens fine motor skills necessary for writing. See *Recommended Materials*.)

BENEFITS OF THE ACTIVITY

- Tearing, wadding, and throwing paper balls improve proprioception, force, and motor planning.
- Preparing paper balls strengthens tactile perception and fine motor skills.
- Aiming paper balls increases visual-spatial awareness.
- Throwing improves balance, gross motor skills, bilateral coordination, and kinesthesia.
- Playing the game improves interaction and communication with others.

◆ Pound Cookies

Searching for an outlet for your child's pent-up energy? The process of pounding cookie ingredients to smithereens will satisfy the need to *beat,* and the product will satisfy the need to *eat.* This activity comes from Marsha Mitnick, Director of The Village Educational Center, an early intervention preschool in Birmingham, Michigan.

DEVELOPMENTAL AGE RANGE All ages

WHAT YOU WILL NEED

- Prepared cookie dough
- Sweet hard candies in small packages
- Gallon size, zip-up plastic bags (one per person)
- Small hammer(s) or wooden mallet(s)
- Baking sheets, spatulas, metal racks, and other cookie-baking paraphernalia
- Optional: Cookie cutters

WHAT YOUR CHILD CAN DO

- Open a package of candies.
- Count out 5 to 10 candies, put them in a plastic bag, and zip up the bag, first pushing out as much air as possible.
- Hammer the candies in the bag until they become sprinkles.
- Help slice or mold cookies and place them on cookie sheets.
- Sprinkle the pounded candies on top of the cookies.
- Help bake cookies and transfer them, when done, to the racks to cool.
- Enjoy!

BENEFITS OF THE ACTIVITY

- Pounding with vigor improves proprioception and force, releases energy, and increases gross motor skills.
- Counting candies, sprinkling sprinkles, and using tools improve tactile discrimination and fine motor skills.
- "Watching what you're doing" strengthens basic eye-motor skills as well as more complex visual-spatial processing skills.
- Baking cookies, sharing tools, and enjoying a snack with friends facilitates language and social skills.

◆ Hammer and Nails

On his fifth birthday, one of my sons received a kit composed of a log, a bag of nails, and a hammer. It was one of his best presents ever, and the fun lasted a long time.

When his supply of nails ran low, we went to the hardware store. He examined many varieties and selected several that he felt had the "just right" length, heft, and glint.

"I know how to hammer now, and I need a lot of nails," he said to the clerk.

"I understand," the kind man said. He let my son scoop the nails from the bins and helped him pour the nails into the scale pan.

Another day, a neighbor cut down a dead tree and set the logs curbside, with a sign that said, "Free Firewood! Take Some!" My little boy chose a big log and tried to move it. He pushed with his hands, nudged with his back, and shoved with his foot, but it wouldn't budge. He tested several other logs, found one that he could control, rolled it home, and got busy with hammer and nails.

DEVELOPMENTAL AGE RANGE 3½ and up

WHAT YOU WILL NEED
- Bag or can of penny nails, about 1 pound
- Seasoned log, about 2-feet tall and with a base about 18-inches or more
- Real hammer (a lightweight toy hammer is unsatisfactory for this job)

PREPARATION
Start the nails for your child, until she gets the hang of it.

WHAT YOUR CHILD CAN DO
Hammer away.

VARIATIONS
Too challenging? Using a toy hammer or wooden crab mallet, your child can reap the same satisfaction and benefits with these modifications:
- Instead of nails, use golf tees.
- Instead of a log, use one of these:
  - Large piece of plastic foam, such as one that comes in a new toaster oven carton

---

Two Mothers Say . . .

Renee Mesh says, "My seven-year-old, Christian, is a crasher basher. After hearing about the play activity of hammering nails, we tried it, and my son loved it immensely. We brought an old tree stump into the garage, gave him a hammer and some big nails, and let him go at it. He hammered for three weeks straight, no joke. He got enormous benefit from it. He said it helped him to think clearly. The smile on his face after a hammering session was so beautiful and content."

Laurie Renke says, "One thousand nails are not enough for Jake. We buy small nails, and he 'writes' his name and makes designs, animals and more with the nails on pieces of wood. He even makes gifts for loved ones."

- Egg carton, turned upside-down
- Pumpkin

BENEFITS OF THE ACTIVITY

■ Grading her movements and controlling the weight of the hammer provides strong proprioceptive input to her muscles and joints.

■ Feeling the rough bark on the tree section, the smoother sawn wood, the lightweight nails, and the heavy hammer increase tactile discrimination.

■ Steadying a nail with one hand and wielding the hammer with the other facilitates bilateral coordination.

■ Hitting the nails on the head improves visual skills including binocularity, fixation, eye-hand coordination, depth perception, and spatial awareness.

COPING TIPS

If your child seeks this kind of proprioceptive input, but poor coordination gets in his way, offer a substitute such as *Playdough* (p. 32), *Pound Cookies* (p. 103), or *Smash and Smell* (p. 190).

✦ Box Sweet Box

Nothing is so calming and comforting as one's own little version of Home Sweet Home. "A *Box Sweet Box* provides a nice, quiet place to go, if the environment is just too much," says Lori Merkel, COTA/L. "By using various sized boxes and some imagination, you and your child can create a wonderful place to play in or relax. I have found that when children help to make a box, they feel more comfortable with this space, like it is their own. It is such a special feeling when some of the really involved children trust you enough to let you in their box! Many times, I have been invited to crawl in, too, where we have had some of the best conversations about their feelings."

DEVELOPMENTAL AGE RANGE Crawlers and up

WHAT YOU WILL NEED

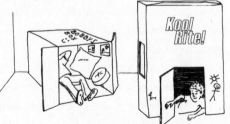

■ Various cardboard boxes large enough for child to crawl in

■ Packing tape or duct tape

■ Scissors or craft knife (for adult use only)

- Crayons, markers, paint, and stickers
- Optional: Flashlight and vibrating pen (see *Recommended Materials*)

PREPARATION

- Inspect boxes for sharp staples and remove them.
- Decide what kind of *Box Sweet Box* the child wants and needs:
  - To make a cave, place the box on its side and open one end. Put blankets, pillows, and books inside for a cozy place away from it all.
  - To make a tunnel, open both ends.
  - To make a playhouse, stand a large box upside down and cut out a door and windows.
  - To make a castle or maze of passage ways, connect several boxes together with tape, helping younger children if necessary.
- Cut in extras such as window shutters, storefront awnings and counters, peep holes, escape doors, and openings in the top so the child can poke his head out to look around.

WHAT YOUR CHILD CAN DO

- Decorate boxes inside and out with crayons, markers, paint and stickers, or vibrating pen.
- Crawl into the cave for some quiet time.
- Crawl through the tunnel and proceed to other pieces of equipment (see *Obstacle Course*, p. 239, and *Barrel of Fun*, p. 67, for related—but more stimulating—ideas).
- Play make-believe: House, Grocery Store, Castle, Rocket, School, Puppet Theater, and so on.
- Use a flashlight to examine pictures drawn inside the big box.

VARIATION

Use the *Box Sweet Box* idea in a mother/child playgroup, each family connecting three or more big boxes in any configuration. Put all the boxes together to form one structure. (Lori says, "At a picnic we made a *huge* box structure with over 60 large boxes. Kids and grown-ups all had a fun time crawling in and exploring the maze.")

BENEFITS OF THE ACTIVITY

- Calculating how her body size relates to the big or small opening of the box ("Can I fit through? or am I too big?") helps her learn about body scheme and improve proprioception, motor planning, and kinesthesia.

- Crawling in and through the boxes improves bilateral coordination.
- Decorating the *Box Sweet Box* with smelly crayons or markers stimulates the olfactory system. (Be aware that smells can be intense when the child colors inside the box.)
- Decorating the cardboard with crayons or wiggle pens causes vibrations that stimulate the tactile and auditory senses. Crayons are especially noisy in the box.
- Using writing implements for pictures, squiggles, or letters increases fine motor skills, prewriting skills, and grasp patterns, especially while working on the box's vertical walls.
- Using a flashlight to locate pictures or stickers placed on the inside walls of a very large box strengthens visual perception.
- The opportunity to rest in a small, quiet place calms and soothes the child for whom the environment can be overstimulating.
- Alternatively, connecting her *Box Sweet Box* with another child's improves social skills and communication and may add to the fun.

◆ Positions, Everybody!

Can you touch your toes? Make the letter "T" with your body? Sit like a pretzel? This funny activity will get you and your offspring into some amazing positions.

DEVELOPMENTAL AGE RANGE 3 and up

WHAT YOU WILL NEED
- Your own bodies
- Optional: a flexible doll or figure, or a wooden, jointed mannequin from a store specializing in art supplies or hobbies

WHAT YOU AND YOUR CHILD CAN DO
- Strike a pose or bend the flexible figure into a position that is physically possible for everybody playing to copy and momentarily maintain.
- Take turns suggesting and imitating positions.

BENEFITS OF THE ACTIVITY

- Arranging his body in different ways improves proprioception, body awareness, postural security, gross motor control, balance, bilateral coordination, extension and flexion, and motor planning.
- Manipulating the figure improves visualization, fine motor skills, and eye-hand coordination.
- Studying the position of the other player or the doll in order to imitate it improves visual perception and attention.
- Playing this game may greatly improve everybody's sense of humor.

Stretchy Bands

This activity lends itself beautifully to luring a non-participant into the play. For example, Sandy, a verbally precocious child with low tone, dyspraxia,[1] and a desperate yearning to be in control, insists he is Spiderman. Superheroes, he claims, do not sing, gallop, shake tambourines, enact *Jack and Jill*, or play *Looby Loo*. Those games are for ordinary children. Sandy will not budge, literally or figuratively.

---

[1] Dyspraxia is difficulty in conceiving of, planning, and carrying out an unfamiliar motor action or series of motor actions.

This year he is my favorite challenge, and I'm working on him. Each morning, I smile and say, "Good morning, Sandy."

"I am not Sandy," he storms. He shakes his Spiderman figure at me. "I am Spiderman. I am the strongest superhero that ever lived! I am not afraid of anything!"

Ordinarily, I ignore or discourage superhero talk, because it tends to be violent, purposeless, and limited. Then I realize that here is a perfect opportunity to deal with Sandy at his level, following his agenda. Maybe if I change my attitude, he can change his and get more in sync with the other children.

The next day, I change my tune and say, "Good morning, Spiderman."

Wary, he pauses, blinks, and lowers the toy. "Hi," he says quietly.

"Look what we're going to play with today, Spidey. Stretchy bands! They are for anyone who likes to be strong. Like superheroes."

Sandy brightens. "Superheroes? Really? Then I guess I'll take one." He fiddles with a band, gingerly at first, and then with some interest. "In fact, it's sort of like a piece of a spiderweb," he says. He has a wonderful time playing with the band, suggesting his versions of "super-strong" ways to stretch, and relating positively to his classmates.

The experience is a breakthrough. (Why didn't I think of this sooner?)

Using stretchy bands gives joints and muscles a workout. This follow-the-leader game also makes every player, whether human or superhuman, feel successful, peaceful, attentive, and part of the group.

DEVELOPMENTAL AGE RANGE All ages

WHAT YOU WILL NEED
- Variety of resistive bands or cords in light, medium, and heavy weights, each about 30 to 36 inches long (see *Recommended Materials*)—or, in a pinch, use pantyhose!
- Recording of pleasant instrumental music, such as "Variations on Twinkle, Twinkle, Little Star," from Don Campbell's *The Mozart Effect—Music for Children, Volume 1: Tune Up Your Mind*
- Several players (although just two can happily play)

PREPARATION
- Stand or sit, facing each other or in a circle.
- Have each player choose a band. Say, "If your muscles are tired today, you may want to play with a light, easy band. If you have energy, try this

medium kind. If you're really strong, this thick and heavy band will feel best."

- Ask, "What can you do with your stretchy band?"
- As the players experiment, observe and imitate them. Enthusiastically comment about their terrific ideas, emphasizing the *what, how,* and *where* of their actions. For example, "Standing on the band with both feet and pulling the ends up and down with both hands makes your arms strong." Or "Stretching the band overhead, from side to side, reminds me of a tree bending in the wind."
- Say, "Let's play. First, watch what I'm doing and follow me. Then it will be Eden's turn to stretch her band a different way, and we'll all follow her. Then Joy will have a turn," and so on.
- When you sense that the children have the gist of the game, start the music.

WHAT THE PLAYERS CAN DO

- Imitate your simple, steady stretching motion for about eight repetitions or until everyone "gets it."
- Take turns as leaders and followers.
- After the game is over, and their proprioceptive system is organized and calm, turn to a challenging task that requires full concentration. They will be ready!

VARIATIONS

- Keep a few bands in the glove compartment so you can play this restorative game when you're out and about, and the kids are getting restless.
- No recorded music? You don't need it: You can sing, or you can just count "One-and-two-and . . . seven-and-eight!"

BENEFITS OF THE ACTIVITY

- Using the resistive band strengthens proprioception, force, bilateral coordination, gross motor control, and kinesthesia.
- Handling the band improves tactile perception.
- Devising new moves builds the child's "movement vocabulary."
- Watching others' gestures and imitating their moves improves attention, focusing, and motor planning.
- This activity is arousing, organizing, and, when it's all over, incredibly calming.

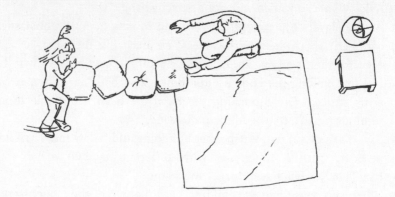

Inside every child is a lovely butterfly waiting to emerge from its cocoon. Melanie Hawke, O.T.R., shows us with this delightful activity how this transformation happens.

DEVELOPMENTAL AGE RANGE 3 and up

WHAT YOU WILL NEED

- Four small pillows, soft cushions, or stuffed animals
- Rug or sheet
- Carpeted floor or large gym mat

PREPARATION

- Place the pillows on the floor or mat in a row, touching one another.
- Spread the rug or sheet out at the end of the row of pillows. The long edge of the sheet should be aligned with the top edge of the pillows.

How to Play *Become a Butterfly*

WHAT YOU CAN DO	WHAT YOUR CHILD CAN DO
1. Say, "Let's pretend you're a caterpillar, about to become a beautiful butterfly." Help the child adjust his body so his head is well above the line of pillows and sheet.	1. Lie flat on his back, with his ribcage touching the first pillow and his arms stretched above his head.

WHAT YOU CAN DO	WHAT YOUR CHILD CAN DO
2. Say, "Caterpillars need to fatten up before making a cocoon. These pillows will make you nice and round."	2. Keeping his body straight, "log roll" toward the pillows, gathering them up one by one and pressing them tightly against his stomach.
3. Hold the sheet to help the child wrap it around his body. Don't let the sheet cover his head or the pillows squash his face.	3. Roll to the end of the sheet to make his butterfly cocoon.
4. Count to three, and then help the child unroll from the sheet.	4. Wriggle out of the cocoon to become a butterfly. Drop the pillows, flap his wings, and fly freely around the room

BENEFITS OF THE ACTIVITY

- Aligning his body correctly, wrapping up tightly in the sheet, and rolling like a log provides deep pressure and proprioception.
- Rolling provides vestibular input.
- Figuring out how to roll, squash the cushions to his chest, wrap himself in the sheet, and burst out of the cocoon all contribute to better tactile perception, body awareness, coordination, force, motor planning, and kinesthesia.

◆ Fabric Tube Tricks

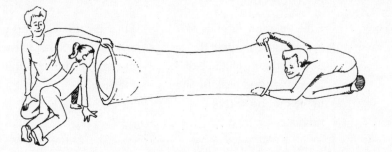

It's amazing how just a few yards of knit cotton tubing can provide so much fun and so many benefits! Most of these suggestions are from Barbara H.

Lindner, M.Ed., O.T.R./L., Director of Therapeutic Integration Services in Bonita Springs, Florida. Thanks also go to "SI Moms," Donna Becker of New Jersey and Rachel Howell of Louisiana.

DEVELOPMENTAL AGE RANGE 3 and up

WHAT YOU WILL NEED

- Tubing (about 4 yards)—knit jersey fabric, sometimes called "knit novelty," used for no-seam dresses and available at the fabric store (an alternative is a ready-made Resistance Tunnel—see *Recommended Materials*)
- 2 hula hoops
- Needle and strong thread, or 12 diaper pins
- Beach ball or therapy ball
- Toys to hide inside
- Jigsaw puzzle

PREPARATION

Secure a hula hoop at each end of the tubing. To do this, fold a few inches of tubing over a hoop. Either sew a hem around the hoop, or make a hem with six diaper pins. (To make getting into the tunnel more challenging for the child— and the preparation easier for you—forget the hula hoops.)

Ways to Play *Fabric Tube Tricks*

TUNNEL GAME	WHAT YOU AND ANOTHER ADULT CAN DO	WHAT YOUR CHILD CAN DO
A. The Crawl	Hold the tunnel's ends so it is taut and resting on the floor. Have the child lie on his tummy and peek through to see the end of the tunnel.	Enter the tunnel on his belly and use his elbows to crawl like an alligator or G.I. Joe in the jungle.
B. The Creep	Have the child enter the tunnel again, this time on hands and knees.	Creep through the tunnel.

TUNNEL GAME	WHAT YOU AND ANOTHER ADULT CAN DO	WHAT YOUR CHILD CAN DO
C. Rockabye Baby	Have child enter the tunnel and stop in the middle. Lift the ends and slowly swing child, as if in a cradle or hammock.	Stop in the middle and enjoy the relaxing side-to-side swinging.
D. Bump and Guess	Purposely bump the child on the floor, *Crash Pad*, beanbag chair, or stuffed animal. Ask, "What do you think you are bumping into?"	Identify what it is that he's bumping against without the aid of vision.
E. Knee or Elbow?	Touch various parts of the child's body and guess what they are. "Hmm, am I touching your knee?" (In this game, you *want* to be wrong now and then!)	Say whether the adult has guessed right, or say what the correct body part is. "Not knee, silly—elbow!"
F. Touchy Feely	Hide toys inside for the child to identify. This game is best inside a dark-colored tunnel, which screens out light.	Feel the toys in the dark and identify what they are, without the aid of vision.
G. The Puzzle Piece	Place a jigsaw puzzle at the exit. Hand the child a piece to fit into the puzzle once she gets to the end.	Hold the piece while creeping or crawling and place it into the puzzle.
H. Push That Ball!	Have the child push the ball through the tube. If the child responds well to hearty voices, encourage enthusiastically: "Push that ball! Way to go!" If he shrinks from loud noises, murmur: "You're getting so strong. We knew you could do it."	Head-butt the ball through the tunnel.

TUNNEL GAME	WHAT YOU AND ANOTHER ADULT CAN DO	WHAT YOUR CHILD CAN DO
I. Tunnel Obstacle Course	Stretch one end of the tube over a big piece of resistive lycra/nylon, or over the mouth of a barrel to extend the play. (See *Barrel of Fun*, p. 67; *Laundromat Game*, p. 75; and *Obstacle Course*, p. 239.	Find new ways to maneuver through the tunnel and other pieces of equipment.

BENEFITS OF THE ACTIVITY

■ Bearing weight on the hands and arms provides proprioceptive input that helps to build upper-body and arm strength and to develop grasping skills.

■ Pushing the ball with the head provides deep joint pressure to the neck and shoulders and improves force.

■ Extending the neck and holding the head up to resist gravity improve muscle tone, gross motor control, and postural stability—all functions of the vestibular system.

■ Crawling left-right, left-right, improves bilateral coordination and kinesthesia.

■ Swinging as if in a hammock stimulates the vestibular system.

■ Brushing against the walls of the tunnel provides touch pressure.

■ Guessing what he's bumping against and touching without the use of his eyes improves tactile discrimination and encourages visualization.

■ Considering what body part is being touched improves body awareness.

■ Pushing the ball and carrying the puzzle piece to the end strengthens motor planning.

A Mother Says . . .

Donna Becker of New Jersey says, "I made a big fabric tunnel for my son to 'climb' through. Go to the sale section at the fabric store and don't worry about the colors. I used four different textured fabrics—taffeta, fleece, bumpy cotton, and corduroy—and sewed them together, selvage to selvage, with the seams on the outside. These fabrics are not so stretchy, so a 6- or 7-year-old may be too big to get through, but they work well for a preschooler. (I always think that the textured fabrics would be nice for a patchwork quilt for a blind person.) We hide stuff in the tunnel, and he has to come out the other end with the items, so he gets lots of proprioceptive and tactile input at the same time. He loves it."

COPING TIPS

The tunnel will stretch with use. If it becomes so long that your child can't see the end, she may be a bit hesitant about going through. To solve the problem:

- Wash the tubing to shrink it back to size.
- Roll up an end to make the tunnel much shorter, and gradually, over time, increase the length.
- Hold one end open and peer in. Beckon the child to crawl to you.

The Shopping Game

Most children love hard work! Kimberly Geary, M.S., O.T.R./L., suggests this game to give young "shoppers" the kind of heavy muscle work that will get their proprioceptive system in sync. Kimberly explains that because proprioception is *the* moderator for all other sensory systems, the game is very organizing and calming.

DEVELOPMENTAL AGE RANGE 3 and up

WHAT YOU WILL NEED

- Plastic beach bucket or laundry tub with solid sides, large enough for a child to sit in—this is the child's "shopping basket"
- Heavy groceries, especially those that are durable, nonperishable, and tightly sealed, such as:
  - Boxes of cereal and oatmeal
  - Bags of beans and rice
  - Plastic bottles of water
  - Kitty litter
  - Cans of coffee
- Heavy telephone books or encyclopedias
- "Coupons": pictures of grocery items—hand-drawn or cut out from magazines, and glued to cardboard

PREPARATION

- "Hide" groceries around the room—put a bag of rice between couch cushions, a box of cereal under a chair, a water bottle on a windowsill, and so on.

- Put the books into the basket, to make it heavier. The size, weight, and number of groceries and books will vary, depending on your child's strength and motor control.
- Spread out the "coupons" within view.

WHAT YOU CAN DO
- Ask child to find the food that matches a "coupon."
- Be there to help load and shove the basket, if necessary.

WHAT YOUR CHILD CAN DO
- Scan the room to locate the groceries.
- Push the shopping basket around to gather the groceries.
- Look at, point to, and talk with you about the "coupons."

VARIATIONS
- Apply Velcro to the backs of the pictures. Make a feltboard by covering a large sheet of cardboard with felt or Velcro cloth. While the child plays the game, stick the relevant pictures to the board.
- Have a sibling or friend be a "ham," "turkey," or box of "detergent," and climb into the basket. Then the shopper has a heavier and more satisfying load to push.
- Have the friend riding in the cart tell the cart pusher what groceries to find first, second, third, and so forth. This becomes a great turn-taking game for playdates!
- Another day, at the real store, offer real coupons to match with food.
- When you're out and about, and your child still needs the deep pressure and proprioceptive input that this activity provides, use a weighted vest. (See "In Your Pocket Designs" in *Recommended Materials.*)

BENEFITS OF THE ACTIVITY
- Pushing heavy loads and feeling the deep pressure of heavy weights provides calming proprioception, while increasing body awareness, gross motor strength, force, and kinesthesia.
- Scanning the room to locate hidden groceries improves attention and visual skills such as focusing, figure-ground, and spatial awareness.
- Moving around the room to pick up one item after another improves sequencing, motor planning, and organizational skills—all important components of praxis.
- Referring to the pictures of grocery items helps your child recall and

organize his shopping. This strategy is especially beneficial for the child with emerging expressive or receptive language skills.

- Playing the game with another child improves communication and social skills.
- Generalizing the activity at the real grocery store, where he can match coupons with food, makes the child feel needed and useful.

◆ Jiggling on the Dryer

Does your little one have low muscle tone and seem considerably less active than other kids? Or is your child easily distressed and difficult to calm? In either case, this quickie experience may help to organize the child's sensory system.

DEVELOPMENTAL AGE RANGE Infancy up to about 40 pounds

WHAT YOU WILL NEED
- Clothes dryer or washer
- Stool or sturdy box
- For a baby, an infant carrier with a non-skid base

WHAT TO DO
Start the machine and let the child sit on it. Supervise this activity closely.

BENEFITS OF THE ACTIVITY
By engaging the proprioceptors, gentle oscillation can both stimulate an underresponsive system and calm an overresponsive one. Ask a therapist to explain how the same experience can affect people in different ways.

◆ Body Length Guesstimation

Estimating distances and quantities is often challenging for the child with poor proprioception. Inaccurate perception of his very own body parts may color the way he functions in daily life.

Where are his feet—somewhere down below? How long is his stride—long enough to cross that puddle? How high should he lift his knee to mount the stair? How far should he squat to sit in a chair? Where are his hands? How many fingers indicate "6"? How much popcorn will fit in his mouth? How close is he to another person?

This activity starts with the child's primary source—his body—to help him measure how far, how many, and how much. When he can "guesstimate" concrete, in-the-flesh relationships to objects and other people, he will be better equipped to understand abstract concepts of arithmetic, algebra, geometry, calculus, and physics.

DEVELOPMENTAL AGE RANGE 3 and up

WHAT YOU WILL NEED
- String
- Brown packaging paper, scissors, and crayons

PREPARATION
- Together, practice walking heel-to-toe. For an extra challenge, hold your child's hand and invite him to walk heel-to-toe with his eyes closed.
- Practice "walking" your hands on a table, with the heel of one hand touching the fingertips of your other hand.
- Bend your thumbs and practice placing them down, nail to knuckle.
- Measure your child's height and cut a piece of string the same length.
- Have your child lie down on the brown paper. Trace around his body.
- Have him cut out the shape and draw his features and clothes on the paper.

How to Play *Guesstimation*

WHAT YOU CAN DO	WHAT YOUR CHILD CAN DO
1. Ask, "How many of your hands do you guess will stretch from my shoulder to my fingertips?" "From the top to the bottom of this picture?" "From this edge of the table to that edge?"	1. Consider the distance and make a guesstimation of how many hands.

WHAT YOU CAN DO	WHAT YOUR CHILD CAN DO
2. Whatever answer he offers, accept it; do not judge. Say, "That's an interesting (or thoughtful, or good) guess. Let's find out!"	2. Place hand to hand, counting aloud.
3. Ask, "How many thumbs from your placemat to your brother's?"	3. Guesstimate the number of thumbs, place them nail to joint, and count how many.
4. Ask, "How many of your feet do you think will stretch from where you are standing to where I'm standing?" "From this wall to that wall?" "Between your bed and the bathroom?"	4. Guesstimate the number of feet, place heel to toe, and count the steps.
5. Ask, "How many of you will fit head to toe from one side of the rug to the other?" Whether he measures the distance with his real body, his paper replica, or the string, mark his body lengths with your toe or a scrap of paper. Better yet, do it at the beach so the child can see his body shapes in the sand.	5. Guesstimate how many body lengths. Then, either: ■ Lie down, get up, lie down again, putting his feet where his head had been, and repeat, ■ Or stretch out the paper figure or string again and again.
6. To extend the activity, measure different forms of locomotion. Ask, "How many jumps between the sandbox and the sidewalk?" "How many scoots across the kitchen floor?" "How many log rolls across the gym mat?"	6. Make guesses and then jump, scoot, and log-roll while counting the repetitions aloud.

HOW MANY THUMBS?

Until measurements began to be standardized in the Middle Ages, people used their own body parts to gauge distances. A foot was the length of a man's foot. An inch was the width of a man's thumb, or the length of the first joint of his index finger. About 12 of these inches were in a foot. The distance from a man's nose to the end of his outstretched arm was a yard. About three of his feet were in a yard. Obviously, this system was imprecise, because every body is different.

In the 1200s, King Edward I of England decided to use his body to standardize measurements. He decreed that his nose-to-fingertip stretch would be the official yard. One third of that would be the official foot, and $\frac{1}{36}$ would be the official inch.

Just for fun, calculate how many of your thumb widths equal your foot length, and how many foot lengths are in your yard. How do you measure up, compared to King Edward I?

BENEFITS OF THE ACTIVITY

- Walking heel-to-toe, hand-to-hand, and thumb-to-thumb improves proprioception and kinesthesia.
- Cutting out his paper body shape and drawing in details promotes fine motor skills and self-awareness.
- Guesstimating the length of his body parts improves body awareness and attention.
- Orienting his body to measure distances strengthens motor control and motor planning.
- Guesstimating distances promotes visual-spatial perception and visualization (visual imagery).
- The activity strengthens academic skills, such as hypothesizing, making mental calculations, and all-purpose problem solving.

◆ Hold Up the Wall!

One of my preschool students with DSI was a hitter-kicker-thrower. Ben's regular target was a sweet, appealing girl. He yearned to play with her and tried to get her attention the only way he knew—by hurling things at her. His inappropriate strategy was a big problem for everyone.

Fortunately, after several sessions with an OT, he began to show progress. One day, he spotted the little girl at the sandbox. He brightened. He picked up

a shovel. He prepared to launch it. Just as three teachers converged on him, he shrugged, dropped the shovel, went to the wall, and pushed his hands against it with all his might. A moment later he stepped away, took a deep breath, and said, "See? I have a new strategy!"

Then he went to the little girl, sat down, and said, "May I be your friend?"

She offered him a spoon, and they proceeded to fill a bucket, the first of many.

DEVELOPMENTAL AGE RANGE 3 and up

PREPARATION

When you want to prevent a meltdown or ease a transition from outdoors to indoors, room to room, or activity to activity, say, "Oh, my goodness, the wall is falling down! Quick! Let's push it with our hands to keep it up!" (If your child tends to take jokes literally or frightens easily, and you don't want to alarm her, say with a smile, "Let's pretend the wall is falling down.")

WHAT YOUR CHILD CAN DO
- Press her hands against the wall with all her strength, for about 15 counts or more.
- Press other body parts against the wall:
  - Head and back
  - Hips and shoulders (one at a time)
  - Buttocks (together or separately)
  - Feet (together, while lying on the floor)

VARIATION

Here's a song to accompany the activity. Piggyback the words to the tune of "If You're Happy and You Know It," or Woody Guthrie's "Put Your Finger in the Air."

Push your hands on the wall, on the wall.
Push your hands on the wall, on the wall,
Push your hands on the wall, and do not let it fall,
Push your hands on the wall, on the wall.

BENEFITS OF THE ACTIVITY

■ Deep joint pressure nourishes the proprioceptive system and has a calming effect.

■ Pressing different body parts strengthens body awareness.

■ The preposterous premise of this activity gives kids the giggles, diffuses tension, and helps them feel in sync with their friends.

More Ideas for Proprioception

Occupational therapists Elizabeth Haber and Deanna Sava have assembled several useful lists of heavy work activities for children. They generously make these lists available to other therapists, teachers, and parents, and have given permission for an abbreviated version to be printed here. Here are some suggestions adapted from their article, "Heavy Work Activities List for Parents," at http://groups.msn.com/DeannaSavasWebsite. Other activities from their list have also been published in Diana Henry's handbook, *Tools for Parents*. (See *Recommended Materials*.)

HEAVY WORK ACTIVITIES LIST FOR PARENTS

Following are activities families can use to provide heavy work activities for the child at home, compiled and edited by Elizabeth Haber, M.S., O.T.R./L., and Deanna Iris Sava, M.S., O.T.R./L. All the activities on this list are "naturally occurring activities." This means they can be provided as part of the child's daily routine. Special thanks to all the therapists who openly shared ideas!

1. Carry, push, and pull heavy items:

   ■ Carry baskets with cardboard blocks, groceries for Mom, cushions, and so on.
   ■ A pillowcase filled with a few stuffed animals in it, for weight—push or pull the pillowcase up a ramp, incline, or stairs.
   ■ Pull other children around on a sheet or blanket.
   ■ When traveling, pull own small suitcase on wheels.
   ■ Fill up a suitcase or box with heavy items (such as books) and push/pull the suitcase or box across the room. Pushing/pulling across a carpeted floor provides more resistance.

2. Perform household chores:

- Sweep.
- Mop.
- Dust.
- Carry the laundry basket.
- Wipe off the table after dinner.
- Push chairs into table after a meal.
- Carry buckets of water to clean with or to water flowers, plants, or trees.
- Clean windows or the front of appliances using a spray bottle.
- Scrub rough surfaces with a brush.
- Pull a heavy trash can out to the curb.
- Bathe the dog.
- Wash the car.
- Put large toys and equipment away.
- Help rearrange his or her bedroom furniture.
- Help change the sheets on the bed (then toss the linens down the stairs).
- Push a child's cart filled with cans and then get on hands and knees (a weight-bearing position) to put the cans away on a low shelf.

3. Perform yard work:

- Mow the lawn.
- Rake the grass or leaves.
- Push the wheelbarrow.
- Shovel sand into a wheelbarrow, push the wheelbarrow to a spot, dump out sand, and use a rake to level it out (functional for filling in low spots in backyard).
- Dig dirt to help plant flowers.

4. Play with friends:

- Have pillow fights.
- Enjoy "play wrestling," a pushing game where two people lock hands facing each other and try to see who can push and make the other person step back first. Use other body parts also, and be sure to have rules (no hitting, no biting, no scratching, and when one person says stop, then both stop).
- Sit on the floor, back to back, with knees bent and feet flat on the floor. The children interlock their arms and then try to stand up at the same time.

5. Participate in sports and other vigorous physical work and play:

- Do gymnastics, karate, and sports activities involving running and jumping.
- Go horseback riding, wrestle, swim, and dive (also dive after weighted sticks thrown in pool).
- Roller skate or in-line skate uphill.
- Make wood projects requiring sanding and hammering.
- Help set up and take down a heavy blanket pulled across a few chairs and go "camping."
- Play catch with a heavy ball, or bounce and roll a heavy ball.
- Open doors for people.
- Do chair push-ups.
- While on hands and knees, color a "rainbow" with crayons on large paper on the floor or with sidewalk chalk outside.
- Play "cars" under the kitchen table, pushing the car with one hand while creeping and weight bearing on the other hand.
- Fill up big toy trucks with heavy blocks and push the trucks with both hands to knock things down.
- Do animal walks (crab walk, bear walk, army crawl).

6. Chew gum, eat chewy or crunchy foods, or sip water from a water bottle with a straw while doing homework.

5

Seeing (The Visual Sense)

Ahmahl, 8, has poor oculomotor skills—the basic ability to move and use his eyes together. One day, he and his Cub Scout den are taking a nature hike along the river. The den leader points toward the rocks and says, "Look, boys! There's a blue heron." Ahmahl looks at the den leader's extended arm a few feet from his nose and then, squinting, attempts to shift his focus to the bird, many yards away. The other boys exclaim, "Oh, man! It's huge!" By the time Ahmahl is looking in the right direction, the bird has spread its wings and is soaring over the river. Ahmahl drops his gaze, because tracking the bird's flight takes too much effort.

Caitlin, 7, has difficulty processing what she sees, quickly and effectively. Her Brownie troop is playing kickball, not her favorite activity. She can see the ball clearly but loses it when it moves toward her. She can't judge properly when it will get to her, or how close it is, so she always kicks too soon or too late. Sometimes she backs away when she should be running forward. If only she could judge distances better, get her timing right, and not get distracted by the movements of the other kids! Then her eyes and feet might work as a team more often, and she could show the other girls that she is really a strong kicker.

Vision is a complex process that enables us to identify sights, to anticipate what is "coming at us," and to prepare for a response. Vision should not be confused with eyesight. Eyesight, the basic ability to see the big "E" on the wall chart, is only one part of vision.

Healthy eyes and 20/20 eyesight are prerequisites for vision, just as hearing is a prerequisite for language skills. Eyesight contributes to our basic visual skills, called oculomotor (eye movement or eye motor) skills. As the child matures and integrates information from the other senses, especially the vestibular sense, more refined visual-spatial processing skills evolve.

Ahmahl and Caitlin's visual skills prevent them from participating fully with the other scouts. When visual dysfunction goes undetected, it can cause reading, learning, physical, emotional, and social difficulties. Some characteristics are listed below.

CHARACTERISTICS OF VISUAL DYSFUNCTION

The child with visual dysfunction may:

☐ Shield her eyes to screen out sights, close or cover one eye, or squint.

☐ Complain of seeing double.

☐ Have difficulty shifting her gaze from one object to another, such as when looking from the blackboard to her own paper.

☐ Turn or tilt her head as she reads across a page.

☐ Turn or tilt her body as she watches television or the teacher at circle time.

☐ Have difficulty tracking or following a moving object, such as a table-tennis ball, or following along a line of printed words.

☐ Fail to comprehend what she is reading, or quickly lose interest.

☐ Confuse likenesses and differences in pictures, words, symbols, and objects.

☐ Omit words or numbers and lose her place while reading and writing.

☐ Have difficulty with schoolwork involving the size constancy of letters, the spacing of letters and words, and the lining up of numbers.

☐ Have difficulty with fine motor tasks involving spatial relationships, such as fitting pieces into jigsaw puzzles and cutting along lines.

☐ Orient drawings poorly on the page, or write uphill or downhill.

☐ Misjudge spatial relationships of objects in the environment, often bumping into furniture or misstepping on stairs and curbs.

☐ Confuse right and left, have a poor sense of direction, and often head the wrong way.

☐ Not understand concepts such as up/down, before/after, and first/second.

☐ Fail to visualize what she reads. It may be hard to call up mental images of objects and people, not relating pictures and words to "the real thing."

☐ Be uncomfortable or overwhelmed by moving objects or people.

☐ Fatigue easily during schoolwork.

☐ Withdraw from classroom participation and avoid group activities in which movement is required.

When visual dysfunction prevents the development of basic oculomotor or complex visual processing skills, SI-based occupational therapy or vision therapy may help. (Vision therapy, or visual training, may improve visual skills and prevent learning-related visual problems. It helps the child integrate visual information with intake from the other senses, such as hearing, touching, and moving.) Here are some Sensory-motor, Appropriate, Fun and Easy activities that your child may enjoy.

Activities for the Visual Sense

◆ Pokin' O's

Pokin' O's is a simple and purposeful vision game. While it may not be as rejuvenating as a weekend in the Poconos (groan), it will help pass the time when your child is restless in a waiting room, sick in bed, or looking for something fun to do.

DEVELOPMENTAL AGE RANGE 6 and up

WHAT YOU WILL NEED
- Marker
- Toothpick or pen
- Newspaper

WHAT YOUR CHILD CAN DO
- Using the marker, color all the O's in a newspaper paragraph or page.
- Poke a hole through the O's with a toothpick or pen.

BENEFITS OF THE ACTIVITY
- Scanning the printed page for O's improves visual discrimination.
- *Pokin' O's* improves eye-hand coordination, bilateral coordination, and fine motor skills.

◆ Schedule Board

"When will Mom come to get me?" "What day is gym day?" "How much time to play before supper?" "When will we go camping?" Many children have a tentative sense of time and space. In addition, many have difficulty with transitions, or with separating from a loving grown-up. This reassuring activity may help them visualize daily events so they can picture how their time is structured and what will happen next.

DEVELOPMENTAL AGE RANGE 2½ to 6

WHAT YOU WILL NEED

- Poster board, dry erase board, or chalkboard
- Ruler, pencil, markers, or chalk
- Camera
- Magazines, catalogs, advertisements
- Optional (to make picture cards): poster board, cut into about 12 rectangles, or large index cards; and tape or glue

PREPARATION

- Measure and mark eight rectangles on the board to make a *Schedule Board*. Decide what daily moments to include, such as difficult transition times or predictably pleasant times. Use a pencil, erasable marker, or chalk so you can change the times and words:

8 a.m.	10 a.m.	Noon	3 p.m.
Get up	Math	Lunch	Bus
4 p.m.	6 p.m.	7 p.m.	8:30 p.m.
Playground	Playdough	Dessert!	Bed

- Discuss various activities and take photographs of your child doing them:
  - Eating breakfast
  - Getting dressed
  - Riding in a car or on a school bus
  - Doing work at school
  - Playing with other children
  - Going to the playground, reading a book, or preparing for bed
  - Receiving treatment at the OT clinic, pool, or with a speech therapist

- Occasional activities: going to the dentist, the zoo, the barber shop, the pumpkin patch, or the shopping center to see Santa
- Additionally, look through magazines together and cut out pictures of other children doing similar activities, or pictures of representative objects, such as a sandwich to represent eating lunch, or a tee shirt to represent getting dressed.
- To make the optional picture cards, glue the magazine pictures to index cards or to rectangles cut from the extra poster board. If you can't find what you want in magazines and have a modicum of artistic talent, you can also draw pictures on the cards.

WHAT YOUR CHILD CAN DO

Before going to school, look at the cards, and place them on the *Schedule Board*. Before going to bed, repeat the activity to prepare for the next day.

VARIATIONS

Make a *Schedule Board* and a set of pictures for specific themes:
- Self-help steps (using the toilet, washing hands, brushing teeth, or making the bed)
- Meal time (setting the table, passing dishes, or eating dessert)
- Seasons, holidays, and celebrations (dressing up, giving presents, or trying new foods)
- Going on a trip (packing, going to the station, or waiting in line)

BENEFITS OF THE ACTIVITY

- Finding magazine pictures promotes visual discrimination.
- Reviewing the child's daily doings improves memory and language skills.
- Cutting with scissors improves bilateral coordination, fine motor skills, and tool use.
- Placing the photographs and picture cards in order on the *Schedule Board* improves sequencing skills and the ability to plan ahead.
- Using a picture schedule helps the child's social and emotional development by:
  - Preparing the child for daily activities and transitions
  - Helping to reduce separation anxiety
  - Increasing independence
  - Decreasing stress (and nagging) at home

Sensational "toys" are already in your kitchen, just waiting for you to look at them in a new light. Offer this multisensory activity when you are trying to fix a meal and the "Underfoot Child" is demanding attention.

DEVELOPMENTAL AGE RANGE 2 to 6

WHAT YOU WILL NEED
- Several citrus fruits, such a kumquat, lime, lemon, clementine, tangerine, orange, or grapefruit
- Bucket
- Paper bag

PREPARATION
- Bring out the fruit and give your child the bucket.
- Set the paper bag or box, open side facing your child, on the floor.

What Your Child Can Do with *Citrus Balls*

Name	Look at and handle the different varieties of citrus "balls" to get a feel for them. Identify them by name, perhaps with your help.
Put in Order	Order them by size or group them by color.
Count	Put the balls into the bucket. Count the pieces, both before and after playing with them (so none disappears under the furniture).

Guess	Without peeking, grope inside the bag, grasp a piece of citrus, and guess by its size, weight, shape, and maybe texture, whether it is a lemon or an orange or a grapefruit.
Roll	Sit on the floor and roll fruit into the paper bag. Or lie tummy-down and roll the fruit. Or face a partner and roll the fruit back and forth. Or use different parts of the body to "putt" the fruit.
Toss	Stand facing a partner and toss a citrus ball back and forth. (If it falls, it may get a bit bruised, but rinds are tough.)
Press and Squeeze	With hand or foot, press firmly on a citrus ball and roll it back and forth. (Rather than damaging the fruit, the pressure actually improves it by breaking down the pulp to yield more juice.) Help a grown-up squeeze juice, and enjoy!
Peel and Eat	Peel off the rind. Pull the sections apart and eat them. (A clementine is probably the easiest, neatest, and sweetest.)

BENEFITS OF THE ACTIVITY

- Naming and counting the fruit promote visual perception, auditory memory, word retrieval, and early math skills.
- Putting the fruit in order strengthens categorization and sequencing.
- Aiming, rolling, and tossing the fruit strengthens basic eye-movement skills of focusing and tracking, as well as more complex eye-hand coordination and visual-spatial skills.
- Lying tummy-down to roll the fruit improves extension, upper body strength, motor control, and grading of movement.
- Rolling the fruit with different body parts increases body awareness.
- Guessing which variety of citrus the piece is, without looking, strengthens tactile discrimination and visualization.
- Playing these games with pals aids communication and social skills.
- Peeling the fruit strengthens hand dexterity and fine-motor skills.
- Smelling and tasting inform the olfactory and gustatory system.

- Pressing and squeezing citrus fruit provides deep touch pressure for the tactile system, and deep joint pressure for the proprioceptive system.
- Helping to prepare juice makes a child feel needed.

COPING TIP

This activity is best played in the kitchen, just in case.

◆ Guesstimation with Objects

In Chapter 3, *Activities for the Proprioceptive Sense*, another *Guesstimation* game (p. 119) intends to help your child use his own body to gauge distances and quantities. Here's a variation, in which the child generalizes that body-measuring skill to apply it to inanimate things.

DEVELOPMENTAL AGE RANGE 4 and up

WHAT YOU WILL NEED
- Two spaghetti boxes or wooden unit blocks
- Several small items, each of the same size, such as:

• Paper clips	• Teaspoons	• Buttons
• Pens and pencils	• Toothpicks	• Dominoes
• Envelopes	• Paper plates	• Legos
• Books	• Paper towel rolls	• Playing cards
• Small boxes	• Plastic tubs	• Pick-up sticks
• String segments	• Sponges	• Building blocks

WHAT YOU CAN DO
- Place two spaghetti boxes side by side, about 5 inches apart. Ask, "How many paper clips (or other small items) do you think could line up between these two boxes?"
- Suggest other objects and distances for the child to consider. "How many paper plates do you think would reach from the door to the sink?" "How many encyclopedias between the bookcase and the sofa?"

- Make estimates and test them.
- Ask you to put your guesstimates to the test.

BENEFITS OF THE ACTIVITY
- Guessing and testing his hypothesis improves visual-spatial awareness.
- Handling objects improves eye-motor coordination, fine motor skills, and tactile awareness.

COPING TIP

Sometimes a visual problem interferes with a child's participation in games. If your child cannot or will not play *Guesstimation with Objects,* a developmental vision evaluation by an SI-trained, behavioral optometrist may be an excellent idea.

◆ Beanbag Jai Alai

Jai alai, a game played with a small ball and wicker baskets, originated in the Basque region of Spain. Pronounced "high lie," the words mean "merry festival," and you will see why when you play *Beanbag Jai Alai* with your child. Thanks to Kathy Winters for suggesting this easy activity. Olé!

DEVELOPMENTAL AGE RANGE 4 and up

WHAT YOU WILL NEED
- Two clean plastic jugs and scissors
- Beanbags, purchased or homemade (see instructions below)

- To make a jai alai basket (like a scoop), turn each jug upside down and cut out a section.
- To make a beanbag, cut out a 5 × 9 inch piece of fabric. Fold right sides together. Sew two seams. Turn the bag right side out, pour in about a cup of beans, and sew up the last seam.

WHAT YOU AND YOUR CHILD CAN DO

Toss a beanbag back and forth with the scoops. Playing this game outdoors, or in a spacious room away from lamps and breakables, is a good idea.

VARIATIONS

- Use the nondominant hand to wield the scoop.
- Toss a variety of balls back and forth.

BENEFITS OF THE ACTIVITY

- Playing the game reinforces eye-hand-foot-body coordination, visual tracking, depth perception, directionality, spatial awareness, and visual figure-ground.
- Stretching to catch and toss the beanbag strengthens balance, proprioception, force, gross motor control, kinesthesia, motor planning, and midline crossing.

Two Mothers Say . . .

Kathy Winters, in Warminster, Pennsylvania, says, "Many children with sensory issues have difficulty catching and throwing balls. Before being diagnosed with DSI, receiving occupational therapy, and playing games like this, my son Eric used to walk around alone at recess. Now he joins the other children in structured play, often involving balls!"

Marta Anders, in Cornwall-on-Hudson, New York, says, "My daughter loves this game and begs to do it. Not knowing it was therapeutic, Lizzie told me it helps her brain. Warning! Causes uproarious laughter!"

◆ Go Fishing

The simple "fishing" game, often used by developmental optometrists during vision therapy, has many beneficial angles. Anne Barber, O.D., Director of Program Services at Optometric Extension Program (OEP), suggests this as a fun, satisfying activity for little tykes.

DEVELOPMENTAL AGE RANGE 3 to 6

WHAT YOU WILL NEED
- For fish: cardboard, construction paper, scissors, crayons, metal paper clips
- For fishing pole: stick or dowel, about 2-feet long; magnet; string, about 2-feet long
- For fishing basket: a wide-rimmed basket, bowl, or box

PREPARATION
On cardboard, draw a fish (about 5 × 3 inches) as a template for your child to trace on the construction paper. Or, if drawing is not one of your talents, use this one, enlarged 200%.

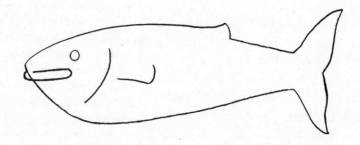

WHAT YOUR CHILD CAN DO
- With help, if necessary—
  • Fold several pieces of construction paper into quarters, trace a fish shape in each quadrant, cut out the fish, and decorate them with eyes, scales, and fins.

- Put a paper clip on each fish head.
  - Tie a magnet to the end of a 2- to 3-foot piece of string and tie the free end of the string to the end of the stick.
- Spread the fish out on the ground or floor.
- Pick up the fishing pole and go fishing!
- Pull the fish off the magnet and place the fish in the basket. A bigger challenge is to jerk the pole to shake the fish off the magnet, right into the basket, without touching the fish.

BENEFITS OF THE ACTIVITY

- Overall visual-motor development improves as the child matches the corners of a paper to fold it, tracks the direction of the crayon tracing the template, watches the outline while cutting, and guides the magnet toward the paper clip.
- Bilateral coordination and fine-motor skills improve as the child folds the paper, steadies the template with one hand and traces around it with the other, holds the paper and cuts it with scissors, and attaches paper clips to fish.
- Tactile discrimination improves as the child uses tools (a crucial skill for human beings!), such as crayons, scissors, paper clips, and the fishing pole.
- Body awareness, proprioception, and gross motor control improve as the child gauges how far to stretch his arm to extend, lower, and raise the pole; and how to steady the pole to prevent the magnet from swinging to and fro.

◆ Peanut Hunt

A *Peanut Hunt* is a low-key, fairly noncompetitive activity to entice kids outdoors, to keep them busy while a picnic is getting organized, or to entertain a group as a party game.

DEVELOPMENTAL AGE RANGE
3 to 10

- Roasted peanuts, in the shell
- Paper lunch bags

PREPARATION

When no one is watching, go outside and sprinkle peanuts all over the yard.

WHAT YOUR CHILDREN CAN DO
- Hunt for peanuts and bag them.
- Open the peanuts and eat them (but not if they are allergic to peanuts).

VARIATIONS

This game is obviously neither safe nor appropriate for a child who is allergic to peanuts or other nuts. As the fun of hunting for small things is the object here, you can still offer the activity by substituting other treasures to look for, such as:
- Individually wrapped candies
- Little party favors
- Pennies, nickels, and dimes
- Poker chips to trade in for a treat
- Large gold and silver "Mardi Gras" coins for a treasure hunt
- Little dinosaurs for an archeological dig in the sandpit

BENEFITS OF THE ACTIVITY
- Scanning the ground for nuts or other small items improves focusing and fixation, depth perception, visual discrimination, spatial awareness, and figure-ground.
- Bending to gather the nuts provides vestibular input and strengthens gross motor skills, motor planning, and kinesthesia.
- Cracking nuts promotes eye-hand coordination and fine motor skills.
- Eating the nuts provides olfactory and gustatory sensations.
- Hunting for peanuts with a group gives a child a sense of belonging.

◆ Billions of Boxes

Hayley, my 5-year-old great-niece, was visiting from Connecticut. One afternoon, we gathered boxes from all over the house and brought them outside to the back deck. "Oh, goody!" Hayley said. "Billions of boxes!"

She made one into a bed for her little stuffed husky dog. She made a house for the bed, and a box street, and a box village. Her play was rich, her conversation delightful, and her happiness contagious. When it was clean-up time, she said, "I wish you were my teacher." I was touched, for I hadn't done anything except be there.

A few weeks later, Robin, one of my favorite preschool students, came to play while his mother and newborn sister napped. Anticipating another lovely and easy afternoon, I brought a load of boxes out to the deck. Robin gave them a quick glance and said, "Boxes? No, thanks. Do you have a hose?"

See? Everybody's different.

DEVELOPMENTAL AGE RANGE 3 and up

WHAT YOU WILL NEED
- Many boxes
- Optional: markers, tape, scissors

PREPARATION
Bring the boxes outside. (Everything is better outside.)

WHAT YOUR CHILD CAN DO
- Nestle the boxes.
- Stack the boxes into a tall tower.

- Arrange boxes into steps to ascend and descend.
- Spread boxes out and step in them (see *Shoe Box Path*, p. 234).
- Sort the boxes into categories:
  - Size: big, little
  - Shape: rectangular, cylindrical, skinny
  - Color: red, brown, multihued
  - Texture: rough-textured, fabric-covered
  - Weight: heavy, light
  - Constitution: wood, plastic, cardboard
  - Fanciness: hinged, beautiful, flowery, satin-lined
- Collect pebbles, seeds, petals, and so forth, classify them, and put them into boxes.
- Pretend the boxes are houses, furniture, planets, spaceships, automobiles, train cars, boats, national monuments, mountains, farmyards, corrals, stores, school desks, sandboxes, animals, robots, people, and so on.

BENEFITS OF THE ACTIVITY

- Looking for the just-right box among a multitude of boxes improves fundamental visual-motor skills, including fixation (aiming one's eyes or shifting one's gaze from one object to another), focusing (switching the gaze between near and distant objects), and binocularity (coordinating the two eyes to work as a team).
- Searching for the right box also improves more complex visual-spatial skills, including visual discrimination (differentiating among objects), visual figure-ground (attending to specific forms or features of an object while simultaneously ignoring unimportant information), and visualization (seeing a bed, street, village, and so on, in the mind's eye).
- Playing with boxes promotes visual integration skills, including eye-hand coordination (using visual perceptual skills along with gross and fine motor movements).
- Handling boxes with different textures, shapes, and sizes promotes tactile discrimination.
- Building box towers and box cities, and stepping in, around, and on boxes strengthen body awareness, force, motor planning, and kinesthesia.
- Tinkering with "beautiful junk," like boxes, can offer hours of open-ended, multisensory play that stretches the imagination and helps the whole child relate to the surrounding world.

◆ Gutter Games

These activities are marvelous fun for one child and even more enthralling when several children play together.

Gutter Track

DEVELOPMENTAL AGE RANGE 3 and up

WHAT YOU WILL NEED
- Four 10-foot vinyl gutters
- Three two-piece joiners, to connect the gutters
- Several already beat-up wheeled vehicles, about 2 or 3 inches wide
- Bucket or box to catch the cars or trucks

PREPARATION
- Outside, connect the gutters with the two-piece gutter joiners. Lay the *Gutter Track* on a slope, or raise one end by resting it on a chair or ledge.
- Slip the bottom end of the *Gutter Track* into the bucket to serve as a garage, train station, or airplane hangar.

WHAT YOUR CHILD CAN DO
- Place trucks at the top of the *Gutter Track* and watch the trucks go.
- Walk or run alongside the trucks.
- Pluck the trucks out of the bucket and carry them back to the top.
- Raise or lower the slant of the track to change the speed of the trucks.
- Place two tracks side by side and have races with other kids.

Gutter Canal

DEVELOPMENTAL AGE RANGE 4 and up

WHAT YOU WILL NEED
- One or two gutters
- Hose (if playing with water is acceptable in your area)
- Sandbox

- Large plastic tub
- Little old boats, sand shovels, scoops, and spoons

- Place the plastic tub in the sandbox, and rest the bottom end of the gutter in the tub. Raise the other end.
- Have the child remove shoes and socks, or wear boots.

WHAT YOUR CHILD CAN DO
- Nestle the hose nozzle at the top of the gutter and turn on the hose.
- Send boats down the canal and into the "ocean" (the water-filled tub).
- Place the *Gutter Canal* directly on the sand. The water will begin to carve out a trench.
- With shovels, scoops, spoons, and hands, enlarge the trench into a river system or a lake.

VARIATIONS
- Instead of gutters, scrape out a trench in the soft sand or mud beside a river or lake.
- Instead of a hose, use buckets full of water.

BENEFITS OF *GUTTER GAMES*
- Watching toy vehicles and water glide down the *Gutter Track* improves basic visual-motor skills, such as tracking, focusing, and binocularity; and more complex visual processing skills such as discrimination, figure-ground, and visual-spatial perception.
- Running alongside the moving toys or water builds gross motor muscles, eye-body coordination, and kinesthesia.
- Constructing a *Gutter Canal* is sensational messy play and tactilely nourishing.
- The *Gutter Canal* activity also encourages visualization, promotes motor planning, and provides hands-on lessons in physics and civil engineering.
- Playing *Gutter Games* with friends fosters communication, social skills, language skills, and emotional security.

On a hot summer night, this activity for two or more players is exceedingly cool. It's another delightful idea from Rondalyn V. Whitney, M.O.T., O.T.R.

DEVELOPMENTAL AGE RANGE 3 and up

WHAT YOU WILL NEED
- Garden hose
- Flashlight for each player
- Colored cellophane or sandwich wrap

PREPARATION
Cover each flashlight's glass with colored cellophane or sandwich wrap.

WHAT THE PLAYERS CAN DO
- Go outside at night.
- One player squirts a stream of water from the hose.
- Other players follow the stream with their flashlights.

VARIATION
Robin's Rainbow
Remember Robin, who prefers hoses to boxes? Robin is 4 years old. On a bright, sunny day, he picks up a hose and points it skyward. He revolves slowly until he finds the just-right angle for the cascading water drops to catch the light and make a rainbow. Radiant, he says, "Isn't that cool? My brother Jesse taught me this trick, and now I'm the teacher, teaching you."

- Watching the stream of water (by night) or the rainbow (by day) encourages eye tracking and binocularity.
- Following the water with the flashlight or aiming the hose accurately to make a rainbow strengthens eye-hand coordination and force.
- Being showered with water nourishes the tactile system.

◆ Squirt Them Down

Squirting a hose on a warm day can be one of childhood's great pleasures. Aubrey Lande, M.S., O.T.R./L., who lives in thirsty Colorado, suggests coordinating this activity with watering the plants and grass. She says, "Try to use a part of the yard that would benefit  from watering so you don't feel like an eco-pariah!" Also, enjoy the activity in the early morning or late afternoon, when less evaporation occurs.

DEVELOPMENTAL AGE RANGE 3 and up (depending on the child's fine motor skills, strength and endurance, and ability to use his or her thumbs effectively)

WHAT YOU WILL NEED

- Empty juice cans or plastic water jugs
- Garden hose with a nozzle that the child can squeeze to affect the flow (the greater the water pressure, the easier the task)

PREPARATION

Line up cans or jugs on the grass or at the edge of a vegetable garden.

WHAT YOUR CHILD CAN DO

- Aim the hose at the cans, squeeze the nozzle, and squirt them down.
- After each knock-down, line up the cans and squirt them down again.

- Aiming at targets improves visual-motor skills, (fixation and binocularity), and visual-spatial skills, (directionality and figure-ground).
- Squeezing the hose nozzle improves grip strength, a major component of handwriting.
- Raising and lowering the hose to position it just right increases body awareness and grading of movement.
- Combining the play with function in an environmentally friendly way teaches children to be mindful of the world's precious resources.

◆ Metronome Code

This game helps elementary school-age children develop rhythm, timing, and eye movement in a coordinated way. Sanford R. Cohen, O.D., F.C.O.V.D., a developmental optometrist practicing in Maryland, says *Metronome Code* is his favorite vision therapy procedure to help children improve their reading skills.

DEVELOPMENTAL AGE RANGE 8 and up (younger children can play too, using two or three symbols)

WHAT YOU WILL NEED

- Chalk and chalkboard, or a marker and big piece of paper on an easel
- Metronome, from a music store or catalog (see *Recommended Materials*)

PREPARATION

- Together, make up a code of symbols to represent body movements. For example:

  X = clap hands   % = pull ear lobes
  / = tap shoulders   # = stamp foot
  ! = cluck tongue   §§ = snatch at an imaginary bug
  + = slap hands on knees ? = shrug shoulders
  * = snap fingers   ~ = wiggle eyebrows

- Make sure that the child knows how to make all these movements. Some children will need practice, as well as verbal or kinesthetic cues, to master complex motions that are not yet in their "movement vocabulary."
- Have the child write the symbols and perhaps the whole code at the top of the board.

WHAT YOU CAN DO

- Write a sentence in code on the board. Start simply, with two symbols. Each group of symbols will represent a word, and each space will represent a pause. Here is an example of a code sentence and its translation into motion:

X /	X X /	/ X	X / X	/ /
Clap, tap, pause	Clap, clap, tap, pause	Tap, clap, pause	Clap, tap, clap, pause	Tap, tap.

- When the child understands the game, add the metronome to increase the challenge. Now the child must clap, tap shoulders, and pause with the beat. Set the metronome first at 30, and then increase the tempo to 45, to 60, and finally to 90 beats per minute.

WHAT YOUR CHILD CAN DO

- Clap, tap shoulders, and pause!
- Try more intricate patterns: clap, tap, snap, slap knees, stamp foot, pause.
- Cross the midline where possible. For example, slap right hand on left knee and left hand on right knee. Tap left shoulder with right hand, and right shoulder with left hand. Pull opposite ear lobes.
- Come up with complex or goofy motions. For example, a triangle could mean "pull an ear lobe with one hand, tweak your nose with the other hand, and stick out your tongue."
- Write sentences on the board and set the metronome to challenge himself—and you, too.

BENEFITS OF THE ACTIVITY

- Moving the eyes ahead of the clapping and tapping makes the child's reading more fluid. In reading, the eyes must be ahead of the word-sound production (pronunciation).

- Reading the symbols and expressing them through movement improves problem-solving skills, eye-hand coordination, and motor planning.
- Engaging various body parts to shrug, stamp, wiggle, and so forth, improves body awareness, gross motor skills, and kinesthesia.
- Moving in time to the metronome improves beat awareness, which leads to smoother overall coordination.
- Playing the game builds auditory-visual integration.
- Writing at a blackboard or easel strengthens postural control, lateralization, fine motor control, and hand position—all ingredients of good handwriting.

COPING TIPS
- Too many symbols? Go back to two or three.
- Tempo too fast? Return to a slower beat.
- Too hard to play with the metronome, even beating very slowly? Then play without a metronome for a while, and then reintroduce it.

Remember: the *F* in **SAFE** activities stands for Fun, not Frustration!

◆ Flashlight Tag

Flashlight Tag is a pleasant activity at bedtime and at many other times. Joye Newman, M.A., a perceptual-motor therapist in Bethesda, Maryland, has ordered the playful interactions in a sequence of difficulty. When you first play the game, begin simply and add more challenges when your child is ready.

DEVELOPMENTAL AGE RANGE 3 and up

WHAT YOU WILL NEED
Two flashlights

PREPARATION
- Have your child lie in a supine position (face up), on the floor or bed.
- Turn out the light.

Ways to Play *Flashlight Tag*

(In Order of Difficulty)

WHAT YOU CAN DO	WHAT YOUR CHILD CAN DO
1. Shine your flashlight on the ceiling and move the light in a slow path. Say, "Follow the light just with your eyes. Keep your head very still."	1. Watch your moving light.
2. Keep moving the light. Say, "Point to the light with your finger or another body part."	2. Point to your light with her finger, elbow, knee, foot, tongue, or nose. (Her head will have to move, of course, when her nose moves!)
3. Give your child her own flashlight. Say, "Hold it in two hands."	3. Holding the light with both hands, experiment with shining her flashlight on the ceiling, walls, and floor.
4. Move your light smoothly across the ceiling.	4. Make her light "jump and land" here and there on your smooth path.
5. "Jump" your light from spot to spot.	5. Make her light jump and land on your jumping light.
6. Make slow, easy paths on the ceiling. Say, "Tag my light—and don't let go!"	6. Keep her light continuously on your smoothly moving light.
7. Make more intricate paths of light, such as a wavy line, zigzag, circle, triangle, square, heart, or figure 8.	7. Keep her light continuously on your intricate path of light.

Variations

1. Shine your light on the floor.	1. Jump on your light with two feet.
2. "Jump" your light from place to place on a wall for your child to "catch." To encourage her to cross the midline, beam the light toward her left side and tell her to catch it with her right hand. Alternate with the other side.	2. "Catch" your jumping light, first with her right hand, then with her left.
3. Tag after your child's light.	3. Take a turn being "It."

BENEFITS OF THE ACTIVITY

- Keeping her head still encourages the eyes to move independently, thereby strengthening visual-motor integration.
- Tracking a moving light improves basic visual-motor skills and directionality.
- "Jumping" her eyes from spot to spot improves her ability to shift her gaze quickly—an important survival skill.
- Holding the flashlight in both hands encourages bilateral integration, which is necessary for crossing the midline.
- Following your light path improves eye-hand coordination and grading of movement.
- Playing *Flashlight Tag* fosters communication and relatedness.

COPING TIPS

- If your child's light misses or "falls off" your light path, slow down. Accurate responses and sustained tracking are the goals here.
- If your child becomes frustrated as the difficulty increases, go back a step.

6

~~~~

Hearing
(The Auditory Sense)

Rasheed, 3, is underresponsive to auditory sensations. He is self-absorbed and pays little attention to most sounds and voices. One day he surprises his father as they stroll around the block. Rasheed alerts instantly when a neighbor's dog, barking fiercely, bolts to the end of its chain. Rather than becoming alarmed, Rasheed grins. He wants to get closer and tugs on his father's hand, but his father wants to protect him and, without discussion, tugs him away.

Marissa, 11, has difficulty processing auditory sensations. She can hear well, but has trouble using what she hears to learn and to relate to others. Her receptive language is poor. For instance, her mother sends her to the store for broccoli, orange juice with no pulp, and chicken wings; Marissa returns with broccoli, yes, but orange juice with pulp and no chicken wings. Her expressive language is also poor. Conversations with classmates are terse, because putting thoughts into words is a struggle. At dinner, when it's her turn to talk about her day, her reports are short, and no one in the family has the energy or know-how to pursue a full answer.

Rasheed and Marissa could use some help to improve their auditory sense.

Audition, or hearing, is the ability to receive sounds. We are born with this basic skill. We can't learn how to do it; either we hear, or we don't.

The ability to hear does not guarantee, however, that we understand sounds. We are not born with the skill of comprehension; we acquire it, as we integrate vestibular sensations. Gradually, as we interact purposefully with our environment, we learn to interpret what we hear and to develop sophisticated auditory processing skills.

Rasheed and Marissa's auditory skills hinder them from using what they hear to respond adaptively. Some characteristics of auditory dysfunction are listed below.

CHARACTERISTICS OF AUDITORY DYSFUNCTION

The child with auditory dysfunction may:

☐ Seem unaware of the source of sounds, and may look all around to locate where the sounds come from.

☐ Have trouble identifying voices or discriminating between sounds, such as the difference between "bear ' and "bore."

☐ Be unable to pay attention to one voice or sound without being distracted by other sounds.

☐ Be distressed by noises that are loud, sudden, metallic, or high-pitched, or by sounds that don't bother others.

☐ Have trouble attending to, understanding, or remembering what she reads or hears. She may misinterpret requests, frequently ask for repetition, and be able to follow only one or two instructions in sequence.

☐ Look to others before responding.

☐ Have trouble putting thoughts into spoken or written words.

☐ Talk "off topic"—talk about her new shirt when others are discussing a soccer game.

☐ Have trouble "closing circles of communication"—that is, responding to others' questions and comments.

☐ Have trouble correcting or revising what she has said to be understood.

☐ Have a weak vocabulary and use immature sentence structure (poor grammar and syntax).

☐ Have difficulty reading aloud.

☐ Have trouble making up rhymes and singing in tune.

☐ Have difficulty speaking and articulating clearly.

☐ Improve her speaking ability after she experiences intense movement.

When interpreting auditory sensations is the problem, speech and language therapy, occupational therapy, or another SI-based therapy such as auditory integration therapy, will help. (Auditory integration therapy is a method of sound stimulation designed to improve a person's listening and communicative skills, learning capabilities, motor coordination, body awareness, and self-esteem.) **SAFE** activities may also be beneficial.

Activities for the Auditory Sense

◆ Slide Whistle Stretch

This activity encourages your child to move his body parts up and down in sync with the rising and falling sound of the slide whistle. The idea to adapt this quickie warm-up exercise as a sit-down activity comes from Pryce, an imaginative and well-liked boy who gets around in a wheelchair. He thrives  on musical, rhythmic, and rhyming activities—and, understandably, shrinks from most gross motor games.

One day, eyeing my slide whistle, Pryce sighs. "Up-and-down stuff is so hard. Can we do something different? Can we just sit?"

Of course! What a great idea! With Pryce in his chair and the rest of us on the rug, we "slide" different body parts up and down, along with the sound. Pryce can't use his legs, but he can lift his arms, shoulders, and head, thanks to years of intensive physical therapy. His agility impresses the other children. "How do you get your arms so high?" one asks.

"Oh, I'm just really good at that." Pryce laughs. He slides from his chair to the floor. "I've got another cool idea. Now, let's lie down on our tummies."

We flip over and arch like cobras. Other children suggest lying on our backs, on our sides, and then face to face with a partner. The game absorbs 30 minutes. The children's creative collaboration, regardless of their differing abilities, is too purposeful and fun to stop.

DEVELOPMENTAL AGE RANGE 3 to 7 to follow you; 5 and older to be the leader

WHAT YOU WILL NEED
Slide whistle (see *Recommended Materials*)

PREPARATION
Sit on the floor, facing each other.

How to Play *Slide Whistle Stretch*

WHAT YOU CAN DO	WHAT YOUR CHILD CAN DO
1. Show the whistle. Say, "Watch and listen. When I blow into this instrument, and the slide is down, the sound is low. As I push the slide up, the sound gets higher." Slowly pull the slide up as you blow.	1. Listen and watch.
2. Say, "Put your hands on the floor. Listen to the sound. When the sound goes up, raise your hands to the ceiling. When the sound goes down, lower them to the floor." Next, have him raise his feet, then his head, and then his hands, feet, and head at the same time. Encourage him to stretch his body parts high and straight.	2. Move his body parts up and down in sync with the rising and falling sound.
3. Vary the way you play: ■ faster ■ slower ■ up and down a scale, note by note ■ with unpredictable bursts and pauses	3. Make adaptive responses to meet the increasing challenges.
4. Ask, "What other positions can we get into while we're on the floor?"	4. Suggest (or show) lying on his back, tummy, and sides.
5. Say, "You are so good at this. Now you be the leader, and I'll follow your slide whistle sound." Clean the mouthpiece, or hand the child his own slide whistle.	5. If able to do so, take the slide whistle and blow into it to control your moves.

VARIATIONS
- Do this while sitting on a therapy ball or a *T-Stool* (see p. 63).
- Squat on your haunches, and say, "Let's stretch up together." Play the whistle and stretch gradually onto tiptoes, along with your child. (See *Scale Songs*, p. 164, for more whole body-stretching ideas.)

BENEFITS OF THE ACTIVITY
- Listening to the rising and falling sound improves attention and auditory discrimination.
- Watching the slide whistle integrates the child's vision with his hearing.
- Making postural adjustments and moving body parts against the pull of gravity, in response to the speed and pitch of the sound, improves the proprioceptive sense, the vestibular sense, and overall sensory integration, from head to toe.
- Blowing on the whistle while pushing the slide up and down strengthens motor planning, force, and bilateral coordination.
- Blowing improves respiration and oral-motor skills.
- Sitting on an unstable therapy ball or *T-Stool* improves posture and balance.
- Playing the game with a group strengthens social skills and a sense of belonging.

◆ Hear, See, and Move

Different noise-makers are necessary for this game. You can purchase rhythm band instruments at any toy or music store. If you want to save money *and* have fun, you and your child may choose instead to make a collection of homemade or natural rhythm band instruments. Suggestions and brief instructions are listed below.

DEVELOPMENTAL AGE RANGE 3 and up

Rhythm Band Instruments

PURCHASED (see *Recommended Materials*)	HOMEMADE/NATURAL
1. Rhythm ("lummi") sticks	1. Two fat dowels, or two branches, about 10 inches
2. Triangle and striker	2. Long carriage bolt dangling from a string, with another bolt or spoon for a striker
3. Woodblock and mallet	3. Wooden block and short dowel; or stones, seashells, or walnuts to strike together
4. Tambourine	4. Jingle bells on a ribbon; or uncooked macaroni or dry beans inside two paper plates, taped or stapled around the rims
5. Shaker	5. Beans or rice in a plastic pill bottle; or dried seaweed, seed pods, leafy branches, or gourds
6. Drum and mallet	6. Oatmeal box or saucepan and pot scrubber or wooden spoon to bang with
7. Slide whistle	7. Your voice, sliding up and down
8. Guiro (Latin American percussion instrument, made from a gourd)	8. Two ears of dried corn-on-the-cob, rubbed together

PREPARATION

- Gather or make rhythm band instruments.
- Go outside, or clear a space indoors for moving around.

Ways to Play *Hear, See, and Move*

(In Order of Difficulty)

WHAT YOU CAN DO	WHAT YOUR CHILD CAN DO
1. Spread the instruments out on a table.	1. Play with the instruments to get a sense of their sound, look, and feel.
2. Say, "Let's play *Hear, See, and Move.*" Strike the triangle and say, "When you hear and see the triangle, that means 'Walk.' Let's walk together." Play and walk for 16 beats.	2. Walk around with you.
3. Next, strike the rhythm sticks together. Say, "When you hear and see the rhythm sticks, walk with your hands in the air."	3. Walk around with you, with hands high in the air.
4. Alternate the triangle/walking combination with the rhythm sticks/ hands-up combination. (You may stay put at the table, although it's more fun for your child if you move, too.)	4. Take simple walking steps when the triangle sounds and walk with hands in the air when the rhythm sticks sound.
5. Add more combinations: ■ Woodblocks = Jump ■ Tambourine = Wiggle and jiggle ■ Shaker = Shake hands in the air ■ Drum, played slowly = March ■ Drum, played rapidly = Run ■ Slide whistle = Kneel down; Stand up ■ Guiro = Turn around	5. Move according to the hear/see/move combinations.
6. Suggest moving at different levels and in different directions.	6. Crouch down low or rise onto tiptoes. Travel backward, sideways, and diagonally.

WHAT YOU CAN DO	WHAT YOUR CHILD CAN DO
7. Increase the challenge by switching instruments after playing only 8 beats instead of 16.	7. Change motions rapidly.
8. Give your child the job of playing different instruments, and do your best to make the appropriate moves.	8. Be in charge of playing the rhythm band instruments and directing your moves.

BENEFITS OF THE ACTIVITY

- Listening to the sounds of the instruments improves auditory discrimination and memory.
- Seeing the instruments provides a visual cue that integrates the senses.
- Moving in different ways enhances beat awareness, body awareness, movement and balance, kinesthesia, bilateral coordination, postural control, and motor planning.
- Playing the instruments improves fine motor skills and grading of movement.
- Being the leader fosters creative thinking, problem-solving skills, communication, and social skills.

◆ Paper Plate Dance

Clean, simple, and dependable, Mozart's music has a powerful effect on the body, mind, and spirit. "Mozart, the prodigy, speaks to the prodigy within each of us," says Don Campbell, music educator and producer of *The Mozart Effect* materials. At his presentations, he scores this point when he conducts the prodigiously popular *Paper Plate Dance*.[1]

---

[1]Based on an exercise that Don Campbell describes in *The Mozart Effect: Tapping the Power of Music to Heal the Body, Strengthen the Mind, and Unlock the Creative Spirit*, Avon Books, New York, 1997, and presented here with his gracious permission.

DEVELOPMENTAL AGE RANGE $3\frac{1}{2}$ and up (adults love this, too)

WHAT YOU WILL NEED

- Two paper plates for each player (no plates? use pieces of construction paper, bean bags, mittens, or clean socks)
- Recorded music (see *Recommended Materials*), such as:
  - "Rondo" from Mozart's *Eine Kleine Nachtmusik*
  - "Papageno's Song" from Mozart's *The Magic Flute*
  - Rossini's *William Tell Overture*
  - Allegro movements from Bach's *Brandenburg Concertos*
  - Stravinsky's *Pulchinello*

PREPARATION

- Show the players how to hold up the plates vertically, one in each hand, and tap the plates' rounded bottoms together to make a gentle sound.
- Sit in a circle and start the music.

WHAT YOU CAN DO

- Tap your plates together in front of you, keeping a steady beat for a count of 8 or 16, or until all the players catch on and copy you.
- Tap your plates together in different positions:
  - Near your feet, at waist-level, at chest-level, and overhead.
  - Behind your back.
  - On your left side, then on your right side. (Always lead with the left hand or foot so your followers will mirror your motions with their right hand or foot. Practicing first with the dominant side may make new movements easier to learn.)
- Move your plates in figure 8s:
  - With both hands doing the same thing side by side—in front of your body, overhead, at your sides, and so forth.
  - With each hand moving in its own direction, mirroring the other.
- Alternate moving your plates on the left and right sides:
  - Swat at imaginary mosquitoes.
  - Tap the left plate on the right knee, the right plate on the left knee.
  - Rub your plates together, holding them vertically or horizontally at different levels—low, middle, and high.
- Hold a plate at each side of your head like elephant ears, and rock side to side.

- Imitate your moves.
- Take over as leader.

BENEFITS OF THE ACTIVITY

- Listening to the music improves auditory processing.
- Following the leader's motions improves eye-ear-hand coordination, proprioception, grading of movement, body awareness, motor planning, and gross motor control.
- Moving the body up and down and from side to side enhances vestibular functioning.
- Using both hands together to tap, wave, flap, and swish the plates promotes bilateral coordination and midline crossing.
- Playing with a group strengthens social skills.

✦ Tapping Tunes

Here's a quickie for any time, anywhere.

DEVELOPMENTAL AGE RANGE 4 and up

WHAT YOU WILL NEED
A pencil to tap, hands to clap, or a drum to beat

PREPARATION
None

- Say, "I'm going to tap out the rhythm of a tune you know. Listen and tell me what the song is."
- Tap, clap, or drum the rhythm of a song your child knows well, such as "Row, Row, Row Your Boat," or "I've Been Working on the Railroad." (Hum the tune, or sing a key word or two, if necessary, to make the game easier.)
- When the child guesses correctly, tap, clap, or drum, and sing the song together.

WHAT YOUR CHILD CAN DO
- Guess the songs.
- Tap, clap, drum, or step to the rhythms.
- Sing along with you.
- Think of a tune and tap, clap, drum, or step its rhythmic pattern for you to guess.

VARIATION
Can't carry a tune in a bucket? Just chant the words rhythmically.

BENEFITS OF THE ACTIVITY
- Listening to the tapped rhythms improves auditory perception and beat awareness.
- Connecting rhythmic patterns with words promotes auditory memory and association, as well as speech and language skills.
- Using the hands to tap, clap, or beat a drum provides tactile and proprioceptive input and improves bilateral coordination and grading of movement.
- Matching body movements to rhythmic beats helps the child internalize the patterns.

◆ Matching Sounds

Each voice and instrument has a distinctive timbre, which is its unique quality of sound. Discerning different timbres may be challenging for the child with an auditory processing problem. This activity makes that task both pleasant and interesting.

DEVELOPMENTAL AGE RANGE 3 and up

WHAT YOU WILL NEED
- Ten empty, identical containers, such as pill bottles or margarine tubs
- Five different kinds of small objects, such as rice, dried beans, kosher salt, paper clips, pennies, buttons, or small pencil erasers

PREPARATION
- Have your child help to partially fill five pairs of shakers: one pair with rice, another with beans, and so on. The preparation process can be a counting-aloud game, with three pennies going into this container and three pennies going into its mate; six buttons into this container and six into its mate, and so on.
- Mix up the pairs and spread the containers on the table.

WHAT YOUR CHILD CAN DO
- Shake a container and guess what is inside.
- Pick up and shake other containers, one by one, until she finds the one with a similar sound. Shake them both at the same time, just to be sure that they match.
- Use the containers as shakers to keep the beat while singing songs or listening to music.

BENEFITS OF THE ACTIVITY
- Counting beans and buttons out loud is a basic language skill.
- Picking up beans and buttons and dropping them into the containers improves eye-hand coordination and fine motor skills.
- Listening to and differentiating the sounds of the containers' contents improves auditory discrimination and auditory memory.
- Shaking the containers improves grading of movement, bilateral coordination, and beat awareness.

◆ Scale Songs

According to a charming myth, when Franz Joseph Haydn, the great eighteenth century C. composer, was a child, he resisted getting up in the morning. His mother struck on a way to rouse him by playing an incomplete musical scale on the keyboard. ("Scale" is from *scala*, Latin for ladder or staircase.) She would begin with middle C, play D, E, F, G, A, B . . . and then stop.

Snuggled under the feather bed, little Franz Joseph would hear the first seven notes. He would wait for the eighth note that would bring resolution to the octave. (An octave, from the Latin *octo*, meaning eight, is a musical series of eight notes.) When the C didn't sound, Franz Joseph would be unable to bear the tension, so he would leap out of bed and run downstairs to hit "C," the final note.

Time for breakfast!

Frau Haydn understood the power of music to restore order and get her son moving. These simple and satisfying *Scale Song* activities may have the same effect at your house.

(Several of these ideas were inspired by the late music educator Peg Hoenack, publisher of MusicWorks materials for teaching xylophone, recorder, and piano to young children. The activities work well with one child or with a group.)

DEVELOPMENTAL AGE RANGE 4 and up

WHAT YOU WILL NEED
- Easel and chalk or marker
- Keyboard, xylophone, or resonator bells (see *Recommended Materials*)
- Eight small stickers, labeled 1 through 8

PREPARATION
- On the board, draw a ladder with eight rungs. Write "1" beside the bottom rung, "2" beside the second rung, and so forth, finishing with "8" beside the top rung. ·
- Place sticker marked "1" on C (middle C on the keyboard, or the first and longest bar on a xylophone or a set of resonator bells). Stick "2" on D, and so forth, ending with "8" on the higher C at the top of the octave.

Playing Scales

<table>
<tr><td>

WHAT YOU CAN DO

1. Stand beside the ladder picture. Put your hand, palm down and flat, next to rung 1. "Step" your hand up the scale, singing the numbers as you go. (Can't sing? In a low voice, say, "One" and raise the pitch of your voice bit by bit as you count up to "Eight.")

</td><td>

WHAT YOUR CHILD CAN DO

1. Place his hand on the floor or on his knee, and, following your lead, move his hand gradually up, one step at a time, until it is stretched over his head at 8.

</td></tr>
<tr><td>

2. Repeat. Pause at 8 and now descend the scale, singing from 8 to 1. Encourage your child to sing the numbers with you.

</td><td>

2. Move his hand up and down, this time singing along with you.

</td></tr>
<tr><td>

3. Turn to the keyboard or xylophone and play up and down the scale, singing the numbers as you go.

</td><td>

3. Crouch, with just his feet touching the floor, and rise inch by inch, stretching to tiptoes until his hands "touch the sky." Return slowly to a crouching position.

</td></tr>
<tr><td>

4. Have your child play the scale while your hand or body follows his lead.

</td><td>

4. Play up and down the scale on the keyboard or xylophone.

</td></tr>
<tr><td>

5. Play and sing "The Pussywillow Song" (below).

</td><td>

5. Crouch and "grow" like a pussywillow. Pause at the top and then descend gradually with each "meow." Wait until the very last moment to fall in a heap at "Scat!"

</td></tr>
<tr><td>

6. Play and sing the scale songs below.

</td><td>

6. Enact the motions the songs suggest.

</td></tr>
</table>

The Pussywillow Song

Play this note:	1 (C)	2 (D)
Sing these words:	I know a little pussy,	His fur is soft and gray,
Play this note:	3 (E)	4 (F)
Sing these words:	He lives down in the meadow,	Not very far away.
Play this note:	5 (G)	6 (A)
Sing these words:	He'll always be a pussy,	He'll never be a cat,
Play this note:	7 (B)	8 (C)
Sing these words:	Cause he's a pussywillow,	Now what do you think of that?
Play this note:	8 (C), 7 (B), 6 (A), 5 (G)	4 (F), 3 (E), 2 (D), 1 (C)
Sing these words:	Meow, meow, meow, meow,	Meow, meow, meow, SCAT!

Ebenezer Sneezer

Play this note:	1 (C)	2 (D)
Sing these words:	Ebenezer Sneezer is a	Topsy-turvy man,
Play this note:	3 (E)	4 (F)
Sing these words:	Sits upon his elbows	Every time he can,
Play this note:	5 (G)	6 (A)
Sing these words:	Dresses up in paper	Every time it pours,
Play this note:	7 (B)	8 (C)
Sing these words:	Whistles "Yankee Doodle"	Every time he snores.
Play this note:	8 (C), 7 (B), 6 (A), 5 (G)	4 (F), 3 (E), 2 (D), 1 (C)
Sing these words:	E— be— ne— zer	Snee— zer! What a man!

Little Bo Peep

Play this note:	8	7	6	5
Sing these words:	Little Bo	Peep has	lost her	sheep and
Play this note:	4	3	2	1
Sing these words:	Doesn't know	where to	find	them.
Play this note:	1	2	3	4
Sing these words:	Leave them a-	lone, and	they'll come	home,
Play this note:	5	6	7	8
Sing these words:	Wagging their	tails be-	hind	them.

Little Bo Peep is a classic "pathètique," a melody based on a descending scale. A pathètique is played with great feeling, or pathos, or, in the case of the inattentive Bo Peep, pathetically.

VARIATIONS

- Take a xylophone to the playground to use near the sliding board ladder. As the child climbs the rungs, play and sing, "1, 2, 3, 4, 5, 6, 7, 8."
- Play a "Body Scale":

  Sing, "1, 1, 1, 1" and tap toes.

  Sing, "2, 2, 2, 2" and tap knees.

  Sing, "3, 3, 3, 3" and tap thighs.

  Sing, "4, 4, 4, 4" and tap belly button.

  Sing, "5, 5, 5, 5" and tap ribs.

  Sing, "6, 6, 6, 6" and tap shoulders.

  Sing, "7, 7, 7, 7" and tap chin.

  Sing, "8, 8, 8, 8" and tap head.

BENEFITS OF THE ACTIVITY

- Scale songs reinforce rhythmic awareness, and they also introduce the concept of musical pitch. (Pitch is the highness or lowness of sounds in relation to one another.)
- Looking at your gestures and the board promotes visual skills, including binocularity, fixation, focusing, tracking, and directionality.
- Matching movements to what he sees and hears promotes eye-ear-body coordination.
- Singing improves auditory awareness, memory, and language skills.
- Changing his head position and maintaining his balance as he moves his body up and down strengthens the child's vestibular system.

- Stretching up and coming down again, inch by inch, improves proprioception, body awareness, gross motor control, force, kinesthesia, and motor planning.
- Refraining from crashing to the floor until the very last note of the scale is played reinforces attention and impulse control.
- Playing the xylophone with the mallet promotes fine motor skills and the use of tools.

◆ Jack and Jill

For the little guys, enacting the brief drama of *Jack and Jill* over and over again is highly entertaining. It's as much fun for two people as it is for a group.

DEVELOPMENTAL AGE RANGE 3 to 5 to enact the story; 5-ish to play the xylophone

WHAT YOU WILL NEED
- Two boards, about 8 feet × 12 inches
- Two blocks, about 12 × 12 × 6 inches
- Two plastic pails
- Gym mat or *Crash Pad* (see p. 90)
- A xylophone or set of resonator bells (see *Recommended Materials*)
- Other rhythm band instruments

PREPARATION
- Practice playing and singing the *Jack and Jill* scale song.
- Place the boards side by side, about 2 feet apart (to prevent crowding).
- Raise the ends of the boards onto blocks to suggest the "hill."
- Spread out the mat or *Crash Pad* near the raised ends of the boards.

WHAT YOU CAN DO
- Show how to play and sing the *Jack and Jill* scale song.
- Let each child play up and down the scale on a xylophone or resonator bells.
- Demonstrate how Jack and Jill will walk slowly up the ramp, and how first Jack, and then Jill, will fall onto the mat.

- Agree who will be Jack and who will be Jill. (A girl can be Jack, and a boy can be Jill, of course. Some children tend to get "stuck" playing the same role, so encourage yours to assume a different persona now and then.)
- If several children are in the audience, distribute xylophones and other instruments among them and help them get ready to play and sing.
- Give Jack and Jill their pails. Or take a pail yourself, if it's just the two of you playing together today.

WHAT JACK AND JILL CAN DO

- Hold their pails, start at the bottom of the "hill," and trudge up slowly while members of the audience play and sing up the scale:

Play this note:	1	2	3	4
Sing these words:	Jack and	Jill went	up the	hill to
Play this note:	5	6	7	8
Sing these words:	fetch a	pail of	wa-	ter.

- Jack first and then Jill tumble onto the mat, while the audience plays and sings down:

Play this note:	1	2	3	4
Sing these words:	Jack fell	down and	broke his	crown and
Play this note:	5	6	7	8
Sing these words:	Jill came	tumbling	af-	ter.

- Pick themselves up, hand over the pails, and be part of the audience while a new cast enacts the story.

BENEFITS OF THE ACTIVITY

- Hearing and singing the song improves auditory discrimination, auditory memory, beat awareness, and speech/language skills.
- Walking up the ramp strengthens movement and balance, motor planning, kinesthesia, and visual-spatial perception.
- Coordinating the actions with the words of the song helps the child pay attention to environmental cues.

- Waiting to take a turn as Jack or Jill and to jump from the hilltop at the right moment develops impulse control, social skills, and team spirit.
- Tumbling gives deep joint pressure input to the proprioceptive system.
- Playing the xylophone or rhythm band instrument strengthens hand dexterity and eye-ear-hand coordination.

COPING TIP

If the child is reluctant to walk up the ramp because of his gravitational insecurity, lay the boards flat on the ground and have him pretend to climb.

◆ Musical Hoops

Competitive games may have little allure for kids whose responses are somewhat slow, or whose coordination is somewhat clumsy. Being the last one picked and the first one out is no fun. To lure kids into the play, offer this noncompetitive game, suggested by Bert Richards, P.T.A., at Abilities Center, in Michigan.

DEVELOPMENTAL AGE RANGE All ages

WHAT YOU WILL NEED
- Four or more players
- Hula hoops, one per person (No hoops? Chalk circles on the floor, tape shapes on the floor, use carpet squares, or see *Recommended Materials.*)
- Musical selections with long pauses "built in," such as:
  - "Musical Chairs," on Wizaublo's *Songames for Sensory Integration*
  - "Wildwood Flower: Start/Stop," on Hap Palmer's *Homemade Band*

PREPARATION
- Arrange hula hoops on the floor in a circle, one hoop per person.
- Say, "When the music plays, we'll all move from one hoop to another, going in a big circle and in the same direction. When the music stops, find a hoop and stand in it. It's okay to stop in a hoop different from the one you started in, because we're sharing the hoops today."
- Start the music. (If you have no start/stop music at hand, choose other lively music and start/stop it manually. An observant child will see what you're doing and integrate that visual cue with the auditory cue—and that is just fine!)

WHAT THE PLAYERS CAN DO (IN ORDER OF DIFFICULTY)

- Go from hoop to hoop around the circle; stop in the nearest hoop when the music stops.
- Jump from hoop to hoop.
- Hop from hoop to hoop.
- Walk backward.
- Watch you remove one hoop each time the music stops and figure out how to share the remaining hoops. (Even when you remove hoops, all players remain in this noncompetitive game, unlike traditional Musical Chairs.)

BENEFITS OF THE ACTIVITY

- Attending to the starts and stops in the music improves auditory discrimination.
- Judging distances between hoops improves visual-spatial perception and directionality.
- Traveling around the circle improves grading of movement, balance, motor planning, kinesthesia, and other functions of the vestibular and proprioceptive senses.
- Jumping into hoops improves bilateral coordination.
- Playing noncompetitive games strengthens social skills and emotional security.

◆ Holiday Rhymes

Any time, anywhere, any number of people can play this rhyming game, suggested by Joanne Hanson, S.L.P.-C.C.C., of Virginia. The simple activity strengthens your child's auditory awareness and tunes the "reader's ear." In fact, an early predictor of good reading skills is the ability to rhyme. So get pencil and pad, and you'll be glad!

DEVELOPMENTAL AGE RANGE 3½ to 12, to think of words and rhymes; 6 to 12, to write them down

WHAT YOU WILL NEED
Paper and pencil

PREPARATION

Together, make a list of words that are related to an upcoming holiday:

- Valentine's Day: red, heart, rose, card, mail, mine, yours
- Independence Day: flag, red, white, blue, parade, corn, melon
- Thanksgiving: friends, food, pumpkin, love
- Hanukkah: candles, lights, pancakes, dreidel, eight
- Christmas: baby, stable, manger, wreath, green, gold, pine, snow

WHAT YOUR CHILD CAN DO

- Write (or dictate) holiday-related words in a column down the left side of the paper. Leave a couple of lines blank between words.
- Think of and write down as many words as possible that rhyme with the holiday words. The rhyming words do not need to be associated with the holiday. For example:
  - red: fed/said/head/bed/thread/led
  - rose: nose/close/chose/those
  - heart: cart/mart/smart/tart
  - card: hard/yard/starred

VARIATIONS

- Suggest made-up words, such as "schmed" to rhyme with "red," or "blart" to rhyme with "heart." Many preschoolers will automatically offer new words that are not yet in our language, and they are welcome contributions to this game.
- Write poems with the rhyming words. For example:

  For you I made a pretty card,
  Very fancy, silver starred.
  I thought about it long and hard.
  Go outside; it's in the yard.

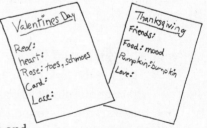

BENEFITS OF THE ACTIVITY

- Rhyming improves important language and reading skills, including auditory processing, memory, and phonemic awareness, which is the ability to recognize "sound bites" called phonemes. Research shows that rhyming games can make it easier for preschoolers to discover similar sounds in spoken words.
- Changing initial speech sounds to suggest more rhymes strengthens oral-motor skills.
- Listing the words on the paper promotes visual-spatial perception, fine motor skills, and handwriting.

◆ Fork and Cork Vibrations

When string players sit down to make music together, they say, "Let's tune." One musician may strike a metal tuning fork that will produce 440 vibrations per second to sound the pitch of "A." Listening carefully to the A, the musicians fiddle with their tuning pegs until their instruments are in tune with one another.

In this multisensory experiment with a tuning fork, you will not only *hear* but will also *see* the pitch of A. This seems almost like magic.

DEVELOPMENTAL AGE RANGE 4 and up

WHAT YOU WILL NEED
- Tuning fork, available at music stores (see *Recommended Materials*)
- Cork
- Needle and strong thread

PREPARATION
Thread the needle and push it through the cork. Tie the thread ends together. Put the cork in your pocket until later.

WHAT YOU CAN DO
- Holding the fork by the handle (the single post), strike one tine on the floor, or on your head or knee. Hold the fork near your ear and listen to its clear, ringing sound.
- Say, "This is a tuning fork. I can hear it ring when I hold it close to my ear, but the sound it makes is too quiet for you to hear. Do you want to hear it?"
- If the child agrees, strike the fork again. Hold it close to her ear. Watch her face light up.
- If she refuses, say, "You can hear it if I put the end of the fork on the table right after I strike it." Touch the handle to a table or other wooden piece of furniture. The sound, resonating through the wood, will fill the room.

- Say, "You can *hear* the sound. Now you will be able to *see* the sound." Take out the cork and dangle it by the thread. Strike the fork again and touch one vibrating tine to the cork. What do you see? The cork dances!
- Say, "The cork vibrates when it touches the vibrating fork. You can really see the vibrations. Now it's your turn to touch the fork with the cork."

WHAT YOUR CHILD CAN DO

- Touch the dangling cork to the fork (after you get it vibrating).
- Make the fork vibrate without help.
- Touch the fork on various surfaces. What happens when it touches hair, skin, or fabric? A box, saucepan, or table? What surface helps it keep ringing, and what makes it stop?
- Hum the note A, matching the A that resonates from the tuning fork.

BENEFITS OF THE ACTIVITY

- Hearing, seeing, and feeling vibrations enhance several sensory systems.
- Handling the fork fosters touch perception, fine motor skills, and bilateral integration.

Buh, Duh, Guh, Blow!

Many children with DSI have difficulty with auditory discrimination. For example, they may be unable to hear the difference between consonants such as *B, D,* and *G.* (For more information, contact a speech/language pathologist or audiologist.)

This **SAFE** activity was created by Laura D. Glaser, M.A., S.L.P.-C.C.C., of Washington, DC. It helps children hone their skills so they have a better chance to become proficient listeners, speakers, readers, and writers.

DEVELOPMENTAL AGE RANGE 5 and up (able to match sounds to letters)

WHAT YOU WILL NEED

- 15 pieces of colored construction paper or white multiuse paper
- Scissors (optional)
- Black crayon
- Blopens™ (markers that you blow through to create pictures—see *Recommended Materials*)

PREPARATION

- Use the paper as is, or to add visual interest, cut each sheet of paper into a snowflake, sunburst, cloud, house, truck, fruit, or large shape.
- On each paper, write one of the sounds listed below. (Sounds that are commonly confused are arranged in five groups. If your child's "specialty" is confusing the "Buh," "Duh," and "Guh" sounds of *B*, *D*, and *G*, you may wish to simplify the game and start with just that group before moving on.)

  1. *B*, *D*, or *G* (pronounced, "Buh," "Duh," and "Guh")

  2. *K*, *P*, or *T* (pronounced, "Kuh," "Puh," and "Tuh")

  3. *F*, *S*, *SH*, or *TH* (pronounced, *Fff* as in "Fun," *Sss* as in "Sun," *SH* as in "SHin," and *TH* as in "THin")

  4. *V*, *Z*, or *Th* (pronounced, *Vvv* as in "Very," *Zzz* as in "Zorro," and *Th* as in "THat")

  5. *M* or *N* (pronounced, *Mmm* as in "Meat," and *Nnn* as in "Neat")

HOW TO PLAY

- Spread out the two, three, or four papers of a sound group.
- Say, "Choose a Blopen and blow some color onto the letter that says, 'Buh.' Now blow some onto the letter that says, 'Duh.' Beautiful!"
- Then let your child decide which letter to decorate. Ask him to tell you what sound he is decorating. Insist on a response. If he really doesn't know, then you pronounce the sound and have him repeat it.

- Depending on your creativity and your child's fine motor skills, you can draw outlines of a snowflake, house, octagon, and so forth, on the paper and have your child cut out the shape. Precision doesn't matter in either the outlining or the cutting.
- Use lowercase letters to challenge your child further. (Usually, children first learn to recognize uppercase letters.)

BENEFITS OF THE ACTIVITY

- Phonics becomes exciting and memorable when the child integrates the sound of the letter, the sight of the brilliant color, and the motion of blowing.
- Blowing stimulates and strengthens the oral musculature (lips, cheeks, jaw, and tongue) and the diaphragm, all of which are needed for speech production.
- Blowing out makes the eyes diverge, widening the child's visual range. (Sucking in makes the eyes converge, bringing near objects into clearer focus). This game gives your child's eyes a healthy workout, thereby strengthening her visual skills.
- Blowing is calming. A calm child is readier to learn and communicate than one who is restless or overexcited.
- Holding and aiming the Blopens improve fine motor skills and motor planning.
- Improving auditory discrimination will, in turn, improve auditory processing, reading, and spelling skills.

◆ "WH" Questions

Learning how to answer *"WH" Questions* is a valuable communication skill. This activity, also from Laura Glaser, S.L.P.-C.C.C., reinforces "WH" concepts while it strengthens auditory processing, movement, and visual skills.

WHAT YOU WILL NEED

- Recordings to inspire kids to move like animals, such as:
  - Ravel's *Mother Goose Suite*
  - Saint-Saëns's *Carnival of the Animals*
  - Hap Palmer's *Animal Antics*
- Paper and pen
- Poster board, ruler, marker
- Scissors and old magazines and calendars featuring animals

PREPARATION

- Put on a recording of music to inspire you to move as animals would. Together, walk, stomp, slither, and so on. Go fast, go slow, reach high, crouch low!
- When you are ready to rest, or on another day, consider the following "WH" questions and make a list of answers, which may be simple or savvy, depending on your child's developmental level. (Some suggestions are offered to get you started.)

    1. WHAT are some animals we can think of?

    - Domesticated animals, or pets: dogs, cats, horses, parrots, goldfish . . .
    - Wild or zoo animals: monkeys, whales, snakes, spiders, owls . . .

    2. WHERE do they live?

    - Close to home: house, garden, aquarium, pet store, farm . . .
    - Out in the big world: beach, ocean, desert, forest, jungle, mountain . . .

    3. WHO pays attention to animals?

    - Boys and girls, men and women
    - Family members: Mommy/Daddy, Sister/Brother . . .
    - Dog groomers, farmers, cowboys, forest rangers, veterinarians . . .

    4. HOW do animals move? (Walk, stomp, creep, leap, slither, stretch . . .)

    5. WHEN do they move? (Day or night; spring or fall . . .)

    6. WHY do they move? (To play, hide, hunt, migrate, warm up . . .)

- Refer to your list of WHERE animals live and have your child choose six animal environments. Divide the poster board into six sections. In each section, draw a symbol or two to suggest a scene where animals may live.

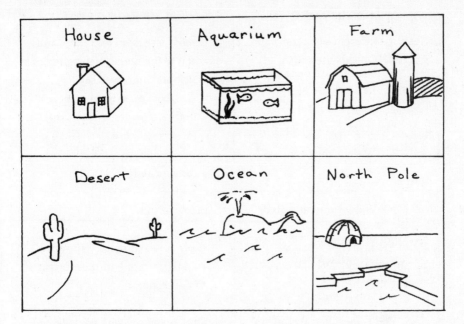

- Together, search through magazines and cut out pictures of:
  - Animals
  - People who pay attention to animals
  - Sun, moon, and stars, and perhaps seasonal foliage or vistas
- Spread the pictures and poster out on a table.

How to Play "WH" Questions

WHAT YOU CAN DO

1. Point to an animal. Ask, "WHAT is this?" If the child can't answer, offer a choice: "Is it a cat or a dog?" (The first choice is the correct answer.) If the child still can't reply, ask a Yes/No question: "Is it a cat?" Give praise for the right answer: "You got it!"

2. Gesture to the poster and ask, "WHERE does the cat live?" (Maybe offer a choice and a Yes/No question.)

WHAT YOUR CHILD CAN DO

1. Pick up the picture and answer, "Cat," or whatever the animal is.

2. Point to the correct scene on the poster and answer, "House" or "Farm." Place the cat in the scene.

WHAT YOU CAN DO	WHAT YOUR CHILD CAN DO
3. Gesture to the cut-out people and ask, "WHO feeds the cat?"	3. Choose a person, pick it up, and add it to the scene. Depending on developmental level, say: • Girl/boy, man/woman, he/she • Pet shop owner, farmer, vet
4. Ask, "HOW does the cat move?"	4. Walk on all fours, stretch like a cat, and arch back.
5. Ask, "HOW does the cat sound?"	5. Meow or purr.
6. Point to the sun or seasonal picture and ask, "WHEN does the cat stretch?"	6. Answer "daytime" or "summer." Add the sun or summery picture to the scene.
7. Ask, "WHY does the cat stretch?" "So it can feel long and strong! Like this!" (Help, if necessary.)	7. Stretch and say with you, "Long and strong!"

VARIATIONS

Transportation "WH" Questions

- WHAT: Bicycles, big wheels, scooters, and other playground vehicles; cars, buses, motorcycles, and 18-wheelers; trains; sailboats, motorboats, tugboats, rafts, and canoes; airplanes, helicopters, and hot air balloons
- WHERE: Playground, backyard, bicycle path; street, highway; railroad track; ocean, river, pond; airport, sky
- WHO: Man/woman; driver, pilot, conductor, skipper, captain, rower
- "WHY does the man drive the car? To go, go, go, go, go!" Roll your hands rapidly in front, like the motion in "The Wheels on the Bus" song.

Clothing "WH" Questions

- WHAT: Sweater, coat, tee shirt, socks, shoes, dress, hat, mittens
- WHERE: Close to home (bed, school, park, party, sledding hill, rain puddle), or out in the big world (North America, Polynesia, Norway, Japan)
- HOW: Child pantomimes putting on sweater, pants, boots
- WHEN: Playing, sleeping, spring, summer, daytime
- "WHY does the boy wear a hat? To feel warm!" (Hug each other.)

Food "WH" Questions

- WHAT: Hamburger, chicken, apple, banana, sandwich, carrots
- WHERE: Kitchen, dining room, picnic table, fast food joint, ice cream parlor, hot dog kiosk, Grandma's house
- WHEN: Valentine's Day, Easter/Passover, Fourth of July, Halloween, Thanksgiving, Christmas/Hanukkah/Kwanza, Birthday
- "WHY does the girl eat? So she can grow, grow, grow, grow!" (Crouch down and stretch up toward the sky, inch by inch.)

BENEFITS OF THE ACTIVITY

- Responding to the music and to "WH" questions benefits auditory processing.
- Making animal sounds and verbalizing answers improves communication and speech and language skills.
- Considering "WH" questions strengthens critical thinking, memory, vocabulary, and categorization, and improves concepts of place, time, and quality of movement.
- Selecting, cutting, and placing pictures on the poster improves visual and fine motor skills.
- Assuming animal-like positions and moving like animals, using different forms of locomotion, strengthens functions of the vestibular and proprioceptive senses, including balance, gross motor skills, bilateral coordination, motor planning, and kinesthesia.

◆ Bird Calls

The calls and songs of wild birds offer a symphony of sound. This activity may be particularly appealing to children with poor vision and superior hearing. Many thanks to Jim Mulholland, a retired teacher and friend, who compiled this list of fairly common birds with distinctive calls. Thank you, Teacher-teacher-teacher! What-cheer-cheer-cheer!

WHAT YOU WILL NEED
- Paper and pencil
- List of birds indigenous to your region, and their distinctive calls.

NE	SE	NW	SE	BIRD	CALL SOUNDS LIKE . . .
*				Ovenbird	Teacher-teacher-teacher
*	*			Northern Cardinal	What-cheer-cheer-cheer
*	*			Eastern Towhee	Drink-your-teee
*	*			White-throated Sparrow	Please-please-Canada-Canada-Canada
*	*			Tufted Titmouse	Peter-Peter-Peter
*		*		Black-capped Chickadee	Chick-a-dee-dee-dee
*		*		White-breasted Nuthatch	Yank-yank-yank
*	*	*	*	Red-winged Blackbird	Konk-la-ree
*	*	*	*	Northern Flicker	Wicker-wicker-wicker/Klee-yer
*	*	*	*	American Goldfinch	PO-ta-to-chip
	*			Northern Bobwhite	Bob-White
	*			Carolina Wren	Tea-kettle-tea-kettle-tea-kettle
	*			Carolina Chickadee	Chick-a-dee-dee-dee
		*		Steller's Jay	Shooka-shooka-shooka
		*		Say's Phoebe	Pee-ee
		*		California Quail	Chi-ca-go
		*		Golden-crowned Kinglet	Tsee-tsee-tsee-tsee
		*	*	Brewer's Blackbird	Ksh-eeee
			*	Common Poor Will	Poor-Will
			*	Scaled Quail	Pea-cos
			*	White-winged Dove	Who-cooks-for-you?

NE	SE	NW	SE	BIRD	CALL SOUNDS LIKE . . .
			*	Cassin's Kingbird	Chi-bew
			*	Cactus Wren	Cha-cha-cha-cha-cha
			*	Oak/Juniper Titmouse	Tschick-a-dee

PREPARATION

Look up regional birds in a reference book, like one of Roger Tory Peterson's *Field Guides*. Knowing how the birds look may help to match sound with sight, although some birds are easier to hear than to see.

WHAT YOU AND YOUR CHILD CAN DO

- Go outside together and listen for bird calls. On the list, check the calls you hear.
- Make note of other birds and their distinct sounds, such as blue jays (a sound like a squeaky swing set) and woodpeckers (rat-a-tat-tat!).
- Make lists of other environmental sounds:
  - Natural—tree branches rustling, squirrels chattering, bees whirring, waves crashing
  - Mechanical—lawn mower, snow blower, air conditioner, car engine, horn, crossing guard's whistle, bicycle bell
- Imitate the calls and ask each other to guess what birds you are trying to imitate.

VARIATIONS

Tape different sounds to identify and perhaps make picture cards for a matching game:
- Other kids' voices
- Rhythm band and musical instruments
- Home sounds—water dripping, footsteps on stairs, computer booting up, toilet flushing
- School sounds—pencil sharpener, stapler, crumpling paper, three-ring binder snapping shut
- City sounds—horn, siren, brakes, whistles, pigeons, coins in a meter, "Taxi!"

BENEFITS OF THE ACTIVITY

- Listening for specific sounds improves auditory discrimination and figure-ground.
- Imitating bird calls and other sounds promotes oral-motor and speech-language skills.
- Matching sounds with sights integrates auditory and visual sensations.

7

~~~~

Smelling
(The Olfactory Sense) and
Tasting
(The Gustatory Sense)

Connor, 5, is not enjoying his first visit to the beach. The smells of low tide, seaweed, fried clams, and mildew in the motel room overwhelm his oversensitive olfactory system. He complains constantly about how the beach stinks. To offer him at least one pleasant beach memory, his parents decide to splurge on a fine dining experience. Everyone puts on shoes, and the family goes to a restaurant that does not feature seafood. Connor is looking forward to plain spaghetti with butter. The waiter, a busy man with strong body odor, comes to take their orders. Connor shouts, "P.U!" He pinches his nose, bursts into tears, and makes such a ruckus that the family leaves. They have soft ice cream for dinner and head for home in the morning. Next summer, they'll return to the mountains.

Mazan, 9, and several buddies share an interest in paper airplanes, kite-flying, and aerodynamics. When the Rocket Club meets, the boys always have to come to Mazan's house. He refuses to go to their homes, because he'll have to eat. He is an extremely picky eater with a narrow range of foods. He won't eat anything with tomatoes or anything green or any fruit. Snacks and meals at his house are not very interesting, so, after a while, the other boys meet at one another's homes without inviting Mazan.

Connor's olfactory sense and Mazan's gustatory sense are atypical. Some characteristics are listed below.

CHARACTERISTICS OF OLFACTORY AND GUSTATORY DYSFUNCTION

The child with olfactory dysfunction may:

☐ Be oversensitive to smells and object to odors, such as a ripe banana, that other children do not notice.

☐ Be undersensitive to smells and ignore unpleasant odors such as dirty diapers.

☐ Be a picky eater.

The child with gustatory dysfunction may:

☐ Be oversensitive to tastes and may strongly object to certain textures and temperatures of foods.

☐ May gag often when he eats.

☐ May lick or taste inedible objects, such as playdough and toys.

☐ May prefer very spicy or very hot foods.

Smell isn't what it used to be. Millions of years ago, creatures depended heavily on this sense to survive. As human beings evolved, the value of smell to help us survive has decreased, as the senses of sight and hearing became more essential.

Still, smell plays an important part in establishing and reviving memories. When we smell something, the olfactory stimulus zips directly to an ancient structure in our brain, the limbic system, without taking a detour. (Other senses send information to the brain through more circuitous routes.)

Our response to familiar smells is immediate. The scent of soap is pleasant, because it instantly evokes a time of being cuddled and cared for, clean and comfortable. Most of us enjoy the effects of soaping up.

Our response to unfamiliar smells is also immediate. Whether or not we have smelled a noxious odor before, we are equipped to alert to it. We sense that offensive odors such as rotten food, gas leaks, and body odor will not improve our well-being. We wrinkle our noses and get away.

Like all the senses, taste helps us survive and provides us with essential information about bitter, salty, sweet, and sour flavors. Is this plum or pill too bitter to swallow? Is this pickle so sour it will cause a stomachache? We spit out what our gustatory sense informs us may be harmful.

Smell and taste are intertwined. In fact, about 75 percent of taste perceptions depend on an efficient sense of smell. That's why a bad cold will decrease your appetite, because food that you can't smell well tastes bland.

DSI may affect smell and taste. Undersensitivity or oversensitivity to smells and tastes often interferes with a child's eating habits and nutrition. Indeed, DSI may be a huge contributing factor to a feeding aversion, leading to a failure-to-thrive diagnosis. (More about eating is in the next chapter on oral-motor development and skills.)

For a problem with the olfactory and gustatory systems, SI-based therapy and nutritional therapy are suggested. Nutritionists provide guidance and dietary supplements to improve a child's development and functioning. Meanwhile, try some **SAFE** activities.

Activities for the Olfactory and Gustatory Senses

◆ Smell and Tell

Whether your child is overly sensitive to smells, not at all sensitive, or somewhere in between, this guessing game may be a pleasant way to inform the olfactory sense.

DEVELOPMENTAL AGE RANGE
4½ and up

WHAT YOU WILL NEED
- Plastic pill bottles, cotton balls, and tray
- Hammer and large nail, or awl
- Wooden board or piece of 2 × 4 inches (like a miniature workbench to hammer on)
- Several strong scent-producers:

(GENERALLY) AROUSING SCENTS

Basil	Garlic	Oregano
Burnt candlewick	Lemon or orange	Pencil shavings
Chocolate	Mint or peppermint	Rubber
Coffee	Mothballs	Sardines
Dirt	Onion or chives	Vinegar

(GENERALLY) CALMING SCENTS

Aftershave	Chamomile	Lily of the valley
Almond extract	Cinnamon	Pine needles
Apple	Crayons	Scented markers
Banana	Hand lotion	Soap
Butter	Lavender	Vanilla extract

PREPARATION
- Holes in each pill bottle lid will allow the scent to escape. Help your child lay the lids on the wood, pick up the hammer and nail, and tap three or four big holes through each lid. (Please use your judgment

about whether this is a safe and appropriate activity for your child. If you are unsure, make the holes yourself.)

■ Array the scent-producing items that you have selected on the tray.

WHAT YOU CAN DO

■ Pick up a pinch of something from the tray. Show it to your child and say, "Here's cinnamon (oregano, lavender, and so on). Umm! Smells good! Just like Granny's apple pie (Dad's spaghetti sauce, Mrs. Stern's perfume, and so on). Want a sniff?"

■ If your child agrees, invite her to sniff the scent. (If she refuses, say, "Okay, maybe another day." Clean up and go about your business.)

■ Say, "Let's put a bit of each smell into its own bottle and play a game."

■ Show how to put a few drops of the liquid smells, such as aftershave or vanilla extract, on a cotton ball.

■ Note your child's alerting and calming responses to different aromas and mark your observations for future reference.

WHAT YOUR CHILD CAN DO

■ Help put some of the items into bottles and snap on the lids.

■ Mix up the bottles on the tray.

■ Choose different bottles, sniff them one at a time, guess what's inside, and tell you what the smell reminds him of.

■ Invite friends and family members to try to identify different smells.

BENEFITS OF THE ACTIVITY

■ Playing the game helps olfactory discrimination.

■ Smelling certain scents may improve memory and attention, while smelling other scents may help the child relax and sleep.

■ Talking about associated memories promotes language and communication skills.

■ Preparing and filling the bottles develops eye-hand coordination, hand dexterity, pincer skills, and the use of tools.

COPING TIP

■ If your child has difficulty guessing the smells, put the items in separate clear plastic bags instead of hiding them in film bottles. Then, integrating what she sees with what she smells, the child may identify the aromas more easily.

■ Do not offer calming and arousing scents at the same time. Strong scents can cause an intense headache.

◆ Pomander

When I was a Brownie, I made a *Pomander* as a Mother's Day gift. It stayed fragrant in my mother's closet for years. When my son's Cub Scout den made them two decades ago, even the boys with fine motor difficulties enjoyed poking the cloves into the fruit.

DEVELOPMENTAL AGE RANGE 5 and up

WHAT YOU WILL NEED
- An orange or apple ("pomander" comes from the Latin, *pomum de ambra,* which means "apple of amber")
- Cloves
- Plastic cup with a rim that is smaller than the diameter of the fruit (so that the fruit won't fall into the cup)
- Pretty ribbon, ½ to 1 inch wide and about 30 inches long
- Two straight pins

WHAT YOUR CHILD CAN DO
- Stick cloves into the orange. (How many? It doesn't matter.)
- Rest the fruit on the cup's rim, to dry and wither.
- Help you measure the ribbon and tie it around the circumference of the dry fruit, and knot the ends together.
- Stick straight pins through the ribbon to secure it to the fruit.
- Hang the pomander in a closet.

BENEFITS OF THE ACTIVITY
- Making and sniffing a pomander, with its fruity and spicy scents, improves olfactory awareness.
- Motor planning, grading of movement, and fine motor skills improve by pushing cloves into the fruit. This action is called "translation movement," according to Mary D. Benbow, M.S., O.T.R./L., a specialist in hand development. A translation movement involves grasping a small item—such as a clove or a push pin—in your thumb, index, and middle fingers and moving these fingers toward and away from your palm.
- Holding the fruit with one hand while poking cloves with the other hand promotes bilateral coordination and tactile awareness.
- Watching what he's doing improves the child's oculomotor skills.

◆ Smash and Smell

This delightfully aromatic activity comes from the fertile imagination of Lori Merkel, C.O.T.A./L. The preparation is pleasant, the process is cathartic, and the product is pretty prints that look lovely when matted and hung on the wall.

DEVELOPMENTAL AGE RANGE 3 and up (possibly younger, if well supervised)

WHAT YOU WILL NEED

- Flowers and other plants of different colors and smells:
  - Pansies, petunias, violets, wild flowers, and three- or four-leaf clovers
  - Petals from marigolds, mums, geraniums, roses, and dandelions
  - Herb sprigs and mint tea sprigs

- Tray
- White construction paper
- Rubber-tipped mallet
- Newspaper or brown paper bags to cover work surface, if done inside

PREPARATION

- Cover a sturdy table with paper, if necessary, or do the activity outside.
- Together, pick and pluck flowers, preferably from your own pots or garden. (It's thoughtful to leave flowers in the wild for others to enjoy.) Lay them on the tray.

WHAT YOUR CHILD CAN DO

- Take a sheet of white paper and arrange flowers or herbs on it.
- Place another piece of paper on top of the flowers and herbs.
- Gently, but firmly, hit the top paper with the mallet, smashing the flowers and herbs below so that the "juices" stain the papers.
- Remove top paper and use fingers to push off any smashed petals and stems that may be sticking to it.

- Smell fingers and paper and look at the pretty designs.
- Later, use dried papers to wrap presents, make cards, mount in picture frames, share with friends, and send to Grandma.

VARIATION
Use a rolling pin instead of a mallet.

BENEFITS OF THE ACTIVITY
- Smelling the flowers and herbs stimulates the olfactory sense.
- Touching, picking, and plucking the flowers and herbs promotes tactile discrimination and improves fine motor skills.
- Arranging flowers improves visual perception and eye-hand coordination.
- Using a mallet with one hand while the other hand stabilizes the paper, or rolling the pin with both hands, improves bilateral integration.
- Hitting the working surface or pressing the rolling pin provides proprioceptive input and improves grading of movement.
- Using the mallet or rolling pin provides beneficial deep pressure input and stimulation to the palms, which may be a very sensitive area for some children.
- Smashing flowers provides auditory stimulation and releases tension.

◆ Scented Flash Cards

Many of the children whom Trude Turnquist, Ph.D., O.T.R./L., treats in her Minneapolis clinic have sensory modulation disorders. She has found that many of these children are very responsive to an *olfactory immersion experience*. For the low arousal kids she sprays the clinic with citrus or spice scents, and for those kids who are anxious, she uses sugar cookie or gingerbread smells that seem to diminish their fears.

Compatible scented markers and scented glues also seem to help the children focus while doing fine motor tasks. Trude's newest discovery is the Harry Potter series of markers, with the strongly arousing "Peppermint Humbugs," the delicious "Chocolate Frogs" and "Grape Marmalade," and, just as popular, the malodorous "Dungeon Dirt" and "Savory Sardine"! (Take care not to mix scents, as many children quickly exhaust their olfactory system and lose attention or can develop headaches.)

Trude follows up her SI activities with TouchMath™ scented flashcards. Here, following her technique, I have designed another touch and smell activity that can help your child learn numbers and letters—and makes perfect scents!

DEVELOPMENTAL AGE RANGE 3 and up

WHAT YOU WILL NEED
- Elmer's 3D scented glue
- File cards and drawing paper

WHAT YOU CAN DO
- Choose a scented stick of glue and squeeze a number of domino-style glue dots on each card.

0 0 0	0 0 0 0 0 0	0 0 0 0 0 0 0 0

- Or write letters on other cards with the scented glue.

- Let the glue dry for one hour.
- Use the number and letter cards as flash cards for the nose and fingers, to reinforce number concepts and letter recognition.

WHAT YOUR CHILD CAN DO WITH *SCENTED FLASH CARDS*:
- Write letters and numbers and draw pictures.
- Stroke, sniff, and read the multisensory number and letter cards.
- Blindfolded, try to recognize the numbers and letters by touch and smell alone.

- Smelling strong odors improves olfactory discrimination.
- Touching and seeing the scented glue numbers and letters integrates tactile and visual sensations with smells, thereby increasing memory, attention, and association.
- Writing and drawing with the glue sticks builds fine motor skills.

◆ Smello

Here's a fragrant new twist on bingo, from Lori Merkel, COTA/L. One child or a bunch of children and adults can play the game.

DEVELOPMENT AGE 2 and up. The game can be adapted for various age levels and abilities. Start with two smells for very young children and add more to increase the challenge.

WHAT YOU WILL NEED
- Blank index cards; or card stock, poster board, or construction paper cut into the approximate size of bingo cards
- Plastic pill bottles
- Cotton balls
- Smells such as lemon juice, cinnamon, and essence oils
- Masking tape or small labels
- Buttons, pennies, or bingo chips

Simple Smello Card   Challenging Smello Card

PREPARATION
- Make *Smello* cards:
  - Decide how many smells you want to use.
  - Divide cards into sections equal to the amount of smells.
  - Place a picture and a word corresponding to the smell in each section.
  - Arrange the smells on each card in a different order, if possible.
  - Optional: Make several copies of each card and laminate them.
  - Make at least two cards for each player.
- Put a cotton ball in each pill bottle and place a drop of juice or oil or a sprinkle of herb or spice on the cotton. Repeat the process until all are prepared.

- Place lids on firmly.
- Write the name of the smell on a piece of tape or label and stick it to the bottom of the pill bottle.

WHAT YOUR CHILD CAN DO

- Pick a card.
- Pick a pill bottle and pry off the lid (with help, if necessary).
- Take a smell and try to describe and identify it.
- Locate the picture or word on the *Smello* card that corresponds to the smell.
- Place a button in the appropriate space on the card.
- "Win" the game by identifying all the smells and filling the card. *Smello!*

VARIATIONS

- Win *Smello* by getting three or four in a horizontal, vertical, or diagonal row, like bingo.
- Play with a group and pass the smells around, so all can smell.
- For a noncompetitive game, make all the cards identical, with all the words/pictures located in the same position on each card for each child.
- Instead of buttons or chips, use a pencil or crayon (or a dry-erase marker on laminated cards) to "X" the word/picture.

BENEFITS OF THE ACTIVITY

- *Smello* helps the child develop smell discrimination.
- The game teaches a new skill: smell/picture/word correspondence.
- Describing smells (sweet, stinky, and so on) improves vocabulary and language skills.
- Removing the lids improves fine motor skills and finger strength.

- Looking at the cards, seeing horizontal, vertical, and diagonal rows, and placing the chip in the appropriate space improve visual skills.
- Using a pencil or crayon promotes prewriting, pencil grasp, and the concept of "X"-ing out.
- Sharing the bottles with other players fosters social skills.

◆ Taste and Tell

While this activity is primarily designed to strengthen gustatory discrimination, it also involves olfactory sensations. Mother Nature intends for us to detect whether the meat is fresh *before* we put it in our mouths.

DEVELOPMENTAL AGE RANGE 3 and up

WHAT YOU WILL NEED
An assortment of food bits, such as:
- Pieces of freshly baked muffins
- Jelly beans
- Small spoonfuls of jam or jelly
- Sections of citrus fruit
- A variety of nut butters
- Popcorn with different seasonings, such as salt, garlic, or curry
- Pieces of food that have a similar appearance and texture, such as:
  - Apple, radish, jicama (a sweet Mexican root vegetable), water chestnut, parsnip, and turnip
  - Nectarine, peach, cantaloupe, and mango

PREPARATION
Set the food bits out on a large plate so the child can see them distinctly and so the flavors stay separated.

WHAT YOUR CHILD CAN DO
Taste and tell!

VARIATION
To make the game harder, try guessing with eyes closed or covered, without the aid of vision.

- Tasting different foods improves gustatory and olfactory discrimination.
- Putting food into the mouth promotes tactile perception.
- Chewing and swallowing improve oral-motor skills and force, which is the ability to judge the motion of the muscles and joints in the mouth in order to bite and chew correctly.
- Guessing what the food is, while the eyes are closed, improves visualization.

COPING TIP

Offer, but do not force this game on a picky eater.

◆ New Taste Sensations

The "just-right" sensory activity before a meal may entice picky eaters to try new foods. Seeing how her son's sensory diet improved his appetite, Angela Gilbert began a program—appropriately named "FedUp!"—for children with DSI and feeding disorders.

Once a month, a group of families gathers together in San Antonio, Texas. Soft background music encourages the toddlers and preschoolers to play and relate to one another. Livelier music encourages them to engage in vigorous sensory-motor activity, and soothing music plays again as they settle down to explore *New Taste Sensations*.

The theme of one meeting was circles and balls. The children played in a ball pit in a tent before moving to the table. Angela says, "All the foods were round to correspond to the ball play. A set of triplets chowed down Spaghettios and peas, which they had never tried before! (My son Gary just ran 'round and 'round . . . oh, well.)"

She adds, "Another program was based on sounds. The children popped plastic bubble wrap and snapped packing peanuts between their fingers. They jumped and rolled on the materials, too. Then they were ready for the transition to noisy foods, such as nuts, seeds, pretzels, and cheese curls. We also showed them how they could let some foods dissolve in their mouths or how 'meltables' like crackers can be eaten quietly by letting them soften in water, juice, applesauce, or soup."

For the families in this unique eating club, the term "fed up" is taking on new and wonderful meaning. *New Taste Sensations* may turn meal time in your home into a pleasant and nourishing experience as well.

DEVELOPMENTAL AGE RANGE 18 months and up

PREPARATION
- ■ Choose a theme for sensory play and foods that are associated with the theme.
- ■ Set the scene.
- ■ Set the table.

WHAT YOUR CHILD CAN DO WITH CIRCLES, BALLS, AND OTHER ROUND MATERIALS	ROUND FOODS
Squeeze, kick, throw, and catch balls and balloons	Spaghettios
	Tortellini
Sit, bounce, and lie on therapy balls	Pita bread
	English muffins, scones
Move around in a ball pit (see *Recommended Materials*)	Pancakes
	Rice cakes
Stack and nestle cans, plastic tubs, and jar lids	Cheerios
	Apple rings
Enjoy other **SAFE**, "round" activities:	Banana slices
• *Barrel of Fun* (p. 67)	Blueberries
• *Chewy Necklace* (p. 209)	Cherries
• *Citrus Balls* (p. 133)	Grapes
• *Inner Tube Sport* (p. 92)	Melon balls
• *The Laundromat Game* (p. 75)	Oranges, clementines
• *Looby Loo* (p. 86)	Carrot, cucumber, and potato slices
• *Musical Hoops* (p. 171)	Lentils
• *Paper Plate Dance* (p. 160)	Olives
• *Peanut Butter Jar* (p. 273)	Peas
• *Pokin' O's* (p. 130)	
• *Pomander* (p. 189)	
• *Sally Go Round the Sun* (p. 84)	
• *Voyage to Mars* (p. 80)	

ACTIVITIES WITH SQUARES, CUBES, AND RECTANGLES	SQUARE FOODS
• *Beanbag Mania* (p. 277) • *Billions of Boxes* (p. 141) • *Box Sweet Box* (p. 106) • *Become a Butterfly* (p. 112) • *Scented Flash Cards* (p. 191) • *Shoe Box Path* (p. 234) • *Toothpick Constructions* (p. 256)	Ravioli Toast and waffles Squared/cubed • turkey, chicken • tofu • cheese • apples, melon, mangoes • potatoes • cucumbers, peppers

STICKY AND MUSHY ACTIVITIES	STICKY, MUSHY FOODS
• *Applesauce Through a Straw* (p. 211) • *Dinosaur Morning* (p. 224) • *Go Away, Glue!* (p. 45) • *Heavy Hands* (p. 34) • *Kiss the Mirror* (p. 223) • *Messing Around with Un-Paint* (p. 26) • *No-Mess Messy Play* (p. 44) • *Slurp Party* (p. 57) • *Tactile Road* (p. 47) • *Touch Pantry* (p. 38)	Applesauce Banana Honey Hummus Cottage cheese Cooked cereal Mashed squash, potatoes Other vegetables Peanut butter Other nut butters

NOISY ACTIVITIES	NOISY FOODS
• *Bubble Wrap Burst* (p. 254) • *Crash Pad*, filled with packing peanuts (p. 90) • *Hammer and Nails* (p. 104) • *Old Lady Sally* (p. 82) • *Swing, Bat and Pitch* (p. 77) • *Wind Competition* (p. 217) • Activities in the Hearing chapter, of course!	Nuts, seeds, and popcorn Rice cakes Pretzels Sliced carrots, radishes, celery, and other crudités Water chestnuts Apples

ACTIVITIES WITH LONG, STRINGY THINGS

- *Applesauce Through a Straw* (p. 211)
- *Fun with a Rope* (p. 96)
- *Hot Dog Roll* (p. 51)
- *Jack and Jill* (p. 169)
- *Mummy Wrap* (p. 50)
- *Simon Says, "Make My Supper!"* (p. 37)
- *Slide Whistle Stretch* (p. 155)
- *Slimy Shapes* (p. 28)
- *Stretchy Bands* (p. 109)

LONG, STRINGY FOODS

Spaghetti, linguini, fettuccini
Ramen noodles
Asparagus
Bean sprouts
Celery
String beans
Julienned carrots zucchini, yellow squash, and peppers
Other vegetables
Licorice string
String cheese

COLORFUL ACTIVITIES

- *Cool and Colorful* (p. 145)
- *Flashlight Tag* (p. 149)
- *Beanbag Mania* (p. 277)
- *Obstacle Course*, with a green, red, or orange theme (p. 239)

COLORFUL

Fruits and vegetables
Tomato sauce
Gelatin dessert

VARIATIONS

- Set out foods that can be dunked, along with mayonnaise, ketchup, cocktail sauce, jelly, hummus, or salad dressing. Baby carrots dipped in ketchup may taste delicious!
- Brainstorm with friends and family members to come up with other themes to use as "hooks." Here are some popular subjects:
  - Animals
  - Construction
  - Dinosaurs
  - Farmers and ranchers
  - Kings and queens
  - Fairy tales/nursery rhymes
  - Transportation
  - Olympics
  - Seasons

BENEFITS OF THE ACTIVITY

- *New Taste Sensations* broadens your child's repertoire of foods and expands his nutritional base.
- Eating engages the gustatory and tactile senses and oral-motor ability.

- Eating new foods promotes social skills, making it easier for your child to go to more places, make new friends, and have new topics to discuss.
- Brainstorming ideas of activities and foods to match improves attention, memory, association, and imagination.

◆ Let Us Eat Lettuce

Even picky eaters will gobble up lettuce that they have grown and garnished with dressings they made themselves. The inspiration for this project comes from Julia H. Berry, M.A., science teacher and assistant director of the nursery school of St. Patrick's Episcopal Day School in Washington, DC.

DEVELOPMENTAL AGE RANGE 4 and up

WHAT YOU WILL NEED
- Plastic containers with small holes in the bottom for drainage
- Potting soil or other medium for growing seeds
- Lettuce or other seeds for edible greens
- Vegetable oil, such as canola, corn, or olive oil
- Vinegar or citrus juice (apple cider vinegar, wine vinegar, balsamic vinegar, or lemon or lime juice)
- Herbs and spices including garlic, chives, dry mustard, salt, and pepper
- Jars and small bowls for each type of dressing

WHAT YOU AND YOUR CHILD CAN DO TO GROW LETTUCE
- Fill the deli boxes with moist potting soil and sprinkle with lettuce seeds. If you are using more than one type of seed, you may wish to

plant them in separate boxes or in rows marked with the type of seed planted.

- Place the boxes in a location that gets lots of light but not direct sun. Cover the boxes loosely with plastic wrap or partially close the box tops until the seeds sprout. Then uncover. Keep the soil moist but not wet.
- Harvest the crop when the plants are bushy and 3 inches or higher (in about 6 weeks).

WHAT YOU AND YOUR CHILD CAN DO TO PREPARE SALAD DRESSINGS

Below are the ingredients for several basic salad dressings. For all of them, the preparation is the same: Put the ingredients in a jar. Shake well. Refrigerate until ready to use, and shake again before serving.

Basic French Dressing

⅓ cup vinegar or lemon juice	3¼ teaspoon salt
1 cup vegetable or olive oil	¼ teaspoon pepper

Optional: 2 tablespoons ketchup or tomato paste

Sweet French Dressing

To Basic French Dressing, add a little honey.

Vinaigrette Dressing

1 tablespoon Dijon mustard	½ cup olive oil
1 garlic clove, minced (or	¼ cup vinegar or lemon juice
¼ teaspoon garlic powder)	2 scallions, sliced thin

Sweet and Sour Dressing (Lemonade Dressing)

⅓ cup lemon juice	1 teaspoon sugar
⅔ cup water	¼ teaspoon salt

Oriental Dressing

3 tablespoons lemon juice	1 tablespoon sugar
3 tablespoons soy sauce	Pinch of ginger

Optional: 1 tablespoon sesame oil

Dressing for Apple and Walnut Salad
Pour this over lettuce tossed with chopped apples and walnuts.

⅓ cup apple cider vinegar   Sprinkle of salt

⅔ cup olive oil   Optional: crumbled blue cheese

WHAT YOU CAN DO

Encourage your child to sniff the herb and spice bottles in your pantry and choose savory herbs such as mint, marjoram, thyme, or citrus peel to add to the basic French or vinaigrette dressings.

WHAT YOUR CHILD CAN DO

- Grow the lettuce and observe the life cycle of plants.
- Measure salad dressing ingredients (with help, if necessary) and shake them.
- Dip lettuce leaves into the dressings and taste the differences.

BENEFITS OF THE ACTIVITY

- Smelling/tasting different dressings promotes olfactory/gustatory discrimination.
- Growing the lettuce and preparing the dressings provides tactile and visual input.
- Eating the fruits of one's labor may make green, crunchy food more palatable.
- This process strengthens social and emotional development as the child feels productive, useful, and connected to growing things.

SAFE Activities for Sensory-Related Skills

8

Oral-Motor Skills

Roberto, 8, is a messy eater. He chews with his mouth open, drools, and spits. The other children who join him at Mrs. O'Brien's house after school don't like sharing a snack with him.

To make snack time more pleasant, Mrs. O'Brien first has the children blow bubbles or blow on whistles or kazoos before settling down to eat. Then she provides straws and cold fruit shakes to "wake up" the children's mouths. She sits near Roberto and makes sure that his food is in manageable bits. Also, she has taught Roberto a secret sign language. When he has crumbs on his face, she pulls her ear. When he dribbles, she taps her nose. When he needs to slow down, she touches her chin. Roberto understands her gestures and tries hard to pay more attention to chewing and swallowing.

Roberto is fortunate to have an after-school caregiver who really cares. She intends to suggest to Roberto's parents that they get professional help for him. First, to learn more about oral-motor skills, Mrs. O'Brien reads an informative booklet, *Out of the Mouths of Babes: Discovering the Developmental Significance of the Mouth—a Book Especially for Parents and Other 'Grown-ups'*. The authors, Sheila M. Frick, Patricia Oetter, Eileen Richter, and Ron Frick, are occupational therapists and parents. (See *Recommended Materials*.)

The booklet explains that most newborns come equipped to master a basic sensory-motor pattern—the coordination of sucking, swallowing, and breathing. This "SSB synchrony" allows infants to eat and to calm themselves. Efficient sucking, the baby's first oral-motor skill, strengthens the muscles in the mouth. Gradually the child learns more oral-motor skills: biting, crunching, chewing, and licking. These oral-motor skills have an enormous influence on the child's overall development.

ORAL-MOTOR SKILLS CONTRIBUTE TO:
- Eating solid food
- Respiration
- Exploring fingers, toes, and toys, with the mouth
- Raising and holding up the head
- Reaching, grasping, writing, and using tools
- Sitting and standing erect
- Crying, cooing, babbling, speaking, and communicating through language
- Binocular vision
- Becoming alert, paying attention, and organizing one's behavior
- Self-regulation and calming

Children with DSI, however, often have poor oral-motor skills. Here are some characteristics discussed in *Out of the Mouths of Babes.*

CHARACTERISTICS OF POOR ORAL-MOTOR SKILLS

The child with poor oral-motor skills may:

☐ Have "oral defensiveness," the term for tactile defensiveness in the mouth. She may have avoided mouthing toys, as most babies do, to learn about them. She may crave certain kinds of oral stimulation, repeatedly sucking or chewing on inedible objects, including herself or other people.

☐ Have feeding and eating problems, including:

  ☐ Difficulty sucking, chewing, and swallowing.
  ☐ Picky eating habits, strongly preferring certain food textures, tastes, and temperatures, while avoiding others.
  ☐ Difficulty with new foods.
  ☐ Difficulty keeping food down and digesting food.
  ☐ Gag, choke, and drool frequently.

☐ Have health problems, including:

- ☐ Chronic diarrhea or constipation.
- ☐ Dental problems, such as slow development of teeth, chronic tooth decay, and irregular alignment.
- ☐ Frequent colds, bronchitis, asthma, and chronic ear infections.

☐ Have problems with motor development, including:

- ☐ Poor postural control.
- ☐ Low muscle tone.
- ☐ Poor proprioception.
- ☐ Poor balance and coordination.
- ☐ Difficulty feeling and staying centered.
- ☐ Difficulty crossing the midline.

☐ Have problems with speech and language development, including:

- ☐ Limited use of gestural "vocabulary" and facial expressions.
- ☐ Use of inappropriate speech sounds.
- ☐ Difficulty with receptive and expressive language.
- ☐ Inappropriate use of inflection and breath when speaking.
- ☐ Inappropriate voice volume, either too loud or too soft.

☐ Have problems with vision and visual-motor development, including:

- ☐ Poor eye-teaming (binocularity).
- ☐ Problems with eye-body coordination necessary to color, draw, write, cut, throw, catch, run, and jump.
- ☐ Difficulty looking straight at what she's doing and where she's going.

☐ Have problems with attention and organization of behavior, including:

- ☐ Inability to calm herself or be calmed.
- ☐ Insistence on elaborate routines before sleeping, eating, or starting an activity.
- ☐ Inconsistent patterns of sleeping, eating, and playing.
- ☐ Difficulty with transitions.
- ☐ Difficulty with familiar, everyday routines.

☐ Have problems with social and emotional development, including:

☐ Difficulty interpreting and responding adaptively to others' emotions and social cues.
☐ Tendency to be isolated from the group.
☐ Tendency to bully or be bossy.
☐ Difficulty communicating and using appropriate ways to get needs met.
☐ Poor self-esteem.

When oral-motor skills are a problem, helpful therapies include SI-based occupational therapy and/or speech-and-language therapy that help with speech skills, voice pitch, and oral-motor control in the muscles of the mouth. Also, the child may enjoy the following **SAFE** activities.

Activities for Oral-Motor Skills

◆ Chewy Necklace

Children with a significant need to suck and chew tend to put inedible things in their mouths, like collars and cuffs. This relaxing activity offers something more appropriate and strengthens oral-motor control, as well as visual and fine motor skills.

DEVELOPMENTAL AGE RANGE
> 1½ and up, to chew the necklace
> 3 to 7, to make the necklace

WHAT YOU WILL NEED
> ■ For a temporary necklace:
>> • Cheerios, other "O" shaped cereal, Gummy Savors, apple and carrot chunks
>> • Licorice strings
> ■ For a permanent necklace:
>> • 2 feet of clear vinyl tubing (often called "aquarium tubing"), available at the hardware store, cut into short sections
>> • Rat tail cord (used for stringing beads for jewelry, available at craft stores) or dental floss
> ■ Plastic tapestry needles, with large eyes and dull tips
> ■ Sponge, to use as a pin cushion

PREPARATION
> ■ Cut cord into lengths of about 30 inches. Thread several needles with cord, because making one chain is often not enough.
> ■ Poke a prepared needle through a Cheerio or tubing piece, and tie it at the end of the cord, like an anchor, to prevent the next pieces from sliding off.

WHAT YOUR CHILD CAN DO
> ■ Pick up individual pieces of cereal or tubing with the nondominant hand, poke the needle through them, and pull them to the end of the cord.

- Stop when about 6 inches of cord are left, to make it easy to knot the ends together.
- Remove the needle and stick it into the sponge "pin cushion."
- Ask for help, if necessary, to tie the two ends of the cord together to make a lovely *Chewy Necklace*.
- Tuck a *Chewy Bracelet* (with just a couple of pieces of vinyl tubing) into a pocket, or latch it to a belt loop, and take it to school and on outings as an on-the-spot stress reducer.

BENEFITS OF THE ACTIVITY

- Some of the possible benefits of gnawing on a *Chewy Necklace* include:
  - Exercising the muscles in the mouth used for speaking
  - Preventing drooling
  - Helping a child "get it together," because the mouth is a great organizer
  - Calming and relieving anxiety
- Selecting, poking, and threading the edible "O's" or the vinyl pieces improve visual discrimination and eye-hand coordination.
- Manipulating Cheerios with just-right pressure develops tactile discrimination and grading of movement.
- Manipulating a needle develops fine motor and pincer skills, which are necessary for grasping a pencil successfully.
- Using both hands to work together improves bilateral coordination.

COPING TIPS

- Do not offer this activity if your child has an intolerance to the cereal ingredients.
- If the child continually pulls the needle off the cord, rethread the needle and knot both ends of the cord together around the anchor piece.

◆ Applesauce Through a Straw

This activity is hard work, as well as silly, fun, and nutritious.

DEVELOPMENTAL AGE RANGE 3½ and up

WHAT YOU WILL NEED
- Pureed applesauce, strained fruit, pudding, yogurt, slush, or slurpie
- About 2 feet of clear vinyl tubing, or regular drinking straws (long, thin straws are harder; short, thick straws are easier)

PREPARATION
- Tie a loop in the vinyl tubing to make a crazy straw.
- Ladle some applesauce into a bowl.
- Tell your child, "Drink your applesauce."

WHAT YOUR CHILD CAN DO
- Suck the applesauce.
- Blow through the straw to make bubbles in the applesauce.

VARIATIONS
- Suck pudding, partially congealed gelatin, or strained pears or apricots.
- Suck a health shake, such as a blended mixture of strawberries, a banana, and vanilla yogurt (or ice instead of yogurt, if your child has a dairy intolerance).

BENEFITS OF THE ACTIVITY
- Sucking thicker-than-liquid foods is a resistive activity that promotes oral-motor development, force, and speech and language skills.
- Sucking and eating applesauce is a gustatory sensation as well as a tactile experience for the lips, mouth, and throat.
- The activity strengthens eye-motor skills, as sucking in makes the eyes converge.
- Sucking is organizing and calming.

◆ Spirited Shepherds

On a dreary December day, Kathleen Morris, M.S., C.C.C./S.L.P., faced the "challenge of teaching Scriptures to an 8th-grade Sunday school class." Undaunted by the teenagers' unfocused energy and aware of how organizing oral-motor experiences can be, she created this divinely inspired activity.

While the process of the game is exciting, the end product is calming. Behold how the shepherds, after corralling the sheep, are ready to focus and attend. Use this moment to present a purposeful task, be it discussing a lesson, or concentrating on a reading, writing, or math assignment. *Spirited Shepherds* may be the answer to your prayers!

DEVELOPMENTAL AGE RANGE 5 to 14

WHAT YOU WILL NEED
- Large, open floor space
- Masking tape
- Cotton balls for "sheep" and "lambs"
- Markers or Blopens™ (see *Recommended Materials*)
- Drinking straws (narrow rather than fat, to increase the challenge)
- Box, bowl, or basket for the "corral"

PREPARATION
- Roll up the rug and clear a space for "shepherds" to move across.
- Put a strip of tape down for a start line.
- Place the "corral" at one end of the room.

WHAT EACH SHEPHERD CAN DO
- Take a handful of cotton-ball "sheep," brand them with a marker or Blopen, and place them on the floor at the start line.

- Take a straw and crouch on hands and knees behind the start line. Blow through the straw to herd his or her flock toward the corral, one sheep at a time or several simultaneously. (The cotton balls will cling together.)
- Suck in through the straw to airlift the sheep and then release them safely into the corral, as quickly as possible.

BENEFITS OF THE ACTIVITY
- Blowing and sucking activities strengthen the respiratory system and speech articulators (tongue, cheeks, and lips), thereby improving speech production.
- Blowing out makes the eyes diverge, widening the child's visual range. Sucking in makes the eyes converge, bringing near objects into clearer focus. This activity gives your child's eyes a healthy workout, thereby strengthening her visual skills.
- Pressing hands and knees against the floor and propelling herself forward improves the tactile sense, proprioception, body awareness, gross motor control, motor planning, kinesthesia, bilateral coordination, balance, and stabilization.
- Moving on all fours changes her head position and stimulates the vestibular sense.
- Playing the game with a group fosters social skills and team spirit.

◆ Puffin' Stuff

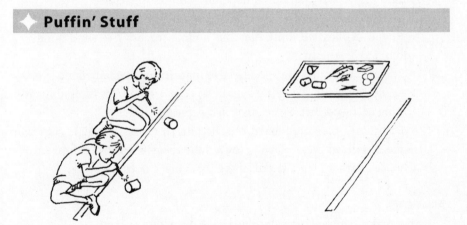

Puffing on objects strengthens oral-motor skills and also teaches valuable lessons about how things move. Information for this activity comes from speech/language therapists Joanne Hanson and Kathleen Morris, and science educators Mary Marcoux, Constance Kamii, and Rheta De Vries.

DEVELOPMENTAL AGE RANGE 3 and up

WHAT YOU WILL NEED
- Straws
- Masking tape
- Objects with different weights and structures, such as:
  - Lightweight—facial tissues, cotton balls, feathers, more straws
  - Cylindrical—empty cans, paper towel rolls, wooden dowels
  - Conical—wooden building block cones, cardboard cones used for string
  - Spherical—Ping-Pong balls, golf balls, marbles
  - Flat—popsicle sticks, plastic container lids
  - Bumpy-lumpy—wooden beads, pebbles, gloves, small blocks

PREPARATION
- Clear a space for blowing—either a large table or smooth floor.
- Put strips of tape down for start and finish lines.

WHAT YOUR CHILDREN CAN DO
- Take a straw, choose an item, and experiment with puffing it across the floor.
- Determine which objects are easy to move, which are hard to move, and which may or may not move, depending on these factors:
  - Weight—heavy objects are more resistant than light objects
  - Shape—cones will only move in a circle unless the wind is strong enough to lift them
  - Force—brief puffs are less effective than strong, sustained blows
  - Angle—blowing straight down on an object is ineffective; finding and aiming at the correct "sweet spot" is necessary
  - Direction—blowing toward the *end* of a straw or a popsicle stick will make it spin, whereas blowing toward the *center* will move it forward
- Choose another object to puff if the first choice does not work.

VARIATIONS
- Try making things move by blowing them without straws.
- Put a bunch of feathers in a large bowl and blow to see what happens.
- Hold up a lightweight tissue, feather, or balloon, and blow underneath it to keep it aloft. Pass it back and forth to a friend just by blowing on it.
- Everyone take a similar object and have a race. Who can blow his feather across the table or floor first?

- Build a miniature obstacle course with blocks, train tunnels, cardboard tubes, and other hindrances to puff items over, around, under, and through.
- Divide into two teams, select an object such as a Ping-Pong ball (for young children) or a golf ball (for older children, 10 and above), and play a game of "Puff Soccer."
- Divide children into two teams. While one team referees, the other blows as many objects as possible across the finish line. If someone's straw touches and pushes an object, he must return to the start line with it and try again. After both teams have had a turn, work together to sort the objects into two groups: those that are moved easily by puffing at them through a straw, and those that are not.

BENEFITS OF THE ACTIVITY

- Puffing promotes oral-motor awareness and exercises cheek and lip muscles.
- Breathing deeply and sustaining long puffs benefits the respiratory system.
- Exploring how to puff "just right" to get various objects going teaches about the movement of objects (mechanics), spatial relationships, logic, physics, and forces that act on objects. Puffing just right also strengthens the child's motor planning and force.
- Handling objects with various properties strengthens tactile discrimination, eye-hand coordination, and fine motor skills.
- Friendly competition with friends builds strong social skills.

COPING TIP

Watch for signs of hyperventilating, as many children with sensory issues have poor feedback and may not recognize when they are actually getting winded.

◆ Magic Garden

Blowing is a wonderful activity to address the respiratory and oral-motor problems often associated with DSI. Adrienne B. Hausman, an activity specialist who leads "Magic Art" workshops for children and adults, suggests this Blopen™ activity as a creative, satisfying, and beneficial experience.

DEVELOPMENTAL AGE RANGE 4 and up

WHAT YOU WILL NEED
- Paper and pencil
- Blopens (see *Recommended Materials*)
- Optional: Stickers
- Newspaper to protect the table

PREPARATION

On a horizontal ("landscape" set-up) sheet of paper, pencil several dots or Xs.

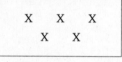

Blowing the *Magic Garden* into Life

WHAT YOU CAN DO	WHAT YOUR CHILD CAN DO
1. Say, "Let's pretend the Xs are flowers. What color do you want them to be?"	1. Suggest any color.
2. Point to an X and say, "Blow color onto one X at a time."	2. Poising the Blopen 2 to 5 inches away above the paper, blow ink onto the Xs.
3. Encourage your child to experiment, giving lavish praise for every puff.	3. Experiment with different intensities of blowing and varying distances from the paper. A light puff from 5 inches away will produce a broad, delicate mist. A hearty blow, closer to the paper, will have a stronger and more precise result.
4. Pencil in vertical lines under each X. Ask, "What color do you think these stems should be?"	4. Suggest green—or whatever other color strikes his fancy.

WHAT YOU CAN DO	WHAT YOUR CHILD CAN DO
5. Help with the Blopens, if necessary.	5. Put away the Blopen and prepare another.
6. Above the Xs, pencil in hearts to represent butterflies.	6. Blow color onto the butterflies.
7. Admire your child's beautiful garden and post it on the refrigerator.	7. Add stickers for even more beauty.

VARIATIONS

- On blank paper, use items like these as stencils:
  - Feathers
  - Leaves, sticks, and grass
  - Buttons and coins
  - Paper clips, bobby pins, safety pins, rubber bands, and string
  - Doilies and plastic forks
- Make a street scene, a moonscape, a family, a house, a magical creature, or an abstract work of art.

BENEFITS OF THE ACTIVITY

- Blowing increases oral-motor awareness.
- Blowing strengthens force and respiration, important for breathing, stamina, muscle strength, posture, and voice volume.
- Blowing and inhaling deeply enhance visual-motor skills as the eyes diverge and converge.
- Preparing Blopens and applying stickers improve tactile perception, motor planning, and fine motor skills.
- Using one hand to hold the Blopen and the other hand to stabilize the paper strengthens bilateral coordination.
- Creating a beautiful picture reinforces the child's artistic ability and self-esteem.

◆ Wind Competition

How long-winded are *you*? In this game, the person with the longest blowing power wins. Kathleen Morris, SLP-CCC, plays this game with one client or with a group of kids. Competition with other players encourages increased and sustained blowing and contributes to the fun.

DEVELOPMENTAL AGE RANGE 5 and up

WHAT YOU WILL NEED
- Stopwatch, or watch with a second hand
- Therapy whistle with movable parts, such as one with a wheel, a train, or a race car (see *Recommended Materials*); or a pinwheel
- Optional: Pen and paper

PREPARATION
- Say, "Let's see who can blow the longest to keep the wheel spinning (train running, car moving)."
- Optional: Make a chart to keep score, like this—

	Mom	Jeremy	Jenny	David	Melissa
1st blow					
2nd blow					
3rd blow					

WHAT YOU AND YOUR CHILD(REN) CAN DO
- Take turns blowing into the toy, competing for the longest spin out of three, four, or five blows.
- Record how long each blow was.

- Mouthing the whistle (or blowing on the pinwheel) improves oral-motor skills.
- Inhaling deeply, blowing out, and sustaining the blowing strengthen respiration, promote calming, and improve force, which is a function of proprioception.
- Both blowing the whistle (or pinwheel) and watching its movement strengthen oculomotor skills.
- Vying with other players promotes social interactions.

◆ Blow Away Blues

Familiar with the "I-can't, I-won't, I-hate-everybody, that's-yucky, nobody-likes-me, I'm-no-good" blues? This antidote is the inspiration of Lucy Jane Miller, Ph.D., O.T.R., who came up the idea when her own kids were young and feeling out of sorts. The activity is simple and effective and will blow you away!

DEVELOPMENTAL AGE RANGE 5 and up

WHAT YOU WILL NEED
Balloons

WHAT YOU CAN DO:
- Ask the child to name the emotion she is feeling. If the child can't identify it, help her recognize and acknowledge it by saying, "I think you're frustrated (angry, disappointed, scared, unhappy, etc.)."
- Say, "I know a magic way to send 'bad' thoughts away."

- Go outside with your child and some balloons.
- Say, "Blow up this balloon. Each puff is another 'bad' or stressful thought for you to push out of your body. When you're done, we'll tie all those thoughts inside the balloon and send them away."

WHAT YOUR CHILD CAN DO
- Take several deep breaths and blow them into the balloon.
- Tie the end of the balloon (with help, if necessary).
- Punch the balloon up to the sky and let the breeze carry it away.
- Search for fallen balloons and pick them up in order to minimize littering.

VARIATIONS
- No breeze? Have your child stomp on the balloon, if the sound is tolerable.
- Write an emotion on a little piece of paper and insert it into a balloon before blowing it up; or use a marker to write the emotion on the blown-up balloon.
- After filling the balloon, have the child let go without tying it. The balloon will do a sputtering little dance, and all the anger or frustration will fizzle out.

BENEFITS OF THE ACTIVITY
- Breathing deeply, in and out, helps regulate the respiratory system.
- Blowing air into balloons develops oral-motor skills.
- Feeling the balloons inflate strengthens tactile perception.
- Watching the balloons inflate and fly away improves visual skills.
- Punching balloons is a resistive activity that provides proprioceptive input and strengthens force and kinesthesia.
- Identifying negative feelings may help to deflate them, and blowing them out and away rechannels the child's energy in a positive way.

COPING TIP
If your child lacks the force to blow up balloons, use paper lunch bags instead. After the child puffs the emotion into the bag, take it outside and "empty" it.

◆ Bubble Gum Blow

Preteens and teenagers savor this old-fashioned bubble-blowing contest, suggested by Kathleen Morris. "Always, always, always let your kids chew gum," she says. *Bubble Blow* will help them get organized, stay on task, and have great fun!

DEVELOPMENTAL AGE RANGE 6 and up

WHAT YOU WILL NEED
- Bubble gum—at least two pieces per person (large wads are easier to feel and less likely to slip down the throat)
- Caliper or small ruler

WHAT THE PLAYERS CAN DO
- Chew on a mouthful of gum to get their wads ready to blow.
- Blow bubbles and hold them.

WHAT YOU CAN DO
Measure the bubbles with the caliper or ruler.

BENEFITS OF THE ACTIVITY
Chewing on a wad of gum—the bigger, the better—strengthens oral-motor skills and provides good proprioceptive input to the mouth, cheeks, tongue, and jaw.

◆ Pumpkin, Pumpkin

Making silly faces is fun and also strengthens speech articulation and communication skills. Thanks to Joanne Hanson, C.C.C.-S.L.P., for contributing her ideas to this delightful activity.

DEVELOPMENTAL AGE RANGE 3 to 7

- ■ Several small pumpkins and markers, or nutritious cookies and cake decorating apparatus
- ■ Large mirror

PREPARATION
- ■ With markers on the pumpkins, or with icing on the cookies, draw different facial expressions such as happy, sad, surprised, angry, scowling, scared, or clownish.
- ■ Discuss the emotions that the faces show.
- ■ Stand side by side in front of the mirror and make silly faces together. Try these oral-motor exercises:
  - • Puff your cheeks out and hold them that way for a few seconds. Release and repeat.
  - • Touch your tongue toward your nose and then toward your chin.
  - • Push your tongue against the inside of one cheek and then the other.
  - • Slowly stick out your tongue as far as it can go and quickly retract it.

WHAT YOU CAN DO
- ■ Stand facing the mirror, and now draw your child close, facing you with her back to the mirror. Gently and rhythmically rub her head (or back), while you chant:

> *Pumpkin, pumpkin, round and fat,*
> *Turn into a jack-o-lantern, just like that!*

> *or,*

> *Cookie, cookie, cookety-cook,*
> *Turn around—now, how do you look?*

> *or,*

> *Child, child, full of grace,*
> *Turn around and make a face!*

- ■ With your hands on her head or shoulders, turn the child 180 degrees to face the mirror.

WHAT YOUR CHILD CAN DO
- ■ Turn toward the mirror and make a pumpkin or monster face, a silly or funny face, or some other highly expressive face.

- Perhaps tell you what emotion she was trying to express—"That was a very scary face!"

VARIATIONS
- Draw pumpkin faces on orange construction paper.
- Do this in front of friends or family members instead of a mirror.

BENEFITS OF THE ACTIVITY
- Making silly faces that engage the lips, cheeks, and tongue improves oral-motor skills that are important for articulating speech sounds and producing language.
- Learning how her own face looks and how she can purposefully assume a different expression teaches self-awareness. The experience may help the child with *dyssemia,* which is a difficulty in using nonverbal signs or signals. (*Dys* comes from the Greek word for "difficulty," and *semia* comes from the word for "signals." Stephen Nowicki, Jr., Ph.D., and Marshall P. Duke, Ph.D., psychologists at Emory University, use this term to denote a nonverbal social communication deficit.) When a child "owns" an expression, she will be better equipped to recognize it in others.
- Being turned halfway around to face the mirror is a gentle vestibular experience that may improve the child's tolerance to passive movement.

◆ Kiss the Mirror

This lovable oral-motor activity is another favorite of Joanne Hanson of Virginia. *Kiss the Mirror,* she notes, is a good activity to do with a child who is a drooler.

DEVELOPMENTAL AGE RANGE 2 and up for mirror-kissing; 5 and up for creating lip-print designs

WHAT YOU WILL NEED
- Old lipstick
- Mirror
- White paper
- Pen

PREPARATION
Help your child put on some lipstick.

WHAT YOUR CHILD CAN DO
- Round his or her lips and plant a kiss or two on the mirror.
- Kiss the paper, and, depending on his or her skill with a pen, add details to the lip-prints to create designs, such as birds and butterflies, manta rays, sporty cars, and lovely tutus for ballerinas.

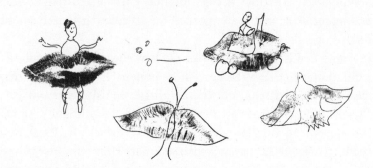

BENEFITS OF THE ACTIVITY
- Lip rounding helps the child develop muscles in the mouth and cheeks that are necessary to articulate sounds.
- Kissing the mirror or paper provides deep pressure and improves force and tactile awareness of the lips.
- Adorning lip-prints with details strengthens visual and fine motor skills.

◆ Dinosaur Morning

Oral/tactile defensiveness may cause many kids with DSI to reject mushy textures, limiting their diet to crunchy foods like dry cereal, crackers, popcorn, and bacon. (Others may prefer a mushy, bland, white diet, rejecting crunchy food.) Laura Glaser, S.L.P., created this imaginative  activity to address the oral-motor skills, language development, and sensory needs of Crunchy-Only Kids.

DEVELOPMENTAL AGE RANGE 3 and up

WHAT YOU WILL NEED
- Large, deep baking pan
- Small, shallow bowl
- Mushy food: applesauce and blueberry yogurt
- Small, crunchy, desirable food: cereal O's, granola, or popcorn
- Chewy food: raisins or grapes
- Toy dinosaurs

PREPARATION
- Wash everybody's hands and the dinosaurs.
- Toward one end of the pan, dump in several cups of mushy applesauce. This is the "swamp."
- Toss in some desirable, crunchy cereal. This is "dinosaur food."
- Put the bowl into the pan, at the other end. This is the "pond."
- Spoon blueberry yogurt into the pond. This is the blue "water."
- Add chewy, not-so-desirable grapes or raisins to the pond. These are "dinosaur eggs," or more dinosaur food.

HOW TO PLAY
- Put the dinosaurs on the table or floor next to the swamp, and get into the play. You could say, "I'll be the Mommy Stegosaurus. Who will you be? Teenage Tyrannosaurus Rex? OK, T Rex, let's start our day with a walk in the swamp." Make your dinosaur trudge over to romp in the swamp. Coax your child to do the same.
- Pluck a cereal piece from the swamp and bring it to your dinosaur's mouth. Smack your lips and say, "Mmm, good! Mommy Stegosaurus sure loves this food. You take some, too, for Teenage T Rex." Encourage the child to pick a piece of cereal out of the mush and feed his dinosaur. (Do not feed your child's dinosaur; that is his job.)
- Say, "This is so good!" Scoop up some cereal and applesauce in your fingertips and eat it. Say, "How about you?" If he resists, say pleasantly, "You don't have to eat it. Just lick it."
- Continue with the scenario. Walk your dinosaur over to the pond. Have your dinosaur bathe in the pond, eat the dinosaur food, and nuzzle the eggs. Encourage the child to do the same.
- After playing for a while—15 or 30 minutes—throw away the food and wash up. The swamp cannot be recycled.

VARIATIONS

■ Add lettuce "grass," celery and carrot "trees," and broccoli "bushes." Just maybe, your child will forget how much he dislikes vegetables!

■ Instead of applesauce, try another strained fruit, custard or pudding, oatmeal or farina, pureed vegetables or salsa. Gelatin dessert may work, too. (Prepare it in a flat pan, using less water than called for so it's firmer than usual. After it has solidified, cut it into cubes.)

■ Instead of a prehistoric swamp, serve these alternatives:

• Beach—Play with toy sharks, dolphins, and lobsters rather than dinosaurs. The mushy food is the sand, the crunchy food is shells, and the chewy food is little sea creatures, like scallops.

• Rainforest—Use jungle creatures, like monkeys, frogs, and snakes. Mushy food is soggy ground; crunchy food is coconuts; chewy food is bird's eggs, roots, branches, or leaves.

■ Vary some aspect of the food:

• Temperature (warm or cool)

• Texture (solid, pureed, chunky, chewy, crunchy, or mushy)

• Taste (tart, sour, spicy, or sweet)

• Color (bright green applesauce may appeal to orally defensive kids!)

BENEFITS OF THE ACTIVITY

■ Mucking around in the applesauce is a beneficial experience for the child with tactile defensiveness. After he becomes more comfortable touching the mush with his fingers, he may be more willing to bring it up to his highly sensitive mouth.

■ Eating any of these mushy/chewy foods will broaden the child's diet.

■ Chatting about the dinosaurs, food, activities, sensations, and feelings improves language skills and imagination.

COPING TIPS

■ If you prefer not to eat from the same swamp, have your own concoction in a bowl nearby. Should the child need additional encouragement to try the food, you can eat the items from your swamp with enthusiasm. Talk about how delicious the food is. Yum, yum!

■ The child may need to experience several Dinosaur Mornings before agreeing to eat the mushy, chewy foods. That's fine, because the initial objective is to "bring the child to the table." The first time, he may only look. The second time, he may touch. The next time, he may lick. Eventually, because the game is so alluring, he may come to the table—and eat.

◆ Jeff Cirillo's Lucky Latté

Jeff Cirillo, third baseman for the Colorado Rockies, is the favorite baseball player of Aubrey Lande, M.S., O.T.R./L. "Why?" she says. "Because this guy realizes that in order to play a good game you need to start off with a good ritual! So, before each baseball game, practice, batting session, whatever, he gets himself a nice, tall, hot vanilla latté. Our kids also love routines,  and the best routines are the ones that help set up the nervous system for success."

DEVELOPMENTAL AGE RANGE All ages

WHAT YOU WILL NEED
The particular food that helps to arouse, organize, or calm your child, according to:
- Texture
  - Chewy—gum, turkey jerky, granola bar, fruit leather, licorice
  - Creamy—pudding, custard, yogurt
  - Crunchy—raw vegetables, apples, cereal, popcorn
  - Smooth and thick—peanut butter, hummus, strained banana or pear
- Taste
  - Salty—pretzels, chips, crackers
  - Spicy—salsa, chili, pizza
  - Sweet—milkshake, grapes, dried fruit
  - Sour—lemon ball, pickle, unsweetened yogurt
  - Tart—cranberry juice, unsweetened grapefruit juice
- Temperature
  - Cold—lowfat ice cream, snow cone, frozen juice bar, ice chips, cold water in a sports bottle, chilled orange slices, or frozen fresh berries, grapes or peas that have been allowed to thaw for 30 minutes
  - Hot—chicken broth, cocoa

PREPARATION
- Establish a "lucky latté" routine to repeat each time your child sets out for a challenging or potentially overstimulating activity.

- Explain ahead of time to the teacher or coach the importance of routine and ritual in your child's life.
- Prepare enough for all the children!

WHAT YOUR CHILD CAN DO

- Enjoy chewing, crunching, sucking, or licking his equivalent of a lucky latté prior to every session of some activity, such as playing soccer, going to gym class, or attending a birthday party.
- Share his snacks with the other kids.

BENEFITS OF THE ACTIVITY

- Oral-motor activity is a great organizer and helps the child focus, attend, and become calm.
- Kids with DSI don't like to be singled out. Bringing enough to share, such as orange slices for the whole team or fruit leather for the whole class, helps the child to be part of the group.

COPING TIPS

- As every child is different, foods will affect children in different ways. A granola bar, for instance, may wake up Little Susie—and put Little Boy Blue to sleep. You may want to consult with an occupational therapist about the most appropriate foods for your child's sensory needs.
- Even on lousy days, keep up the routine. Use your child's lucky latté not as a reward, but as a foundation for success.

9

~~~~~~

Motor Planning

Brittney, 9, is clumsy in fact, but in her fantasy she is an Olympic gymnast who earns perfect 10s. She is thrilled when the P.E. teacher introduces gymnastics into the 4th grade curriculum. Brittney is positive that if she works hard enough, she can be beautiful on the parallel bars and balance beam. Unfortunately, simple movement activities are demanding enough, and the gymnastics classes are so demanding that they almost break her spirit. At home, she says, "Mom, if I can't do gymnastics, I've got to do something!"

Her mother and teacher confer about Brittney's mismatched body and spirit. The teacher suggests perceptual motor therapy to benefit motor planning and boost self-esteem. Brittney finds that the therapy is similar to the gymnastics of her dreams. She loves it. Her body and spirit get more in sync as her coordination and motor planning abilities begin to improve.

Motor planning is getting organized to do something novel and rather complicated, such as put on a seatbelt in a friend's car or use the spiral playground slide for the first time. (Motor planning is often used as a synonym for *praxis*, although motor planning is one component of praxis. Praxis includes *ideation*, which is conceiving of a complex sequence of unfamiliar movements; *motor planning*, which is organizing oneself to do these actions; and *execution*, which is carrying out the movements.)

Some children motor plan best after seeing someone else get on the merry-go-round or after hearing the steps involved in blowing up a balloon. Seeing and hearing are not enough, however; the most important part is doing.

The more a child actively touches and moves, the better his motor planning and motor skills become. Mastering one motor skill leads to the ability to generalize what he has learned and apply it to another, more challenging, task. For instance, after gaining confidence on a jungle gym, a child may generalize his skills to hang upside down from a monkey bar. This is adaptive behavior.

Motor planning is necessary for gross motor control, the smooth coordination of the large muscles, and for fine motor control, which a child develops after establishing gross motor control. It is necessary for eating, writing, crossing the street, succeeding at home and school, playing, and feeling emotionally secure. We all need to integrate the senses effectively so we can motor plan to do what we set out to do.

Before Brittney begins therapy, poor motor planning, a part of dyspraxia, interferes with almost everything she does or tries to do. Some characteristics of motor planning problems are listed below.

CHARACTERISTICS OF POOR MOTOR PLANNING

The child with poor motor planning may:

☐ Have trouble planning and organizing the steps involved in a sequence of body movements, such as cutting with scissors or riding a bicycle. Novel experiences as well as familiar activities may be difficult, especially if the child can't see what she is doing.

☐ Have difficulty positioning her body, as when someone is helping her into a coat, or when she is trying to get dressed or undressed.

☐ Have difficulty knowing where her body is in relation to objects and people, frequently falling, tripping, and bumping into obstacles.

☐ Show fear when moving in space.

☐ Be unable to generalize what she has already learned to accomplish a new task.

☐ Have poor self-help skills.

☐ Have poor gross motor control for running, climbing, jumping, and going up and down stairs.

☐ Have poor fine-motor control of her fingers for precise manual tasks, her toes for gripping sandals or walking barefoot, and her mouth for chewing and speaking.

☐ Have poor eye-hand coordination.

☐ Have low self-esteem.

When motor planning is the problem, SI-based occupational or physical therapy or another treatment such as perceptual motor therapy will be beneficial. Perceptual motor therapy provides integrated movement experiences that remediate problems with gross motor, fine motor, visual, and motor planning skills. The **SAFE** activities here may be helpful, too.

Activities for Motor Skills

◆ Hands on Toes, Fingers on Nose

Preschoolers usually love this activity. They "get it" right away and enjoy responding to the increasingly complex commands. Playing with one child is good, and, of course, playing with a bunch of kids is better.

DEVELOPMENTAL AGE RANGE 3 to 5

WHAT YOU WILL NEED
- Percussion instrument, such as a pair of rhythm sticks, a drum, or a tone block (i.e., a mallet and wooden block)
- Optional: a 12-inch plastic hoop for each person

PREPARATION
- Place the hoops in a circle.
- Have everyone sit in his or her hoop.

WHAT YOU CAN DO
- Say, "In this game, I'll say something like, 'Put your hands on your toes,' or 'Put your fingers on your nose.' And when you hear this sound [strike the instrument], that will be the signal to change your body position as quick as a wink."
- Chant a series of verbal commands, slowly and rhythmically. Use different prepositions—on, over, under, through, beside, and so on.
- After each command, rap on the instrument. Allow plenty of time for the children to change their body position.
- Praise each original idea! The children's motions need not be identical nor what you would expect. Bringing the chin *down* to the knee is as appropriate as bringing the knee *up* to the chin. Independent thinking and creative movement are great.
- For an extra challenge, add a little bit of background noise. This will sharpen foreground/background perception, which is good for auditory processing.

SAMPLE COMMANDS

(accent the names of body parts as you speak)

"Put your HANDS on your HEAD." *Rap!*

"Put your CHIN on your KNEE." *Rap!*

"Put your THUMBS under your CHIN." *Rap!*

"Put your FINGERS on your NOSE." *Rap!*

"Put your FINGERS through your FINGERS." *Rap!*

"Touch your TOES to your TOES." *Rap!*

"Touch your ELBOW to your ELBOW." *Rap!*

"Put your THUMBS on your ELBOWS." *Rap!*

"Put both HANDS on one HIP." *Rap!*

"Touch your FINGERS behind your BACK." *Rap!*

"Put a HAND on your EARLOBE and a hand on your ANKLE." *Rap!*

MORE SAMPLE COMMANDS, WHEN YOU USE THE HOOPS

"Put your ARM in the hoop." *Rap!*

"Put your EAR in the hoop." *Rap!*

"Put your ELBOWS in the hoop." *Rap!*

"Put your HEAD in the hoop." *Rap!*

"Put the hoop behind your HEAD." *Rap!*

"Put your HEELS in the hoop." *Rap!*

"Put your WAIST in the hoop." *Rap!*

"Put the hoop between your LEGS." *Rap!*

"Put your LEGS through the hoop." *Rap!*

"Put a HAND and a FOOT in the hoop." *Rap!*

"Stand up in the hoop." *Rap!*

"Put your whole body under the hoop." *Rap!*

WHAT THE PLAYERS CAN DO

- Listen for the rap and follow your directions.
- Take turns as the leader making the commands.

BENEFITS OF THE ACTIVITY

- Mastering this game strengthens motor planning, body awareness, grading of movement, and kinesthesia.
- Responding to verbal directions with the correct body position promotes auditory discrimination, language skills, and visual-spatial awareness.
- Learning what prepositions mean improves receptive and expressive language.
- Using both body sides improves bilateral coordination and crossing the midline.
- Playing the game with a group fosters social interactions.

Children who process language slowly or have poor body awareness may need to watch others for clues about which body parts to move and touch. Give them plenty of time to observe and copy others' motions.

◆ Shoe Box Path

This mini-obstacle course, suggested by Lynne Israel, O.T.R./L., is an ideal rainy-day activity.

DEVELOPMENTAL AGE RANGE 3 and up

WHAT YOU WILL NEED
- Shoe boxes (8 or more)
- Textured items, such as buttons, cotton balls, sand, shag carpet, fake fur, yarn, rice, lentils, beans, paper, or foam packaging

PREPARATION
- Put a different material into each shoe box and line up the boxes for the child to step into, one after the other. Place some boxes very close, and some farther apart—but not so far apart that the child must step on the floor or crush the edges of the box while attempting to step inside.
- Have the child remove shoes and perhaps socks, too.

WHAT YOUR CHILD CAN DO IN INCREASING ORDER OF DIFFICULTY
- Step into boxes lined up in a straight row.
- Step into boxes arranged in a serpentine (S-shaped) line.
- Cross one leg in front of the other before stepping into the next box.
- Walk backwards.

BENEFITS OF THE ACTIVITY
- Traveling successfully through the *Shoe Box Path* develops motor planning.
- Grading his leg movements to stretch for the boxes strengthens proprioception.
- Moving his body through space improves balance and kinesthesia.
- Getting his feet "in touch" with a variety of textures improves tactile perception.

- Watching where his feet are going improves visual skills, such as eye-foot coordination, depth perception, and spatial awareness.

COPING TIPS
- If your child's balance is an issue, take the child's hand or offer a finger for him to grasp or touch for support.
- If your child finds a particular texture uncomfortable to step on, remove the box. It may be more tolerable on another day.

◆ Push-Me-Pull-You

Remember the animal family described in Hugh Lofting's *Dr. Dolittle* books? This activity is named for Dr. Dolittle's Pushmi-Pullyu, the most vigilant and versatile animal of all. *Push-Me-Pull-You* activities benefit children who need a physical boundary (the rolling tub) to help them attend to where they are going and how they are moving.

Push-Me-Pull-You experiences, literally loaded with benefits, are tons of fun! They are inspired by Teri Kozlowski, O.T.R., who has also provided the instructions for making a rolling tub. If you are not handy with tools, try to find someone to help you make this fabulous piece of equipment.

DEVELOPMENTAL AGE RANGE 2 and up

WHAT YOU WILL NEED
- Rolling tub (see *instructions* below)
- Big stickers
- Weights, such as beanbags, stuffed animals, bags of rice, pillows—or another child

- For the obstacle course:
  - Traffic cones, blocks, hoops, wastebaskets, cans, boots
  - Chalk or tape
  - Water squirter or spray bottle, or large sponge or brush

For a Passive *Push-Me-Pull-You* Experience

WHAT YOU CAN DO

- Help your child into the tub.
- Put a few pounds of weight on the child's lap. Gradually increase the weight.
- Pull the child slowly, in straight lines. This linear movement, especially when the child's lap is loaded with weights, may be extremely calming.
- Pull the child fast, in wavy, angular, and circular lines. This kind of movement may arouse the child's vestibular system.
- Slow down or stop if the child indicates that this is not fun.

WHAT YOUR CHILD CAN DO

Sit in the rolling tub and tell you when to start, where to go, what direction to go in (forward or backward, straight or zigzag, or turning in circles), how slowly or fast to push, and when to stop.

For an Active *Push-Me-Pull-You* Experience

WHAT YOU CAN DO

- To guide the child with poor body awareness, place stickers on the lip of the tub as reminders for where his hands should stay.
- Stand by and pay attention.

WHAT YOUR CHILD CAN DO

- Load the tub with weights—a few pounds at first, increasing the load gradually. Instead of weights, another child can climb into the tub.
- Propel the loaded tub, slowly or fast:
  - By tugging on the rope, with his hands behind him.
  - By pushing or pulling the dowel.
  - By placing his hands on the stickers and shoving the tub.
- With a buddy, work cooperatively to push or pull the tub.
- Use the rolling tub for doing chores, such as moving groceries from door to kitchen, recyclables from house to curb, laundry from dryer to dresser, toys from floor to shelf, and so on. An occupational therapist

working with your child may include tasks such as these in a home program called ADLs (Activities for Daily Living).

▪ Incorporate pushing/pulling activities into make-believe play, such as pretending to ride in a horse and buggy; take a car, train, or airplane trip; or shop for groceries.

For a *Push-Me-Pull-You* Obstacle Course

WHAT YOU CAN DO

▪ Place two or more obstacles on the floor or pavement. Start with a distance of about 4 or 5 feet apart. Gradually move the objects closer, to about 3 feet apart.

▪ Mark a "road" with two parallel lines of tape (indoors) or chalk (outdoors), about 1½ yards wide and 5 yards long, at first. As the child improves his skill in negotiating the obstacles, narrow and elongate the road. You can also make a one-line road, with obstacles on either side.

WHAT YOUR CHILD CAN DO

▪ Push/pull the loaded tub in a straight line between the obstacles.

▪ Push/pull the tub in a figure 8, around the obstacles.

▪ Pick up obstacles, load them into the tub, haul them around, unload them, and reposition them according to his own strategic plan.

▪ Outdoors, spray, squirt, sponge, or brush water on the chalked road to make the lines disappear, just like a magician.

VARIATION

Substitute a regular garden wheelbarrow or a child's wagon for a rolling tub.

BENEFITS OF THE ACTIVITY

▪ Being moved passively in the tub provides vestibular input as your child makes righting responses to stay in equilibrium.

▪ *Actively* pushing and pulling a loaded tub are calming and organizing experiences that benefit the proprioceptive system.

▪ The deep pressure input of handling and sitting under mounds of weight calms and organizes the child's somatosensory system.

▪ Negotiating the obstacle course integrates tactile, vestibular, proprioceptive, and visual sensations and strengthens motor planning.

▪ Pushing/pulling heavy weight with both hands improves bilateral coordination, body awareness, and gross motor skills.

▪ Squirting water and scrubbing chalk improves eye-hand coordination, motor planning, and crossing the midline.

Instructions for a Rolling Tub

- Large plastic tub, about 2 feet tall and 2 feet in diameter, available from large hardware stores and home/housewares stores
- Piece of ¾-inch plywood, about 2 × 2 foot
- Casters (4 will do; 8 are best)
- ½-inch wood screws
- Drill and ¼-inch drill bit
- 1¼-inch bolts with nuts
- Stretchy exercise tubing (see *Recommended Materials*) or rope
- Small hoop or rubber ring, or a dowel, about 2 inches in diameter and 2 feet long

PREPARATION

- Turn the tub upside down, trace its circumference onto the plywood, and saw around the circle. (Making the plywood base the same circumference as the tub's top, rather than the narrower bottom, provides more stability.)
- Draw two lines across the diameter of the circle, intersecting at 90 degrees.
- Position casters 2 inches from edge, on the lines. Attach them with ½-inch screws. (For maximal support, add another intersecting cross and use eight casters rather than four.)
- Place the tub upside down and put the plywood circle on it. Drill holes, about ¼ inch in diameter, equidistant between the casters and through the plywood and the tub. (To line up the holes correctly, it helps to push a bolt temporarily through the holes as you work.)
- Flip the plywood and tub over. Connect them with 1¼-inch bolts and nuts.
- To make a handle for the child to grip:
  • Tie one end of a 2- to 3-foot length of rubber tubing or rope to a handle of the tub, and tie the other end to a hoop or rubber ring, or
  • Drill holes in the ends of the dowel. Thread 6 to 8 feet of rubber tubing or rope through one of the handles of the tub. Tie the ends of the tubing through the holes in the dowel ends. Now the child can pull or push against the dowel to propel the rolling tub.

◆ Obstacle Course

Everybody loves an obstacle course. Like their typically-developing peers, children with DSI also have the inner drive to master physical challenges. They need manageable obstacles and plenty of time to practice moving their bodies through space.

A well-designed obstacle course will involve many kinds of movement: bending, straightening, balancing, alternating hands and feet, crawling, creeping, climbing, somersaulting, scooting, swinging, sliding, ascending and descending inclines, leaping, jumping, pulling and reaching, and taking big steps.

For children with poor coordination and poor motor planning skills, an obstacle course is an ideal activity. Build it, and they will come.

DEVELOPMENTAL AGE RANGE 2½ and up

WHAT YOU WILL NEED (PICK AND CHOOSE FROM THESE COMPONENTS)
From the Landscape/Garden Center

- Landscape timbers (railroad ties)—These sturdy lengths of wood are about the width of a gymnast's balance beam or of a sidewalk curb.
- Rocks or aggregate stones—Flat rocks, about 1-foot across, are good stepping stones.

- Flower pots—Unbreakable pots, about 8 or 10 inches high, make fine "traffic cones."
- Picnic table and benches—Outdoor furniture can be obstacles to clamber over.

From the Neighborhood

- Tree sections—Look for tree sections with a base of about 1 foot or wider and a height between 1 and 2 feet. You may find some curbside after a tree-trimming job in the neighborhood. Enlist your child's help to load a few tree sections into his little red wagon and haul them home. Imbed them into the ground, if necessary. If their bases are broad enough, you won't need to imbed them to make them secure, and you will then have the freedom to rearrange them at whim.
- Logs—A whole log would be a terrific substitute for a railroad timber. Maybe you can figure out a way to get one to your yard.

From the Hardware Store or Home Building Supply Center

- Rope—Get some thick rope, about 2 inches wide, for kids to walk on or swing on like Tarzan. (Also see *Fun with a Rope*, p. 96.)
- Ladder—A simple ladder with round rungs is best, as a folding or extension model may pinch small fingers and toes.
- Milk crates—Plastic, strong, lightweight boxes are excellent for stepping into, onto and around, and they double as indestructible storage boxes for outdoor toys.
- Boards—Smooth, finished boards, approximately 12 inches × 8 feet, make great ramps and bridges. Screw a wood strip, about 1 × 2 × 10 inches, near each end of the board to secure it when you rest it over a ladder rung or a sawhorse.

From the Toy Store, Sporting Goods Store, or Catalog Company (see Recommended Materials)

- Tunnel—Use a homemade tunnel (see *Fabric Tube Tricks*, p. 113; *Inner Tube Sport*, p. 92; and *Barrel of Fun*, p. 67), or get a crawling tunnel that can be collapsed for easy storage. Some tunnels have "windows" for children who don't like being in the dark.
- Gym mat—A vinyl-covered, folding, 1½-inch-thick gym mat has many uses.
- Hula hoops—Hula hoops of different sizes are versatile toys.

- Traffic cones—Colorful traffic cones, the sort employed by soccer coaches, make useful visual cues, as in, "See that cone over there? When you get there, you'll be halfway through the course."
- Climbing gym—A jungle gym with ladders, bridges, ropes, and monkey bars is an excellent investment. Get the best you can afford.

From the House

- Blankets or tablecloths—They should be old enough so you don't care what happens to them. Shower curtains and painters' tarpaulins also work.
- Mixing bowls—Large, colorful, unbreakable bowls from the kitchen cupboard can substitute for traffic cones.
- Flour—This is useful to mark the course. Flour offers no obstruction to the lawn mover and will vanish with the first rain. A whimsical alternative is making a path with pebbles or bread crumbs.
- Cardboard boxes—Large cartons from new appliances that are big enough to sit in are creative additions, although they do not age gracefully, especially after the rain. (See *Shoe Box Path*, p. 234.)

PREPARATION

- The simplest course, to build and to go through, runs in a great, linear circle. The first obstacle leads directly to the second, the second to the third, and eventually, the last right back to the first. A logical order of obstacles will help children understand the sequence and will keep them moving.
- Alternate the obstacles so that the children must vary both their body position and kinesthesia, or body movement, as they proceed from one challenge to the next. As you lay out a course, mutter prepositions to yourself: *up, down, in, out, under, over, across, through, between, beside, alongside, into, upon,* and *around.*
- Let your youngsters help with the layout, because they know what they like and need. Make a game of it. Ask, "How many prepositions did we set up here today? Do we have too many 'unders'? Should we add another 'between'?"
- Be vigilant about safety. Allow sufficient space between obstacles for the child to readjust his posture. Check the obstacles frequently for stability. Always be available to help when asked, and never leave the child alone.
- Get ready to observe your child move in imaginative ways. Don't tell him how to approach an obstacle; let him figure it out, all by himself. That's what motor planning is all about!

Sample Arrangement of an *Obstacle Course*

Obstacle 1—Up and Across

Mark the beginning of the obstacle course with a traffic cone. For the first obstacle, rest one end of a board on the ground and the other end on a short tree section or stepping stone, for a gentle upward slope. Offer the child a hand or finger, if necessary.

Obstacle 2—Down and Across

Spread the mat (or blanket) on the ground on the other side of the tree section for the child to step or jump down onto. The child may cross the mat any way he chooses, by somersaulting, rolling, crawling, walking, jumping, or running.

Obstacle 3—Into

Lay a few hoops on the ground for the child to step or jump into.

Obstacle 4—Through

The tunnel is next. Crawling (with the body close to the ground) and creeping (moving forward on hands and knees) are forms of cross-lateral locomotion. This movement, in which opposite arms and legs move forward at the same time, helps the left and right hemispheres of the brain "talk" to each other. When brain parts work smoothly together, the whole child functions better, often with noticeable improvements in social skills, motor skills, and cognitive ability.

No tunnel? How about a refrigerator carton? (See *Box Sweet Box*, p. 106.)

Children with DSI often seek quiet, cozy spots, where they can get away from it all. Your child may go into the tunnel and stay there for a while.

Obstacle 5—Across

Place one end of a railroad tie at least a yard away from the tunnel exit. The child will need space to straighten up and get stabilized.

Here are some of the ways a child can traverse a railroad tie:

- One foot in front of the other, as on a balance beam
- Sideways, with both feet pointed in the same direction
- One foot on the tie and the other foot down on the ground
- Both feet on the ground, straddling the tie

A popular obstacle with the little guys is two ties, side by side, with about an inch of space between them. Parallel beams may help the child feel safe and successful.

Obstacle 6—Up, Across, and Down

If you have a climbing gym, here's a good place for it.

Climbing up a ladder encourages the use of alternate hands and feet and strengthens bilateral coordination. Crossing a bridge or gangway engages the tactile, proprioceptive, vestibular, and visual senses. Hand rails and a board stretched across the rungs are best for the child with visual problems or gravitational insecurity.

Climbing down from a jungle gym requires more motor planning than climbing up a ladder. Many children need help here. Remind the child to turn to look at the rungs while descending and to "feel" for the rungs with his feet.

Some children will skip the climbing up and climbing down parts and stay below, swinging underneath the rungs, hand after hand, like monkeys. This maneuver is excellent for developing upper body strength, necessary for sitting at the table or desk to eat or write.

Obstacle 7—Alongside

Next is weaving "in and out the window" alongside a series of flowerpots, mixing bowls, or traffic cones. Set down five pots, about 18 inches apart, in a gentle "S" curve. Sprinkle flour on the ground to make a serpentine path for the child to follow. A visible path is very helpful, because changing direction is challenging for many children, especially those with visual-spatial difficulties.

No pots, bowls, or cones? Other options are rocks, plastic jugs, laundry detergent bottles, or cardboard boxes.

Obstacle 8—Up, Across, and Down

Now introduce *Matthew's Teeter-Totter* (see p. 65), if you have an extra grown-up or older child to serve as spotter. Someone must be there.

Obstacle 9—Between

Place two large objects side by side, about a foot apart, for the child to walk between. The large objects may be railroad ties, logs, garbage cans, patio chairs, window boxes, or large boxes.

Obstacle 10—Into

Set the ladder on the ground. The obstacle here is stepping into the spaces between the rungs, a super activity for strengthening eye-foot coordination, muscle control, grading of movement, and attention.

No ladder? Incorporate *Shoe Box Path* (p. 234) instead.

Obstacle 11—Up and Over

Station the picnic table and benches next so the child can climb up and over. No picnic table? Build shallow steps with four stepping stones by placing one on the ground, then a stack of two, followed by the fourth. No stepping stones? Use milk crates or cardboard boxes that are sturdy enough to support the child's weight.

Obstacle 12—Under

Drape a blanket over a folding table, such as a bridge table. Arrange the blanket so that it makes "walls" on the sides, leaving the entrance and exit wide open.

Obstacle 13—Upon

Lay the thick, heavy rope on the ground in a straight or curvy line. Walking across it is a wonderful activity to develop attention and balance.

Obstacle 14—Across

Spread another blanket out for the child to lie down on and roll across. Rolling feels good all over. And now—back to the beginning for another round!

VARIATIONS

- Railroad ties—Line up two or more, end to end, to make a long balance beam. Or use three to make a triangle, or four to make a square, in the center of the obstacle course. Children will use the triangle or square as a getaway, where they can rest and think, or as a make-believe house, spaceship, or wigwam.
- Boards—Vary their position each time you build an obstacle course so that the children always have the fun of working through new patterns.
- Rope—Tie it to two trees to make a roof line for a makeshift tent. Throw a blanket over the rope, anchor it to the rope with clothespins and to the ground with stepping stones, and you offer your child an instant retreat or clubhouse.

- Hoops—Press the edge of a hoop into a piece of Styrofoam for the child to pass through.

BENEFITS OF THE ACTIVITY
- An obstacle course rich in prepositions helps children understand spatial relationships. For instance, after moving their bodies through the tunnel and between the chairs, the children may grasp the abstract meaning of "through" and "between" more clearly.
- Proceeding through an obstacle course, children improve motor planning, exercise kinesthetic muscle sense, sharpen problem-solving skills, integrate most of their senses, and learn that they have skills to master new challenges set in their path.

◆ Metronome Workout

The human heart beats at about 60 to 80 beats per minute. No wonder, then, that a metronome set to a slow, steady beat helps us all restore order.

This rhythmic, imitative activity is one that Kimberly Geary, M.S., O.T.R./L., plays frequently with her clients and highly recommends. Practicing this game can help prepare your child for music classes, dance, martial arts, and other sports where imitation, bilateral coordination, rhythm, and timing are necessary for success.

DEVELOPMENTAL AGE RANGE 3 to 12

WHAT YOU WILL NEED
Metronome, available from a music store
(also see *Recommended Materials*)

PREPARATION
- Sit on the floor, facing your child.
- Set the metronome to 60 beats per minute and place it between you.

WHAT YOU CAN DO AND YOUR CHILD CAN IMITATE (IN ORDER OF DIFFICULTY)
1. To the slow beat of the metronome, tap your knees (or chest, shoulders, head, etc.) in a symmetrical pattern. That is, use both hands to tap both knees simultaneously and rhythmically. Tap for 8, 12, or as many counts are necessary for your child to "catch" and copy your motion and rhythm.

2. Tap asymmetrically, one hand and knee at a time: left hand on left knee, right hand on right knee, left hand on left knee, right hand on right knee.
3. Cross the midline: Tap right hand on left knee, left hand on right knee.
4. Stand and jump up and down.
5. Do modified jumping jacks, just opening and closing legs (no arms).
6. March in place: left, right, left, right.
7. Jump and cross feet:

   * Jump in place, with feet side by side.
   * Jump and land, with right foot crossed in front of left foot.
   * Jump in place, with feet side by side.
   * Jump and land, with left foot crossed in front of right foot.

8. Add arms to jumping motions.
9. Increase the challenge with "sensory loading":

   * Set the metronome to a faster tempo, or
   * Fade how many times you repeat the pattern, to encourage the child to take over the rhythmic motions without being able to watch and imitate you.

10. Increase the challenge with "cognitive loading":

   * Say an alphabet letter or number as you tap, clap, or jump:

     "A" (tap), "B" (tap), "C" (tap)
     "One" (jump), "two" (jump), "three" (jump)

   * Add a speech/language challenge by showing pictures of objects to the child and having her say what she sees:

     "Heart" (tap), "square" (tap), "circle" (tap)
     "House" (clap), "daisy" (clap), "giraffe" (clap)

   * Suggest a category, such as food, animals, or cartoon characters, and have the child think of and say individual category items:

     "Pizza" (tap), "apple" (tap), "hamburger" (tap)
     "Gazelle" (clap), "beagle" (clap), "panda bear" (clap)
     "Mickey Mouse" (jump), "Donald Duck" (jump)

BENEFITS OF THE ACTIVITY

■ Meeting the increasingly challenging demands of this game improves ideation (the process of forming, entertaining, and relating ideas), motor planning, sequencing, imitation, and timing.

- Using both sides of the body together reinforces bilateral coordination, and using both sides of the body in alternation strengthens lateralization skills.
- Mirroring the adult's gestures improves visual skills, proprioception, body awareness, and grading of movement.
- Tuning into the beat and pattern strengthens auditory attention and focusing skills and helps the child inhibit, or tune out, distractions in the environment.
- Thinking of individual category items before tapping, clapping, or jumping also promotes ideation and benefits speech and language development.

◆ Mrs. Midnight

This game—a variation of "Mother, May I?"—is fitting to play at Halloween, when black cats and spooky nights are exciting to think about. Of course, you can play this noncompetitive game any time, anywhere, and with almost any number of players.

DEVELOPMENTAL AGE RANGE 3 to 9

WHAT YOU WILL NEED
- Black cat hand puppet (see *Recommended Materials*)
- Masking tape or chalk
- *Crash Pad* (see p. 90) or gym mats

PREPARATION
- At one end of the room or yard, use the tape or chalk to draw a box, about one yard square. This is Mrs. Midnight's Safe Place, in which she stands alone.

- At the other end of the space, draw a start line for the Movers to stand on. Behind the start line is their Safe Place. Place a *Crash Pad* on the floor or gym mats on the ground for the children's safe landing.
- Hold the puppet, step into Mrs. Midnight's Safe Place, and demonstrate what to do. (See How to Play *Mrs. Midnight,* below.) Then, select a child to be the next Mrs. Midnight. (This game moves quickly; everyone gets a turn. Sometimes it helps to assign numbers to the kids so they'll know when their turn will be.)

HOW TO PLAY *MRS. MIDNIGHT*

- Any one—or all—of the Movers call out, "What time is it, Mrs. Midnight?"
- Mrs. Midnight answers, "It's 1 o'clock." (She's the boss for the moment, so she may also answer, "It's 7 o'clock," or any other o'clock she wants, from 1 to 11.)
- At first, the Movers take walking steps. Once the children get the gist of the game, Mrs. Midnight (or a Mover) can suggest a different form of locomotion:

  - Marching
  - Taking baby steps
  - Jumping
  - Hopping
  - Skipping
  - Rolling like a hot dog
  - Leaping like a frog
  - Leaping like a deer
  - Crab-walking (sideways, on all fours)
  - Creeping on hands and knees
  - Slithering like a snake
  - Waddling like a duck
  - Scooting (sitting down, sticking feet out, and moving bottoms forward)
  - Taking scissors steps (moving with elbows up and hands on one's shoulders, to look like the finger holes at the top of the scissors, and with one foot crossed in front of the other)
  - Pirouetting (placing one finger on one's head, spinning on one foot, and somehow propelling oneself forward at the same time)
  - Moving sideways or backward in any of the above ways

- Counting aloud, the Movers take one big step over the start line.
- This call-and-response pattern continues: the Movers ask again, Mrs. Midnight answers, and the Movers count aloud and take the correct number of steps.
- When the Movers' toes are at—but not over—Mrs. Midnight's Safe Place, they ask one last time, "What time is it, Mrs. Midnight?"
- Mrs. Midnight whispers dramatically, "It's . . . midnight!"
- All the Movers run back to the start line and tumble onto the *Crash Pad*

or mats. (Mrs. Midnight, greatly relieved, stays in her Safe Place and doesn't chase them.)

BENEFITS OF THE ACTIVITY

- Moving in different ways improves functions of the proprioceptive and vestibular systems, including motor planning, body awareness, gross motor skills, bilateral coordination, force, and kinesthesia.
- Moving with the group promotes visual skills, such as eye-ear-body coordination, directionality, depth perception, peripheral vision, and spatial relationships.
- Handling the puppet provides a soft and benign tactile experience.
- Counting aloud helps children regulate their movements, coordinate what they do with what they say they will do, and improve impulse control.
- *Mrs. Midnight* has the kind of tension and release that is extremely emotionally satisfying for most young children.

COPING TIPS

Tactile defensiveness may cause some Mrs. Midnights to rebuff the puppet or to pronounce, "It's midnight!" when the Movers have scarcely set out from the start line. These responses help the children with DSI cope—and stay in the game. Fine!

10

Fine Motor Skills

Khalid, 12, has mild DSI, which cause poor fine-motor skills. In preschool, he avoided cutting, drawing, pasting, puzzles, and xylophones. In elementary school, he received so-so grades because of poor handwriting. He shirked written assignments, and when he did turn in papers, they were usually late and always illegible. He could hunt and peck with one finger on the keyboard, but mechanical word processing was not much easier than struggling with a pencil.

Now in middle school, Khalid's hands are the right size for him to learn typing—a fine solution for many people with fine motor problems. The typing teacher suggests that Khalid master the Dvorak rather than the QWERTY keyboard. He explains that the QWERTY keyboard, named for the first six letters in the top row, was deliberately designed in the nineteenth century to slow down typists so they wouldn't jam the keys. The Dvorak keyboard was devised by August Dvorak, a twentieth century American professor of education. It is designed to increase speed, decrease fatigue, improve accuracy, and reduce frustration. Furthermore, Dvorak is perfectly compatible with twenty-first century computer keyboards.[1]

So Khalid learns to type. Now, he completes written assignments on time, and his teachers are finding what a fine mind he has. Khalid is fortunate that modern technology provides a solution that lets him express his thoughts and compensate for some of his fine motor woes.

---

[1]Many websites on the Internet provide information about the Dvorak keyboard, how to switch your computer to the system, and tutorials, all for free. (See *Recommended Materials*.)

Fine motor skills depend on efficient gross motor skills. With typical integration of tactile, vestibular, and proprioceptive sensations, a child develops effective large muscle, or gross motor, control in the torso, neck, arms, and legs. Good gross motor control is the foundation for small muscle, or fine motor, control.

Fine motor activities require the precise use of small muscles. These muscles are throughout the body—in the fingers and hands, in the toes, in the eyes, and in the tongue, lips, and muscles of the mouth and jaw.

Fine motor skills are requirements for good eye-hand coordination so a child can draw, write, turn pages, use utensils and other tools, build with Legos, and do jigsaw puzzles. Fine motor skills are necessary for precise eye-motor (oculomotor) movement, and for articulating speech and expressing language. They are also instrumental in retrieving a dropped pencil with the toes, wiggling the earlobes, raising an eyebrow, dilating the nostrils, and urinating into the toilet.

The child who has opportunities every day to run and play in open spaces is more likely than a "couch potato chip" to become skillful with scissors, screwdrivers, and measuring spoons. For various reasons, including tactile defensiveness and poor motor coordination, children with DSI may lag in the development of fine motor abilities.

Khalid's difficulties prevent him from doing everything he would like to do. Some characteristics of poor fine-motor skills are listed below.

CHARACTERISTICS OF POOR FINE-MOTOR SKILLS

The child with poor hand coordination may:
☐ Avoid ordinary classroom activities such as writing exercises, art projects, and science experiments.
☐ Avoid the use of tools, such as crayons, pencils, scissors, hole punches, staplers, screwdrivers, rulers, compasses, or tweezers.
☐ Have poor handwriting.
☐ Have poor self-help skills.
☐ Be a messy eater.

The child with poor oral-motor skills (also see chapter 8) may:

☐ Mouth and chew food in unusual ways.

☐ Have poor articulation and immature language skills.

☐ Use more gestures than words to communicate, because of inadequate control of the tongue, lips, and jaw.

The child with poor oculomotor control (also see chapter 5) may:

☐ Have difficulty with basic binocular skills such as visual tracking and focusing.

☐ Have poor eye-hand coordination.

When the child's problem is poor fine-motor skills, seek therapy that addresses large-muscle as well as small-muscle development. **SAFE** activities may be helpful, too.

Activities to Strengthen Fine Motor Skills

◆ Clothespin Togs

Dressing up is fun—and so is dressing up another person. This funky and funny activity, devised by Barbara Bassin, O.T.R./L., B.C.P., gives children the chance to be the boss of someone else's get-up in an acceptable way. Adorning another person strengthens kids' fine motor skills and simultaneously boosts their proprioception, problem-solving abilities, artistic expression, and sense of humor.

DEVELOPMENTAL AGE RANGE 3½ and up

WHAT YOU WILL NEED
- Clothes basket
- Bucket of plastic or wooden clothespins with springs
- Scarves, gloves, ski caps, nightgowns, socks, tee shirts, neckties, and so on
- A shiny penny or two

PREPARATION
- Hand your child the clothesbasket.
- Together, go on a treasure hunt throughout the house for clothes and accessories suitable for dressing up. If the child can follow directions, he may be able to gather the clothes himself. For example, you may say, "Go to my bedroom, open the top drawer in the bureau, and find the blue scarf. Put it in the basket." After he accomplishes that task, say, "Now go look in your bedroom closet. Find the Batman cape and put it in the basket. Then . . ."
- Have the child set down the loaded basket and pick up a "lucky penny." Show him how to press it against his palm with his ring finger and pinkie. Separating the two sides of the hand in this way frees the thumb, index finger, and middle finger so the child can manipulate the clothespin correctly, using the tripod grasp (described below).

- Practice manipulating a clothespin.
- Select a scarf, mitten, necktie, or other dress-up item.
- Take a clothespin out of the bucket, and, using the tripod grasp, pin the item to the clothes you are wearing. A scarf can hang from the back of your collar. A mitten can decorate a trouser cuff. A ski cap can dangle from your shoulder. The sillier, the better.
- Continue, until the basket is empty, your child is ecstatic, and you look positively ridiculous!

BENEFITS OF THE ACTIVITY

- Manipulating the penny and clothespins promotes the tripod grasp, needed for effective use of common "tools," including forks, pencils, and paintbrushes. In a tripod grasp, the wrist is bent up, or extended. The thumb pad is on the bottom of the item being grasped, and the pads of the index and middle fingers are on top. The hand leaves an open circle between the fingers, as if making an "okay" sign.
- Following directions improves auditory processing skills.
- Searching for the "blue scarf" amid other articles of clothing helps develop the visual skill of figure-ground perception.
- Lugging a heavy basket of clothes provides proprioceptive input.
- Using both hands to carry the load improves bilateral coordination.
- Collecting clothes, carrying the basket from room to room, using the clothespins, and pinning on the items improve motor planning.
- The open-ended activity may free your child to try something new. There are many funny ways to attach a glove to somebody's shirt.

COPING TIPS

If the child has difficulty grasping the clothespin, offer it with the two pieces "stacked" vertically. Then it will be oriented in a way for him to grip it properly.

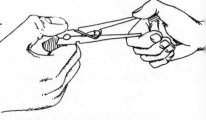

◆ Bubble Wrap Burst

Try this noisy bubble wrap game to release pent-up energy.

DEVELOPMENTAL AGE RANGE 3 and up

WHAT YOU WILL NEED

- Bubble wrap with the biggest bubbles
- A number dice and a color dice
- Six permanent ink markers with the same colors as are on the color dice

WHAT YOUR CHILD CAN DO

- Mark some bubbles and let the colors dry for a few minutes.
- Shake and throw the two dice.
- Pop the corresponding number and color of bubbles.
- Jump on the bubbles, with or without shoes and socks.

VARIATIONS

- For bouncier jumping, secure a large sheet of bubble wrap (with strapping tape) on top of a trampoline pad.
- Instead of bubble wrap, use packing peanuts to color and snap between the fingers. Jumping on packing peanuts is fun, but too messy.

BENEFITS OF THE ACTIVITY

- Coloring and popping the bubbles improves pincer skills, use of tools, hand dexterity, tactile perception, and eye-hand coordination.
- Shaking and throwing the dice and popping the bubbles promotes bilateral coordination.
- Jumping promotes proprioception, balance, bilateral integration, and motor planning.
- The linear movement of jumping up and down sends strong messages to the vestibular system through the inner ear. This kind of stimulation often improves the child's speaking skills, as many speech/language pathologists have learned when they use OT strategies in their treatment.
- Jumping on bubble wrap sends significant input to the auditory system through the outer ear, as well. The noise may delight sensory seekers.

COPING TIP

If the explosive sound of the popping bubbles dismays your sensory avoider, this activity may be more pleasing outdoors on the sidewalk.

◆ Toothpick Constructions

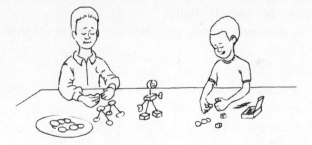

This multisensory activity is usually a big hit at any time, especially with siblings or a group of buddies. Who can make the funniest construction?

DEVELOPMENTAL AGE RANGE 3 and up

A Mother Says . . .

Laurie Renke says, "One of Jake's favorite activities that is gluten-free and milk-free is mini-marshmallows and toothpicks. He builds all types of things—animals, buildings, shapes. He built a model of a jungle gym and wants to sell the design to his school so they can get in the *Guinness Book of World Records* for having the largest play gym. I think he used 1,000 toothpicks and two bags of mini-marshmallows. He had a ball! It was the centerpiece on our table for about a month. Everyone that came into the house would be amazed and ask lots of questions. He got a big boost of self-esteem. We plan to use the idea to make little skeletons for his class Halloween party. This is a good activity for little ones learning their numbers and letters, and it is great for shapes, too!"

WHAT YOU WILL NEED
- Box of toothpicks
- Food chunks, such as:
  - Grapes, berries, pieces of banana, apple, melon, or cucumber
  - Lima beans, kidney beans, peas, corn kernels, popcorn
  - Cubes of cheese, tofu, chicken, turkey, or ham
  - Marshmallows

WHAT YOUR CHILD CAN DO
Stick toothpicks into food chunks to construct houses, scaffolding, robots, spaceships, people, monsters, porcupines, sea urchins, and other creations.

BENEFITS OF THE ACTIVITY
- Constructing creatures and objects improves pincer skills, translation movement, hand dexterity, and bilateral coordination.
- Manipulating the materials improves tactile perception.

- The activity improves visualization (the ability to picture something in the mind's eye), eye-hand coordination, and visual-spatial skills.
- Conceiving of creatures and objects to construct stretches the child's attention span, memory, imagination, and sense of fun.
- Playing with food may encourage the picky eater to try new foods.

✦ Squirting Race

Little squirts and big squirts will love this easy game of competition, suggested by Rondalyn V. Whitney, M.O.T., O.T.R.

DEVELOPMENTAL AGE RANGE 5 to 13

WHAT YOU WILL NEED FOR EACH PLAYER
- Large, clean squirt bottle (for mustard, ketchup, detergent, and so on)
- Plastic milk or water jug
- Ping-Pong ball

PREPARATION
- Fill the squirt bottles with water.
- Cut the tops off the plastic jugs so they are all the same height.
- Fill the jugs equally, with about 6 cups of water.
- Put a Ping-Pong ball into each jug.

WHAT THE PLAYERS CAN DO
Squirt water from their bottles into their jugs. Whoever gets the Ping-Pong ball to fall out first is the winner!

VARIATIONS

- Squirt water to "write" letters and "draw" figures on the sidewalk.
- Chalk letters and figures on the sidewalk or blackboard. Race with a friend to squirt away the chalk.
- Squirt shaving cream on an upright dry-erase board, and then squirt water to rinse off the shaving cream.
- Put lemonade powder into large ketchup bottle, fill the bottle with water, and shake the bottle to mix the drink. Squirt lemonade into small cups for family and friends.
- Squirt air (not water) and race with a friend to push cotton balls or scraps of lightweight tissue paper, medium-weight construction paper, and heavy-weight cardboard across the floor or table. (See *Spirited Shepherds*, p. 212, for a similar game that strengthens oral motor skills.)

BENEFITS OF THE ACTIVITY

- Squeezing and squirting develops fine-motor skills, hand function, and bilateral coordination.
- Squeezing and squirting with "just-right" force improves proprioception.
- Messy play with water improves tactile perception.
- Squirting water accurately into the jug and holding the eyes on a target strengthens focusing, visual attention, and eye-hand precision.
- Friendly competition builds social skills.

◆ Squeeze a Breeze

This imaginative game requires a pod of whales, a fleet of ships, and a strong sea breeze—all produced from "beautiful junk." Both the preparation and the play will amuse a crew of young sailors and whalers, simultaneously improving their fine motor skills. Mary Marcoux, a science teacher at Beauvoir in Washington, DC, and OT Rondalyn Whitney contributed to this activity.

DEVELOPMENTAL AGE RANGE 3 to 10

WHAT YOU WILL NEED

- Large squirt bottle (ketchup or detergent bottle)
- Construction paper or light cardboard

- Plastic foam meat trays
- Toothpicks
- Markers and scissors
- String or rope

- Have your child cut out paper whales and Styrofoam ships, using these templates, enlarged 150 percent:

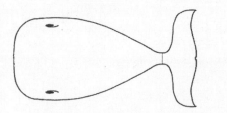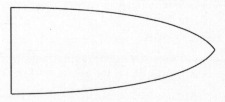

- Bend up the whales' tails a bit, to help them catch the "sea breeze."
- Cut out paper triangles to be the "sails." Stick a toothpick in and out of each sail and then into the Styrofoam.
- On the floor, arrange the string or rope in a circle to represent the ocean.
- Put the whales and sailing ships into the ocean.

WHAT YOUR CHILD CAN DO
- Kneel, squat, or lie near the ocean. Point the top of the bottle toward the ocean.
- Squeeze air from the bottle toward the whales and boats. Propel them around and across the ocean.
- With a friend, race your whales and boats or have them chase one another.

BENEFITS OF THE ACTIVITY
- Preparing the whales and boats encourages fine motor skills, the use of tools, tactile perception, and eye-hand coordination.
- Squeezing with both hands improves hand dexterity and bilateral coordination.
- Squeezing hard, squeezing lightly, and hovering over the "ocean" (without falling in) improves balance, force, gross motor control, motor planning, and kinesthesia.

◆ Bunny Ears

"My wonderful OT, Heather Miller-Kuhaneck, has a great idea for tying shoes," says Sara, an SI Mom. "Use two different laces of different colors. That way, explaining which one goes where is more obvious to the child. Pretty simple. Pretty neat."

DEVELOPMENTAL AGE RANGE 5 and up

WHAT YOU WILL NEED
- Two pairs of short shoe laces of different colors (let's say red and blue)
- Shoes

A Mother Says . . .

Raena, in Oklahoma, says, "A great demonstration of the *Bunny Ears* method is in Harrison Ford's movie, *Regarding Henry*. He's a lawyer who gets shot in the head and has to relearn/reinvent his life. His little daughter teaches him how to tie his shoes. My son and daughter (who both have sensory integration issues and resulting dyspraxia) might never have learned to tie their shoes if I hadn't seen that movie. When my son was 5 or 6, we sang the songs, recited various cute little stories, practiced ad nauseum, and he just couldn't figure out the usual method of shoe tying. I bought Velcro shoes and dropped the whole subject. It's so tough on a kid to try and fail, try and fail. When I saw that movie, I thought, 'There it is. THAT is what we're going to do.' He learned the *Bunny Ears* method immediately, and, at 14, uses it to this day."

PREPARATION
- Knot the ends of a red lace and a blue lace together.
- Lace up a shoe and leave the ends dangling.

WHAT YOU CAN SAY TO TALK YOUR CHILD THROUGH THE TYING PROCESS
- "Criss-cross the laces across the shoe to make an X."
- "Which one is on the bottom? Yep, Blue (or Red) is on the bottom. Take Blue (or Red), bring it toward your tummy and then back through the hole where he came from. Pull tight."
- "Near the knot, make a red loop and a blue loop, like two bunny ears."
- "Criss-cross the bunny ears to make an X."
- "Which one is on the bottom? Yep, Red (or Blue) is on the bottom. Bring Red (or Blue) toward your tummy and back through the hole he came from. Pull tight."
- "You did it! Now you know how to tie your shoes. Let's do the other shoe."

Use pipe cleaners to get started, if laces are too frustrating. Graduate to laces later.

BENEFITS OF THE ACTIVITY
- Tying one's own shoes is a fine motor activity that most children are driven to master. This self-help skill makes a kid feel big, successful, and independent, and it prevents teasing and tears. (The number one thing that gets kids with DSI singled out and teased on soccer teams is untied shoes!)
- Tying shoes promotes eye-hand coordination, bilateral coordination, grading of movement, and motor planning.

◆ Tor-Pee-Do

This activity is a "guy thing." Sorry, girls!

DEVELOPMENTAL AGE RANGE 2½ and up (boys only)

WHAT YOU WILL NEED
- Cereal O's or biodegradable peanuts used for packages or crafts
- Sense of humor

PREPARATION
Toss a handful of cereal into the toilet.

WHAT YOUR LITTLE BOY CAN DO
Get ready, aim, and fire away.

VARIATIONS
If playing with food this way seems inappropriate, use paper, instead:
- Give your boy a hole puncher and a piece of paper. He can punch out paper circles, called "chad," toss them into the toilet bowl, and use them as targets.
- Have your son tear off squares of toilet paper and twist them into bow shapes, or scrunch them into wads, or rip them into shreds. Toss them into the toilet bowl and *Tor-Pee-Do* away!

- Aiming for and hitting Cheerios is very much fun, apparently. The activity may motivate late-bloomers to become quickly toilet-trained.
- This activity improves bilateral coordination, force, and motor planning.
- Sinking Cheerios helps the child focus visually, and it fosters . . . shall we say "eye-um" coordination?
- Punching out chad (instead of using cereal) improves fine motor skills and hand dexterity.

COPING TIP

Rondalyn Whitney suggests this solution for failures in toilet training: Buy a small waste can with a swing lid. Draw a funny face on the lid. Fill the can halfway with water and some bleach. Every pair of "accident" undies gets fed to the waste can character. The underwear gets a good soaking until laundry time, and there's no embarrassing issue for the child.

◆ Doodle-Doo

There are many ways to doodle. If you are having difficulty luring your child to use the toilet, try this art project. It comes from Susan Keeley of Chicago, who quickly toilet-trained her two sons with this ingenious method.

DEVELOPMENTAL AGE RANGE 2 and up

WHAT YOU WILL NEED
- Plastic bag
- Marker
- Large metal washer or fishing weight
- String, about 2 feet long

PREPARATION
- Slip the plastic bag over toilet seat lid.
- Tape one end of the string to a marker. Tie the washer to the other end of the string. Lift the toilet tank lid and drop the washer in. (This little trick will prevent the marker from dropping into the toilet.)

WHAT YOUR CHILD CAN DO
- Sit backward on the toilet seat, facing the lid.
- Doodle on the plastic bag.
- Meanwhile, "doo-doo" into the toilet!

- Drawing or doodling at the impromptu easel (the toilet seat lid) improves postural control, hand dexterity, fine motor skills, arm movements, and eye-hand coordination, all of which benefit handwriting.
- This activity fosters tactile awareness and interoception, which is the sense involving both the conscious awareness and the unconscious regulation of bodily processes of internal organs.
- Sometimes distraction will help the child relax and get the job done.

COPING TIP

A child may resist sitting on the toilet because of gravitational insecurity. She needs to feel her feet grounded before she can do anything else. To help her feel safe and comfortable, place two boxes of the same height under her feet, on either side of the toilet, if she's facing backward, or a footstool under her feet if she is facing forward.

◆ Piggy Toe Pick-Up

This fine motor activity for the toes combines water play and one-foot standing balance. Lori L. Merkel, COTA/L, of Pennsylvania, says, "This is a favorite of many of my clients in OT sessions or in playgroup settings. We play the game often with successful results, and it is a lot of fun."

DEVELOPMENTAL AGE 3 and up (depending on variations used)

WHAT YOU WILL NEED

- Large dishpan or tub (like one you would use to bathe a baby or small dog)
- Water (warm or cool, depending upon the child's tolerance)
- Small items that sink, such as marbles, smooth rocks, stringing beads, and so on.
- Carton or dishpan, for storage
- Towels for drying off
- Tarp or shower curtain, if playing indoors

PREPARATION

- Fill tub with water, about one-third full.
- Together, place small items in the tub.
- Have child take off shoes and socks.

- Standing next to the tub, place a foot into the water.
- Holding an adult's hand, if necessary, grope around with her toes to find an item.
- Trap the item in her toes and try to pick it up and out of the water.
- Bring her foot up to her hand and pluck the item from her toes. SUCCESS!
- Place the item in the box or dishpan.
- Alternating feet, try again until all items are removed.

VARIATIONS TO INCREASE THE CHALLENGE

- Do the activity with eyes closed.
- Do the activity again in colder or warmer water.
- Do the activity in soapy water.
- Trap floating objects, such as acorns and pecans, grapes, popsicle sticks, corks, packing peanuts, and so forth.
- Capture stringing beads and then string them.
- Work with a partner, one child on either side of the tub (bound to cause giggles).

VARIATIONS TO DECREASE THE CHALLENGE

- Do the activity sitting on a chair.
- Pick up an item and just place it on the floor, without bringing foot to hand.
- Do the activity without water, or even without a tub.

BENEFITS OF THE ACTIVITY

- *Piggy Toe Pick Up* exercises fine motor muscles in the toes.
- Picking up items with the toes in a fun way may help to decrease over-sensitivity in some children's feet.
- Playing in water is a tactile experience.
- Practicing one-foot standing balance improves postural control and equilibrium, functions of the vestibular sense.
- Looking for objects in the water and directing the toes toward them promotes eye-foot coordination and depth perception.
- Stretching the foot to reach objects in the tub strengthens proprioception, grading of movement, motor planning, and kinesthesia.
- Bringing the left foot to the right hand, or right foot to left hand, improves the ability to cross the midline.
- Stringing beads fosters bilateral integration.
- Working with a partner improves social interactions and communication skills.

11

Bilateral Coordination and Crossing the Midline

Billy's DSI affects several areas of development, particularly bilateral coordination and crossing the midline. At his 4th birthday party, this problem becomes evident. The party activity is enacting the story of "The Three Billy Goats Gruff," a story dear to Billy's heart. Miss Bonnie, the Birthday Party Lady, comes to his house and sets up chairs and tables as a makeshift bridge. She settles the children down and teaches them a song, with accompanying motions, to the tune of "Five Little Ducks."

"THREE BILLY GOATS GRUFF" SONG	ACCOMPANYING ACTIONS
Three billy goats went out one day,	Hold up three fingers.
Over the hills and far away.	Stretch the arm up and across the body.
Their little feet went, "Trip, trop, trip, trop."	Alternate stamping feet.
The big troll hollered, "Stop, stop, stop!"	Hold up both hands, palms front, and on each "Stop," thrust them toward the left, the right, and the left again.

Miss Bonnie demonstrates the story of the brave billy goats and the hungry troll. She shows how the troll dismisses the first two goats, too small for his big appetite, with a sweeping gesture across his body and the words, "Be off with you!"

Imitating her motions befuddles Billy. Poor bilateral coordination means that he can't stamp his feet rhythmically and with equal force. Difficulty with crossing the midline means that he can't move his arm easily across his body to accompany "Over the hills and far away" and "Be off with you!" He can't use both hands to gesture "Stop!" on his left and right sides. He isn't getting the motions right, and he looks worried.

Billy's mother is worried, too. Watching the group of children, she notices how her son is not moving as smoothly as his playmates. She wonders if it matters and decides to speak with his teacher to find out if Billy shows coordination problems that need to be addressed.

Bilateral coordination develops as babies learn to move their torsos and limbs. Some movements are symmetrical, such as waving both arms at the same time; other movements are asymmetrical, such as kicking feet in an alternating pattern. Babies who are placed in different positions, including tummies and sides, have a decided advantage over babies who are always placed on their backs.

Research shows that many babies who have difficulty learning to crawl have not had sufficient opportunity to experience being in different positions. (Remember: the "Back to Sleep" suggestion to prevent Sudden Infant Death syndrome is intended just for sleeping.) Wide-awake babies must have plenty of time on their stomachs in order to explore what their bodies can do and to develop strong motor skills and bilateral coordination.

Bilateral coordination is the ability to use both sides of the body simultaneously. Sometimes, a person uses the two sides to do the same action such as jumping, or using a rolling pin, or tossing a beach ball. Other times, the person uses reciprocal, or alternating, movements—using each side to perform the same motion at different times—such as creeping on hands and knees, or climbing stairs. Another function of bilateral coordination is using the two sides of the body for different purposes, such as balancing on one foot to kick a soccer ball with the other, stabilizing a paper with one hand while writing with the other, playing the guitar, and learning phonics.

Crossing the midline depends upon efficient bilateral coordination. Crossing the midline is using the eye, hand, or foot of one side of the body in the space of the other eye, hand, or foot. We have three midlines: sagittal, transverse, and frontal.

1. The *sagittal midline* is vertical. It divides the left side of the body from the right. An infant can cross the sagittal midline when he learns to throw one arm across his chest and turn from his back to his tummy. A preschooler can cross the sagittal midline when she paints a horizontal stripe across the paper, from left to right or from right to left, without switching the brush from hand to hand. She can cross her arms to tap her left shoulder with her right hand, and vice versa. She can sit on the floor with her legs crossed in an "X." By the time she is in first grade, she can track words smoothly across a page as she reads from left to right.

2. The *transverse midline* is horizontal. At the waist, it divides the upper and lower parts of the body. When a 5-month-old plays with his feet, he crosses the transverse midline (and when he grabs his left big toe with his right hand, he crosses the sagittal midline, too). A 4-year-old crosses the transverse midline when she can bend at the waist and touch her toes. Holding a ball in one hand over her head, she can lean forward to put her weight on the opposite foot, bend slightly at the waist, and throw the ball.

3. The *frontal midline* is vertical, dividing the front of the body from the back. When an 18-month-old stands on the bed and falls backward onto the pillows, he can cross the frontal midline. As he grows, he learns to walk and run with smooth coordination, while swinging his arms front to back. He can also walk backward and swing his arms simultaneously, and he can hop forward and jump backward.

Billy's coordination problems hinder his ability to move and play with as much fluidity as his peers. They also suggest that the two hemispheres of his brain may not be communicating with each other to pass information back and forth. Some characteristics of these difficulties are listed on page 268 .

CHARACTERISTICS OF POOR BILATERAL COORDINATION AND OF DIFFICULTY CROSSING THE MIDLINE

The child with poor bilateral coordination may:

☐ Not have crawled or crept as a baby.

☐ Have poor body awareness.

☐ Have poor gross-motor skills and frequently stumble and trip, or be clumsy at sports and active games. She may have "two left feet."

☐ Have difficulty making both feet or both hands work together, such as when jumping up and down on a trampoline, jumping from a ledge, jumping rope, using a rolling pin, or throwing and catching a ball.

☐ Have trouble using both hands in a smooth, alternating manner, as when skipping, going up and down stairs, or clapping hands and striking rhythm instruments together to keep a musical beat.

☐ Have difficulty using one foot or hand to assist the other, such as when standing on one foot to kick a ball, or steadying the paper to write.

☐ Not have an established hand preference by the age of 4 or 5. The child may use either hand to color, draw and write, or may switch the crayon or pencil frequently between hands.

☐ Have poor fine-motor skills and difficulty using tools such as eating utensils, crayons, pencils, and combs.

☐ Have difficulty learning to play a musical instrument.

☐ Have a hard time with organization and structured activities.

The child with difficulty crossing the midline may:

☐ Switch the brush from hand to hand while standing at the easel and painting a horizontal line.

☐ Have trouble tapping a hand on the opposite shoulder or elbow in games such as Simon Says.

☐ Have trouble reading a line smoothly from left to right, needing to stop in the middle of the line to blink and refocus.

☐ Have trouble visually tracking a moving object, such as a ball.

Activities for Bilateral Coordination and Crossing the Midline

Fence Painting

This one is as old as time . . . and so good for crossing the midline.

DEVELOPMENTAL AGE RANGE
2½ to 12

WHAT YOU WILL NEED
- Pail, large brush, and water
- A wall or fence

WHAT YOUR CHILD CAN DO
"Paint" the house or fence.

BENEFITS OF THE ACTIVITY
- Side-to-side brushstrokes promote crossing the midline.
- All brushstrokes promote gross-motor skills, motor planning, grading of movement, and eye-hand coordination.
- Playing with water is the kind of "clean" messy activity that may entice a child with tactile defensiveness into the play.

Going on a Bear Hunt

Remember this old standby? It still does the job admirably to pass the time and to help children develop good bilateral coordination.

DEVELOPMENTAL AGE RANGE 3 to 6

How to Play *Going on a Bear Hunt*

WHAT YOU SAY	WHAT YOU AND YOUR CHILD DO
"Let's go on a bear hunt. Come with me."	Sit in a circle—on the floor, seated in chairs, or balancing on *T-Stools*.
"Let's walk. Walk, walk, walk, walk, walk, walk."	Drum your hands on your thighs, or "walk" your feet: left-right, left-right.
"Here we are in the tall grass. We'd better push the grass aside so we can pass through. Swish, swish, swish."	Bring the backs of your hands together. Press them to the sides, as if pushing apart tall grasses.
"Uh-oh, here's a river. Guess we have to swim. Swim, swim, swim."	Make swimming motions: • breaststroke • butterfly • crawl • side stroke • backstroke • doggy paddle
"Let's dry off. Shake, shake, shake."	Shake your head, arms, and legs to flick off the water drops.
"Let's look around. Do you see a bear anywhere? I don't see one, do you?"	Bring your hands to your brow, like a sun visor, and look left and right.
"Oh, look, a big tree. Maybe we can see a bear from the treetop. Climb, climb, climb, climb."	Make climbing-up-the-tree motions, left-right, left-right. Stretch your arms higher each time. At the top, stretch your neck and look around.
"See anything? No? Me, neither. Let's go down again. Down, down, down."	Begin with arms high. Lower them as you climb down.
"My goodness, another stream! Here is a rowboat. Oars, too. Come on, let's get in and row. Row, row, row."	Row your boat with two oars.
"We must drag this boat onto shore. Here's a towline for you. Pull, pull."	Hand each child a pretend rope. Pull on your ropes to haul in the boat.

WHAT YOU SAY	WHAT YOU AND YOUR CHILD DO
"Any bears in sight?"	Look around.
"I don't see any, either. We are in a muddy swamp. We'll have to slog through it somehow. Squish, squish, squish."	Lift your feet heavily, left-right, left-right, left-right, left-right, and make a slurpy sound.
"Here's a big mountain . . . and here's a cave. Should we go in? Yes? Okay, but I'm a little scared. Are you?"	Shiver with pretend fear.
"Wow, it's too dark in this cave to see. We'll have to feel our way."	Grope in front with both hands, as if you're feeling around in the dark.
"Hmmm, what's this? It's big, and warm, and furry . . . Yikes, it's a bear! Come on, let's run! Run, run, run."	Drum your hands rapidly on your knees, or make running motions with your feet: left-right, left-right.
"Hurry! It's after us! Let's get through the swamp! Squish, squish. Here's the boat. Let's pull it to the river. Pull, pull. Let's row. Row, row. Here's the tree. Let's climb up to see where the bear is after us. Climb, climb. Oh, I see it! Let's get down!"	Continue retracing your steps and repeating the appropriate motions.
"We're home! Open the door! Slam the door! Run upstairs! Hide under the bed! Whew, we're safe! . . . and I wasn't scared at all, were you?"	Sag with relief.

- Bilateral coordination improves when children use both sides of the body in a cooperative manner:
  - In repetitive, alternating motions (walking, swimming the crawl or backstroke, climbing, and squishing through the swamp)
  - In tandem (pushing apart the grass, rowing, shielding the eyes)
- Using the body in different ways improves body awareness, gross motor coordination, grading of movement, motor planning and kinesthesia.
- For kids with poor body awareness, sitting in a circle enables them to watch and imitate other children's actions and to learn from them.
- Participating improves auditory awareness and speech and language skills.
- Imagining the tall grass, river, boat, tree, cave, house, and so on, promotes visualization.

◆ Clapping Bubbles

For a quick and easy bilateral coordination game, *Clapping Bubbles* is about as good as it gets. This multisensory, old-fashioned activity gives every child the sweet satisfaction of success.

For an extra challenge, bring out a teeter-totter. Rocking and clapping at the same time will really help to get both sides of the child's brain and body in sync.

If, however, simultaneous rocking and clapping is difficult for the child with gravitational insecurity or poor coordination, do not complicate the activity with a teeter-totter. For this gleeful activity, the bilateral clapping is more important than balancing.

DEVELOPMENTAL AGE RANGE 2 and up

WHAT YOU WILL NEED

- Bubbles, which you can make by mixing 4 cups water, ½ cup light corn syrup, and 1 to 1½ cup dishwashing liquid (let the mixture settle for several hours)

- Bucket of water for rinsing hands
- Optional: Rocking board or *Matthew's Teeter-Totter* (see p. 65)

WHAT YOU CAN DO
Blow bubbles toward your child.

WHAT YOUR CHILD CAN DO
- Clap at the bubbles to make them pop.
- Alternating hands, punch the bubbles with fists, or poke the bubbles with pointed index fingers.
- Tip and balance on the rocking board while clapping.

VARIATION
Play catch with a beach ball, balloon, or large beanbag. Do this every day!

BENEFITS OF THE ACTIVITY
- Stretching and reaching in different directions to clap bubbles with both hands strengthen bilateral integration and midline crossing.
- Clapping improves balance, gross motor control, grading of movement, and motor planning.
- Focusing on the floating bubbles—especially while moving on the teeter-totter—improves visual processing.
- Tipping from side to side gets both sides of the brain "talking" to each other and calms and organizes the vestibular system. One positive end-result may be increased speech and language output.
- *Clapping Bubbles* is messy play that the child with tactile defensiveness may tolerate.

Peanut Butter Jar

Need a quick fix for a stressful day or a play-date that isn't going well? Call the kids to the kitchen and have them spread room-temperature peanut butter on toast.

DEVELOPMENTAL AGE RANGE 3 and up

WHAT YOU WILL NEED

- Peanut butter in a plastic jar (for the child with an allergy to peanuts, try a substitute such as apple butter or soy nut butter)
- Butter knife, craft stick, or other dull blade
- Apple slices, crackers, bread, or toast

WHAT YOUR CHILD CAN DO

- Twist open the jar.
- Spread peanut butter on the crackers, apples, bread, or toast.
- Screw the lid back on the jar.

VARIATIONS

- Put a little toy that your child most wants into a clear jar. Leave the jar out, and sooner or later, the child will get it open.
- Put an apple slice in a clean jar, go outside on a midsummer night, and catch fireflies—another activity that requires both hands and promotes bilateral coordination. Put the fireflies in the jar. Watch them flash and glow for a while and then let them go. (Punching holes in the jar lid is unnecessary. For the short time fireflies are in the jar, they will have plenty of oxygen. Furthermore, fireflies prefer moist air, and holes release moisture.)

BENEFITS OF THE ACTIVITY

- Opening the jar requires two hands—one to hold the jar, the other to twist the lid. Loading a knife with peanut butter requires two hands— one to hold the jar, the other to handle the knife. Spreading peanut butter requires two hands—one to hold the bread, the other to move the knife.
- Spreading peanut butter fosters grading of movement, fine motor skills, tool use, and eye-hand coordination.
- Spreading room temperature peanut butter on warm toast is a soothing, quiet, and calming experience.
- Preparing her own snack makes a child feel useful, teaches self-help skills, and may even make the food taste better.

COPING TIP

If your child has an intolerance to peanut butter, substitute it with another spreadable food.

◆ Marble Trails

The process of making these artistic paintings is excellent for bilateral integration. When the product is used as a party invitation or little book cover, it becomes a lovely keepsake. Lori Merkel, C.O.T.A./L., has perfected this old favorite and added *Tire Trails* as an imaginative variation.

The project is fairly certain to make a mess, because marbles and little cars tend to zoom off the pan in all directions. Be sure to do it in a place that's easy to clean up.

DEVELOPMENTAL AGE RANGE 3 to 8

WHAT YOU WILL NEED
- Jellyroll pan, cafeteria tray, or shallow cardboard box, such as a pizza box or soda tray
- Construction paper
- Washable paint in several colors, or in gold and silver for a holiday look
- Marbles
- Paper cups or tuna fish cans
- Plastic spoons
- Smock or big old tee shirt to cover clothes

PREPARATION
- Pour about ½-inch of paint into paper cups or cans (one for each color).
- Place one marble into each cup or can.
- Cover the bottom of the pan, tray, or box with paper.

WHAT YOUR CHILD CAN DO
- Use a spoon (one for each cup) to stir the marble and coat it with paint.
- Carefully spoon the marble out of the cup and onto the paper.
- Holding its short sides, tip and tilt the pan slightly to move the marble about on the paper, leaving trails of paint.
- Repeat steps with other marbles until satisfied with a completed project.

VARIATIONS

- Use several marbles at the same time.
- Add glitter to the paper while paint is still wet.
- Work with another child, facing each other, both holding the same tray.
- Stand in a variety of positions to work on balance, such as on one foot or with one foot placed in front of the other.
- Sit to do this activity.
- When the paint has dried, fold the paper to make the cover of a little book, holiday card, or invitation.

Tire Trails

- Instead of marbles, use small cars or trucks with an interesting tread. Put a blob of paint on a paper plate. Holding onto the roof of the vehicle, the child runs only its tires through the paint, places the car in the pan, and tips the pan to make *Tire Trails* on the paper.
- For a greater challenge, older children can do this activity with their eyes closed. Have them use a truck with tread. Using only their ears to tell where the truck is on the pan, they must figure out how to react with their body movements to move the truck back and forth on the paper. (FUN!)

BENEFITS OF THE ACTIVITY

- Stirring with a spoon while the other holds the cup and using two hands to hold and move the jellyroll pan strengthens bilateral coordination.
- Using paint offers a tactile experience.
- Watching the marble or vehicle move about the paper improves eye-hand coordination and visual tracking.
- Tipping the pan with just-right force so the marble stays on the pan improves proprioception, motor planning, flexion, and extension.
- The activity can address tolerance to smells depending on the type of paint used, as some paints can be very smelly.
- Working with another child increases awareness of movement and builds social skills and communication.

Beanbag Mania

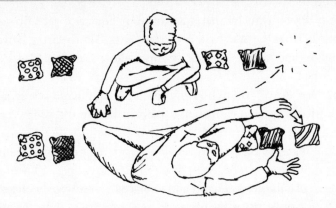

For the child who has difficulty with crossing the midline, visual-spatial aware-ness, proprioception, and motor planning, this game is one of the best. Joye Newman, perceptual-motor therapist, and one of her young clients invented it years ago. It has become a favorite at her clinic, Kids' Moving Company, in Maryland.

DEVELOPMENTAL AGE RANGE 3½ and up

WHAT YOU WILL NEED
6 matching pairs of beanbags (12 in all)

PREPARATION
- Sit on the floor, facing each other.
- You each select six different beanbags. You might say, "OK, I'll take a blue, and you take a blue. I'll take a red, you take a red. You take a plaid, I'll take a plaid."
- You each place three beanbags to your right and three to your left. Arrange them as if in a mirror so that the reds, the blues, and the plaids, are opposite each other.

WHAT TO DO (IN ORDER OF DIFFICULTY)
- Raise your left arm. Say, "Do what I do," or "Be my mirror." Your child will raise his right arm.
- Place your left hand on your left ear, shoulder, and knee. Repeat motions with your right hand. Your child will mirror your movements.
- Use movements that cross the midline, such as placing your left hand on your right ear, shoulder, and knee. Repeat with the right hand.

Encourage him to use smooth movements across his midline as he imitates you.

- Slowly, reach your left hand across your body and pick up your green beanbag from the floor near your right knee. Slowly, bring it over to your left side and deposit it next to the yellow beanbag. (Do not switch hands!)

- Say, "Your turn!" Your child will reach his right hand across his body to pick up his green beanbag and place it beside the yellow bag on his right.

- Continue, reaching sometimes with your left hand and sometimes with your right. Put each beanbag down in a different place. Encourage your child to use the correct hand and to place his beanbags with accuracy.

- Pick up two or three beanbags at once and place them on your other side.

- Challenge your child with a sequence of movements to copy:
  - Arrange the beanbags at your side in a triangle, a vertical row, a three-dimensional heap, or another spatial configuration.
  - Pick up two or three beanbags and arrange them in an unpredictable configuration on the other side.

- When you both have the hang of the game, go faster. The goal is to become so adept at copying the other's moves that you work in tandem, as if facing a mirror.

- Take turns being the leader and the follower.

VARIATION

For tactile and visual interest, use beanbags with different textures (corduroy, velvet, fake fur, burlap, satin, flock, or flannel) and patterns (plaids, polka dots, stripes, flowers, teddy bears, boats, and so on).

BENEFITS OF THE ACTIVITY

- Moving his hands from one side of his body to the other improves the ability to cross the midline. This skill is important for smooth movement and reading.

- Grading his movements to pick up the beanbag and deposit it on the other side of his body improves proprioception and body awareness.

- Matching beanbag pairs, tracking the other player's motions, and placing his beanbag accurately fosters visual motor skills, including spatial awareness and eye-hand coordination.

- Organizing his body to do what he wants to do improves motor planning.

- Anticipating, observing, and responding to each other's motions improves gestural communication, which is an essential component of relating to others. (Gestures account for about 70 percent of all communication.)

COPING TIPS

- If crossing the midline is hard, and your child wants to switch hands, gently place your hand on his hand holding the beanbag to help him complete the movement.
- If using one hand alone is hard, gently hold the other hand in yours to keep it still.

Conclusion

This is not the end of **SAFE** activities; this is the beginning! Hundreds, thousands of other wonderful ideas are waiting to be written down and shared.

Do you have some great activities that other children would enjoy? Activities that you or your child invented, or that a therapist suggested, or that are geared especially for preteens and teenagers? If so, let's collaborate to put them into another book, *The Out-of-Sync Child Has More Fun*. These are the ingredients:

1. Activity title
2. Introductory comment
3. Developmental Age Range
4. What You Will Need
5. Preparation
6. What You Can Do
7. What Your Child Can Do
8. Variations
9. Benefits of the Activity
10. Coping Tips
11. Your name, address, and e-mail
12. Name, address, and e-mail of person who gets the credit (if it is not your idea)
13. Photograph or stick drawing of your child playing, if possible, to aid the illustrator

PLEASE SEND YOUR IDEAS BY "SNAIL" MAIL TO:	PLEASE SEND YOUR IDEAS BY E-MAIL TO:
Carol Kranowitz c/o Perigee Books Penguin Putnam Inc. 375 Hudson Street, 4th floor New York, New York 10014	sheila.oakes@us.penguingroup.com Subject line: *Out-of-Sync Child Has More Fun*

Thank you—and have fun!

Warmest wishes,
Carol Kranowitz

Appendix

GLOSSARY

With grateful acknowledgment to the following experts:

Sally Abruzzese, M.Ed., O.T.R./L., B.C.P.; A. Jean Ayres, Ph.D., O.T.R.; Sheila M. Frick, O.T.R.; Laura D. Glaser, M.A., S.L.P.-C.C.C.; Barbara Hanft, M.A., O.T.R./L., F.A.O.T.A.; Sharon Heller, Ph.D.; Diana Henry, M.S., O.T.R./L.; Catherine C. Hostetler, O.T.R.; Amy McLean, O.T.R./L.; Lucy Jane Miller, Ph.D., O.T.R.; Heather Miller-Kuhaneck, M.S., O.T.R./L., B.C.P.; Patricia Oetter, M.A., O.T.R., F.A.O.T.A.; Eileen Richter, M.P.H., O.T.R., F.A.O.T.A.; Trude Turnquist, Ph.D., O.T.R.; Julia Leigh Wilbarger, M.S., O.T.R.; Patricia Wilbarger, M.Ed., O.T.R., F.A.O.T.A.

Adaptive behavior: the ability to respond actively and purposefully to changing circumstances and new sensory experiences.

Adaptive response: an adjusted behavior or action that effectively and efficiently meets an environmental demand or challenge. A simple adaptive response may be initiating eye contact; a complex adaptive response may be diving from the high board for the first time.

Arousal: a state of the nervous system ranging from sleep to awake, from low to high. The optimal state of arousal is the "just-right" midpoint between boredom and anxiety where we feel alert and calm.

Auditory discrimination: the auditory-language processing skill of differentiating among sounds.

Auditory memory: the ability to remember what has been said and to repeat a sequence of sounds.

Bilateral coordination: the ability to use both sides of the body together in a smooth, simultaneous, and coordinated manner.

Bilateral integration: the neurological process of integrating sensations from both body sides, the foundation for bilateral coordination.

Binocularity: the basic oculomotor skill of forming a single visual image from two images that the eyes separately record.

Body awareness: the perception of one's own body parts, where they are, how they interrelate, and how they move.

Brain Gym™: a movement system to promote integrated visual, auditory, and kinesthetic functioning.

Central nervous system (CNS): the part of the nervous system, consisting of the brain and spinal cord, that receives sensory impulses, sends out motor impulses, and coordinates the activity of the entire nervous system.

Cortisol: a stress hormone linked to a person's level of self-regulatory behavior and to expressions of distress and aggression.

Crossing the midline: the ability to use one side or part of the body (hand, foot, or eye) in the space of the other side or part.

Depth perception: the visual-spatial processing skill of seeing objects in three dimensions and judging relative distances between objects, or between oneself and objects.

Directionality: the visual-spatial skill of being aware of right/left, forward/back, up/down, and diagonals, and the ability to move oneself in those directions.

Dyssemia: a difficulty in using nonverbal signs or signals.

Dysfunction in sensory integration (DSI): the inability to modulate, discriminate, coordinate, and/or organize sensations adaptively, leading to difficulties in learning, development, and behavior.

Dysfunction in sensory discrimination: a problem in interpreting the characteristics of sensory stimuli and in differentiating among and between sensory stimuli.

Dyspraxia: dysfunction in praxis; difficulty in conceiving of, planning, and carrying out a novel motor action or series of motor actions; often related to poor somatosensory processing.

Extension: the pull of the muscles away from the front of the body; straightening or stretching.

Extensor: a muscle that serves to extend a limb or other body part.

Eye-hand coordination: the efficient teamwork of the eyes and hands, necessary for activities such as playing with toys, dressing, and writing.

Figure-ground: a complex processing skill of differentiating between objects seen in the foreground and in the background (visual figure-ground), or between sounds heard in the foreground and in the background (auditory figure-ground).

Fine motor: pertaining to movement of the small muscles in the fingers, toes, eyes, and mouth.

Fixation: the basic oculomotor skill of aiming one's eye at an object or shifting one's gaze from one object to another.

Flexion: movement of the muscles around a joint to pull a body part toward its front or center; bending.

FloorTime: a systematic technique, based on the work of Stanley I. Greenspan, M.D., that fosters children's healthy emotional development through intensive, one-on-one interactions with adults who are literally on the child's level.

Focusing: the basic oculomotor skill of accommodating one's vision smoothly between near and distant objects.

Force: the body's ability to judge the motion of the muscles and joints in relation to objects in the environment; a function of proprioception.

Foreground/background (see **Figure-ground**).

Grading of movement: the flexion and extension of muscles according to how much pressure is necessary to exert.

Gravitational insecurity: extreme fear and anxiety that one will fall when one's head position changes or when one is moving through space, resulting from poor processing of vestibular and proprioceptive information.

Gross motor: pertaining to movement of the large muscles in the arms, legs, and trunk.

Hyper-responsiveness (also **Hypersensitivity**): observable behavior involving a quick or intense response to sensory stimuli that others usually perceive as benign; characterized by exaggerated responses ("fight or fright") or withdrawal from stimuli ("flight or freeze").

Hyper-reactivity and **Hyporeactivity:** exaggerated neurological and physiological processes that we cannot observe and that may be the cause of hyper-responsive and hyporesponsive behavior.

Hyporesponsiveness (also **Hyposensitivity**): behavior involving a slow response to sensory stimuli, requiring high intensity or increased duration of the stimuli to invoke an observed behavioral response; and characterized by a tendency either to be sensory-seeking, or to withdraw and be difficult to engage.

Hyperventilation: involuntary, rapid, shallow breathing, which may lead to dizziness, light-headedness, and shortness of breath.

Ideation: the process of forming, entertaining, and relating ideas; the first component of praxis.

Impulse control: difficulty in restraining one's actions, words, or emotions.

Inhibition: the useful neurological process that reduces unnecessary connections in the brain and checks one's overreaction to sensations.

Inner drive: every person's self-motivation to participate actively in experiences that promote sensory integration.

Interoception: the sense involving both the conscious awareness and the unconscious regulation of bodily processes of internal organs.

Joint pressure: pressing the bones of a joint together (or pulling them apart) to stimulate the sensory receptors in the joint to help organize and calm a person.

Just-right challenge: An experience that encourages a person to stretch beyond her abilities—to reach a little farther, swing a little longer, climb a little higher—without causing frustration or an ineffective response.

Kinesthesia: the conscious awareness of the movement of body parts, such as knowing where to place one's feet when climbing stairs, without looking. Sometimes called "conscious proprioception," it is based on information coming from visual, proprioceptive, tactile, and vestibular input.

Lateralization: the process of establishing preference of one side of the brain for directing skilled motor function on the opposite side of the body, while the opposite side is used for stabilization; necessary for establishing hand preference and crossing the body midline.

Linear movement: a motion in which one moves in a line, from front to back, side to side, or up and down.

Low (muscle) tone: the lack of supportive muscle tone, usually with increased mobility at the joints; the person with low tone seems "loose and floppy."

Meltdown: the process, usually caused by excessive sensory stimulation, of becoming "undone" or "unglued," accompanied by screaming, writhing, and deep sobbing.

Modulation: the brain's ability to regulate and organize the degree, intensity, and nature of the person's response to sensory input in a graded and adaptive manner.

Motor planning: the ability to plan, organize, and sequence a complex and unfamiliar body movement in a coordinated manner; a piece of **praxis**.

Muscle tone: the degree of tension normally present when one's muscles are relaxed, or in a resting state; a function of the vestibular system, enabling the person to maintain body positions.

Occupational therapy (OT): the use of activity to maximize the independence and the maintenance of health of an individual who is limited by a physical injury or illness, cognitive impairment, a psychosocial dysfunction, a mental illness, a developmental or learning disability, or an adverse environmental condition. OT encompasses evaluation, assessment, treatment, and consultation.

Oculomotor skills (eye-motor skills): movements of muscles in the eyes, including binocularity, fixation, focusing, and tracking.

Oral defensiveness: hypersensitivity in the mouth to certain food textures or tastes.

Oral-motor skills: movements of muscles in the mouth, lips, tongue, and jaw, including sucking, biting, crunching, chewing, and licking.

Oscillation: up-and-down or to-and-fro linear movement, such as swinging, bouncing, and jumping.

Perception: the meaning that the brain gives to sensory input.

Perseverate: to continue an activity or behavior when no longer appropriate.

Pincer grasp: picking up and holding an object with the thumb and index finger.

Physical therapy (PT): a health profession devoted to improving a person's physical abilities, involving activities that strengthen muscular control and motor coordination, especially of the large muscles.

Postural stability: the feeling of security and self-confidence when moving in space, based on one's body awareness.

Praxis: the ability to conceptualize (or "ideate"), to plan and organize, and to carry out a sequence of unfamiliar actions; to do what one needs and wants to do in order to interact successfully with the physical environment.

Prone: referring to the "tummy-down," horizontal body position.

Proprioceptive sense (proprioception, or the position sense): the unconscious awareness of sensations, coming from receptors in one's joints, muscles, tendons, and ligaments, that provides information about when and how muscles contract or stretch; when and how joints bend, extend, or are pulled; and where each part of the body is and how it is moving.

Proprioceptor: a sensory nerve terminal that provides information about movements and position of the body.

Sensory-motor: Pertaining to the brain-behavior process of receiving messages from sensory stimuli and producing physical responses, thoughts, and feelings.

Self-regulation: the ability to control one's activity level and state of arousal, as well as one's emotional, mental, or physical responses to sensations; self-organization.

Sensory defensiveness: a tendency to respond to certain harmless sensations as if they were dangerous or painful; the overactivation of one's protective senses.

Sensory diet: the multisensory experiences that one normally seeks on a daily basis to satisfy one's sensory appetite; a planned and scheduled activity program that an occupational therapist develops to help a person become more self-regulated and at the optimal state of arousal.

Sensory integration: the modulation, discrimination, coordination, and organization of incoming sensory information received from the body and the environment in order to produce adaptive and purposeful responses; or, more simply, the organization of sensory input for use in daily life.

Sensory integration dysfunction (see **Dysfunction in sensory integration**).

Sensory integration therapy: therapeutic intervention with the goal of improvement in the way the brain processes and organizes sensations. The emphasis is on improving sensory-motor processing rather than on skill training.

Sensory modulation dysfunction (SMD): a problem in the capacity to regulate and organize the degree, intensity, and nature of response to sensory input in a gradual and adaptive manner.

Sensory-motor: pertaining to the brain-behavior process of receiving sensory messages (sensory input) and producing an adaptive response (motor output).

Somatosensory: referring to tactile-proprioceptive perception of touch sensations and body position; body-sensing.

Suck/swallow/breathe (SSB) synchrony: a sensory-motor pattern in which sucking, swallowing, and breathing are coordinated so that a person can eat and breathe without choking.

Supine: referring to the "face-up," horizontal body position.

Tactile defensiveness: a type of dysfunction in which the tendency is to react negatively and emotionally to unexpected, light touch sensations.

Tactile sense (the sense of touch): the sensory system that receives sensations of pressure, vibration, movement, temperature, and pain, primarily through receptors in the skin and hair. Protective receptors respond to light or unexpected touch and help a person avoid bodily harm; discriminative receptors provide information about the tactile qualities of the object or person being touched.

Touch pressure: the tactile stimulus that causes receptors in the skin to respond.

Tracking: the basic oculomotor skill of following a moving object or a line of print with the eyes.

Translation movement: an action that involves grasping a small item, such as a push pin, in one's thumb, index, and middle fingers and moving these fingers toward and away from one's palm.

Tripod grip: the grasp of a pencil or crayon using three fingers (thumb, index, and middle).

Vestibular sense (the balance and movement sense): the sensory system that responds to changes in head position, to body movement, and to the pull of gravity. It coordinates movements of the eyes, head, and body, affecting balance, muscle tone, visual-spatial perception, auditory-language perception, and emotional security. Receptors are in the inner ear.

Vibrotactile: referring to the therapeutic effect of vibrating appliances when used on skin surfaces. or: when applied to skin surfaces.

Vision therapy: treatment to help a person improve visual skills and to prevent learning-related visual problems: optometric visual training.

Visualization: the act of forming mental images of objects, people, or scenarios.

Visual-motor: referring to one's movements based on the perception of visual information.

RECOMMENDED MATERIALS

Below are four lists:
- *SAFE Activities Toy Chest*: Basic equipment and materials that are good to have handy and are easy to find in stores or around the house.
- *Special Items*: Materials that may be less easy to locate, with *Suggested Sources*.
- *Suggested Books and Other Media*: Some of the books, audiotapes, videos, and CDs dealing with sensory integration and activities for children.
- *Where to Find Recommended Materials and More*: Addresses of catalog companies and organizations that provide equipment, information and support.

SAFE Activities Toy Chest

HOUSEHOLD ITEMS
Bowls, cookie cutters, cookie sheets
Rolling pins, eating utensils, kitchen gadgets
Cooking pots, roasting pans, pie tins
Cake decorating supplies
Cafeteria trays, plastic placemats
Clear plastic jars
Spray bottles
Sponges
Buckets, dish pans, laundry tubs
Trash cans
Small objects including coins, keys, paper clips, buttons, toothpicks, poker chips
Bedding/linens, including pillows, pillowcases, sheets, comforters, bedspreads, towels, washcloths, bath mats, sleeping bags
Tarpaulin, oilcloth, or shower curtain

Clothes basket
Clothespins
Clothing accessories
Shoelaces
Dress-ups
Large mirror
Magnifying glass
Rope
Flashlights
Magnets
CD player or tape deck
Stopwatch

GROCERIES AND DRUGSTORE ITEMS TO PLAY WITH
Cereal O's
Corn syrup
Cornstarch
Dry beans, rice, oatmeal, popcorn, peanuts, spaghetti, and other pasta
Flour
Food coloring
Dishwashing liquid
Drinking straws
Lunch bags
Resealable plastic bags
Paper/plastic plates and cups
Cotton balls
Diaper pins
Kitty litter
Shaving cream, bath foam, hand lotion
Tweezers
Vinyl gloves, finger cots

SUPPLIES FROM THE ARTS/CRAFTS/HOBBY STORE,
STATIONERY AISLE, AND FABRIC SHOP
Beads
Sequins, sparkles, stickers
Colored cellophane
Construction paper, tissue paper, crepe paper
Brown packaging paper
Drawing/writing paper
Envelopes of different sizes
Index file cards
Corrugated cardboard, poster board
Large plastic or cardboard storage boxes
Scissors, stapler, ruler

Masking tape, duct tape
Glue
Crayons, markers, pens, pencils
Fingerpaint, tempera paint
Paintbrushes
Smocks
Chalk, chalkboard
Easel
Fabric tubing
Fabric swatches of different textures
Rat-tail cord
Ribbons
Sewing needles, tapestry needles
Thread, yarn
Velcro strips

HARDWARE STORE/GARDEN STORE ITEMS
Dowels
Wooden and plywood boards
2 x 4s
Railroad timbers
Stepping stones
Wood screws
Hammers, nails
Long metal carriage bolts
Wooden mallets, rubber-tipped mallets
Flower pots
Hose, spray nozzle
Gutters, gutter joiners
Milk crates
Rope
Sand
Sandpaper
Vinyl aquarium tubing
Washers

MISCELLANEOUS CONSUMABLES AND "BEAUTIFUL JUNK"
Balloons
Bottle caps
Boxes of all sizes
Bubble gum
Bubble wrap, packaging "peanuts," foam packaging material
Cardboard cylinders (from wrapping paper and paper towel rolls)
Carpet samples or squares
Coffee and orange juice cans, margarine tubs, deli containers

Corks
Empty detergent or ketchup squirt bottles
Egg cartons
Film canisters
Old lipstick
Old telephone books, magazines, catalogs
Paper and plastic grocery bags
Plastic water jugs and one-liter soda bottles
Popsicle sticks
String
Plastic foam meat trays
Shells, pebbles, acorns
Tree-trunk sections, logs, sticks, twigs

TOYS AND PLAY EQUIPMENT
Blocks
Balls of all sizes
Plastic baseball bat or T-ball bat
Koosh balls, squeeze toys, hand "fidgets"
Beanbags
Hula hoops
Climber and swing set; tire swing
Drums
Bubbles
Finger puppets, hand puppets
Stuffed animals
Bendable doll
Dice
Dominoes
Foam letters and numbers
Jigsaw puzzles
Marbles
Small cars, boats, dinosaurs, people, bears, and other figures

SPECIAL ITEMS
(and chapters in which they are first mentioned)

SUGGESTED SOURCES
(For full addresses, see *Where to Find Recommended Materials*)

CHAPTER 1: KIDS GOTTA MOVE!

Background information on DSI

The Out-of-Sync Child: Recognizing and Coping with Sensory Integration Dysfunction, at bookstores everywhere and through catalogs and organizations, such as **Sensory Resources, LLC**, and **Developmental Delay Resources**

SPECIAL ITEMS	SUGGESTED SOURCES
"Over-the-counter" OT strategies	*Tools for Parents* and *Tool Chest for Teachers, Parents and Students,* by D. Henry, **Henry Occupational Therapy Services, Inc., Integrations,** or **Southpaw Enterprises**

CHAPTER 2: TOUCH	
Recipe for gluten-free playdough	*Unraveling the Mystery of Autism and Pervasive Developmental Disorder,* by K. Seroussi, from bookstores, catalogs, and **Autism Network for Dietary Intervention**
Therapy putty, or Theraputty™	**Abilitations, Sammons Preston Pediatrics,** or **Therapro**
Gluten-free pretzel dough	**Miss Roben's**
Latex-free, stretchy exercise bands	**Abilitations, The Therapy Shoppe, Inc.,** or **Therapro**
Therapy ball	**Abilitations** or **Sammons Preston Pediatrics**
Vibrating massager	**Integrations**

CHAPTER 3: BALANCE AND MOVEMENT	
T-Stool	**Sammons Preston Pediatrics, Southpaw,** or **Therapy Shoppe**
Physio-Roll™ "Peanut" ball	**Sammons Preston Pediatrics** or **Therapro**
Trampoline	**Abilitations** or **Integrations**
Gym mat	**Abilitations** or **Early Childhood Direct/Chime Time**
Beanbag chairs/cushions	**Abilitations** or **Therapro**

SPECIAL ITEMS	SUGGESTED SOURCES
Jump-rope chants and poetry	*Anna Banana: 101 Jump Rope Rhymes*, by J. Cole, and other rhyming books, videos and DVDs, at children's bookstores or www.geometry.net/sports/jumprope.html
Barrel	**Abilitations, Sammons Preston Pediatrics**, or **Southpaw Enterprises**
Activity songs	*Wee Sing* series (books, DVDs, videos), by P. Beall & S. Nipp, at kids' bookstores; also see www.kididdles.com for lyrics, and www.kidsongs.com or www.kiddomusic.com
Body Sox™	**Dye-namic Movement Products, Inc., Abilitations**, or **Early Childhood**
Plastic Ballpit™ balls	**Abilitations, Sammons Preston Pediatrics**, or **Southpaw**
Rainy Day Indoor Playground™ with chinning and trapeze bars	**Abilitations, Playaway Toy Company, Inc.**, or **Sensory Comfort**
Streamers, ribbons and scarves	**Early Childhood, Environments, Inc.**, or **Pocket Full of Therapy**
Traffic cones	**Therapy Shoppe, Sportime**, or **U.S. Games**

CHAPTER 4: BODY POSITION

Crash pad, or Cloud Nine	**Abilitations** or **Southpaw**
Carpeted scooter board	**Abilitations** or **Therapro**
S'Cool Moves for Learning	**Therapro**
Fabric tube, or Resistance Tunnel	**Southpaw**
Vibrating pen, or Squiggle Wiggle Writer	**Pocket Full of Therapy** or **Sensory Comfort**
Weighted vest	**Abilitations, In Your Pocket Designs, Sensory Comfort**, or **Therapy Shoppe**

SPECIAL ITEMS	SUGGESTED SOURCES
CHAPTER 5: SEEING	
Metronome	**Integrations** or **West Music**
CHAPTER 6: HEARING	
Slide whistle	**Kindermusik, PDP Products, Pocket Full of Therapy,** or **West Music**
Rhythm band instruments, xylophones and resonator bars	**Early Childhood, Environments, Kindermusik, MMB Music,** or **West Music**
Mozart & other classical recordings	**Abilitations, MMB Music,** or **The Children's Group, Inc.**
Songames for SI	**DDR** or **Sensory Resources, LLC**
Hap Palmer recordings	**Educational Activities, Inc.,** or **Environments**
Hoops	**Therapy Shoppe** or **U.S. Games**
Tuning fork	**West Music**
Blopens™	**Magic Art & More** or **www.blopens.com**
CHAPTER 7: SMELLING AND TASTING	
Koosh balls	**Integrations, Pocket Full of Therapy,** or **Therapro**
Touchmath®	**Touchmath**
CHAPTER 8: ORAL-MOTOR SKILLS	
Out of the Mouths of Babes	**PDP Products**
Therapy whistles	**Abilitations, Integrations,** or **Therapro**
CHAPTER 9: MOTOR PLANNING	
Crawling tunnel	**Early Childhood, Environments, Integrations,** or **U.S. Games**
Climbing gym	**Early Childhood**

SPECIAL ITEMS	SUGGESTED SOURCES
Exercise tubing	**Abilitations, Southpaw,** or **Therapro**
Black cat hand puppet	**Environments** or **Playful Puppets**

CHAPTER 10: FINE-MOTOR SKILLS

Information on Dvorak Keyboard	**Dvorak International** or www.mwbrooks.com/dvorak

Suggested Books and Other Media

With exciting momentum, new publications are leaping onto the Sensory Integration bookshelf. The bibliography here includes some of the best books, videos, audiotapes, and CDs. Many materials, which may be hard to find in bookstores, are available through catalogs (see *Where to Find Recommended Materials,* the next list below) or organizations devoted to offering information about DSI and other developmental disabilities, such as:

Developmental Delay Resources, www.devdelay.org
and
Sensory Resources, LLC, www.SensoryResources.com

BOOKS

A Parent's Guide to Understanding Sensory Integration (1991). Torrance, CA: Sensory Integration International.

Ames, Louise Bates, Frances L. Ilg, Sidney M. Baker, & Carol C. Haber (1980–1997). Series about typical child development, beginning with *Your Two-Year-Old: Terrible or Tender; Your Three-Year-Old: Friend or Enemy;* and so forth, through *Your Ten- to Fourteen-Year-Old.* New York: Dell.

Ayres, A. Jean (1979). *Sensory Integration and the Child.* Los Angeles: Western Psychological Services.

Beall, Pamela Conn, & Susan Hagen Nipp. *Wee Sing* series (books, DVDs, videos). Los Angeles: Price Stern Sloan.

Bissell, Julie, Jean Fisher, Carol Owens, & Patricia Polcyn (1998). *Sensory Motor Handbook: A Guide for Implementing and Modifying Activities in the Classroom.* San Diego: Academic Press.

Brazelton, T. Berry (1994). *Touchpoints (The Essential Reference): Your Child's Emotional and Behavioral Development.* Reading, MA: Addison-Wesley.

———— & Stanley I. Greenspan (2000). *The Irreducible Needs of Children: What Every Child Must Have to Grow, Learn, and Flourish.* New York: Perseus.

Buck-Murray, Marian, & Ralph Butler, Illus. (1998). *The Mash and Smash Cookbook: Fun and Yummy Recipes Every Kid Can Make!* Indianapolis: John Wiley.

Campbell, Don G. (2000). *The Mozart Effect for Children: Awakening Your Child's Mind, Health, and Creativity with Music.* New York: William Morrow.

Cheatum, Billye Ann, & Allison A. Hammond (2000). *Physical Activities for Improving Children's Learning and Behavior: A Guide to Sensory Motor Development.* Champaign, IL: Human Kinetics.

Clements, Rhonda L., Ed. (2000). *Elementary School Recess: Selected Readings, Games, and Activities for Teachers and Parents.* Boston: American Press.

Cole, Joanna, & Alan Tiegreen, Illus. (1989). *Anna Banana: 101 Jump Rope Rhymes.* New York: William Morrow.

Cooke, Jackie (1996). *Early Sensory Skills.* Oxfordshire, England: Speechmark Publishing (formerly Winslow Press).

Davolos, Sandra R., Ed. (1999). *Making Sense of Art: Sensory-Based Art Activities for Children with Autism, Asperger's Syndrome and Other Pervasive Developmental Disorders.* Shawnee Mission, KS: Autism Asperger Publishing.

Eliot, Lise (1999). *What's Going on in There? How the Brain and Mind Develop in the First Five Years of Life.* New York: Bantam.

Dennison, Paul E., & Gail E. Dennison (1994). *Brain Gym: Simple Activities for Whole Brain Learning.* Ventura, CA: Edu-Kinesthetics.

Flowers, Toni (1992). *Reaching the Child with Autism through Art: Practical, Fun Activities to Enhance Sensory Motor Skills and to Improve Tactile and Concept Awareness.* Arlington, TX: Future Horizons.

Frick, Sheila, Ron Frick, Patricia Oetter; & Eileen Richter (1996). *Out of the Mouths of Babes: Discovering the Developmental Significance of the Mouth—a Book Especially for Parents & Other "Grown-ups."* Hugo, Minnesota: PDP Press.

Getz, Donald J., & Lora G. McGraw (1999). *Seeing Is Achieving: Improve Your Child's Chances for Success.* Visual Edge, Inc.

Greene, Ross W. (1998). *The Explosive Child: A New Approach for Understanding and Parenting Easily Frustrated, "Chronically Inflexible" Children.* New York: HarperCollins.

Greenspan, Stanley I. (1995). *The Challenging Child: Understanding, Raising, and Enjoying the Five "Difficult" Types of Children.* Reading, MA: Addison-Wesley.

———— with Jacqueline Salmon (1993). *Playground Politics: Understanding the Emotional Life of Your School-Age Child.* Reading, MA: Addison-Wesley.

———— & Serena Wieder, with Robin Simons (1998). *The Child with Special Needs: Encouraging Intellectual and Emotional Growth.* Reading, MA: Addison-Wesley.

Hannaford, Carla (1995). *Smart Moves: Why Learning Is Not All In Your Head.* Arlington, VA: Great Ocean Publishers.

Hanson, Joanne (1998). *Progress with Puppets: Speech and Language Activities for Young Children.* Arlington, VA: Building Blocks Therapy.

Healy, Jane M. (1999). *Endangered Minds: Why Children Don't Think—and What We Can Do About It.* New York: Simon & Schuster/Touchstone.

———— (1994). *Your Child's Growing Mind: A Practical Guide to Brain Development and Learning from Birth to Adolescence.* New York: Doubleday.

———— (1999). *Failure to Connect: How Computers Affect Our Children's Minds.* New York: Simon & Schuster/Touchstone.

Heiberger, Debra Wilson, & Margot C. Heiniger-White (2000). *S'cool Moves for Learning: A Program Designed to Enhance Learning Through Body-Mind Integration.* Redding, CA: Integrated Learner Press.

Henry, Diana (1998). *Tool Chest for Teachers, Parents & Students: A Handbook to Facilitate Self-Regulation.* Accompanies two videotapes: *Tools for Students: OT Activities for Classroom & Home,* and *Tools for Teachers: an Overview of School Based Occupational Therapy.* Youngtown, AZ: Henry Occupational Therapy Services.

———— & Tammy Wheeler (2001). *Tools for Parents: A Handbook to Bring Sensory Integration into the Home.* Youngtown, AZ: Henry Occupational Therapy Services.

Hickman, Lois, & Rebecca Hutchins (2000). *Seeing Clearly: A Synergistic Blend of Behavioral Optometry & Occupational Therapy Focused on Enhancing Visual Perception.* Boulder: Belle Curve.

Hong, Chia Swee, Helen Gabriel, & Cathy St. John (1996). *Sensory Motor Activities for Early Development.* Oxon, England: Winslow Press.

Huebner, Ruth A., Ed. (2001). *Autism: A Sensorimotor Approach to Management.* Gaithersburg, MD: Aspen.

Kasser, Susan L. (1995). Inclusive Games: Movement Fun for Everyone! Champaign, IL: Human Kinetics.

Kelly, Marguerite (1994). *Marguerite Kelly's Family Almanac/The Perfect Companion for Today's Family: A Helpful Guide to Navigating through the Everyday Issues of Modern Life.* New York: Fireside.

Kohl, MaryAnn F. (1992). *Mudworks: Creative Clay, Dough, and Modeling Experiences.* Bellingham, WA: Bright Ring Publishing.

Koomar, Jane, Barbara Friedman, & Elizabeth Woolf, illus. (1992). *The Hidden Senses: Your Muscle Sense,* and *The Hidden Senses: Your Balance Sense.* Rockville, MD: AOTA.

Kranowitz, C. S. (1995). *101 Activities for Kids in Tight Spaces.* New York: St. Martin's Press.

———— (1998). *The Out-of-Sync Child: Recognizing and Coping with Sensory Integration Dysfunction.* New York: Perigee.

Kurcinka, Mary Sheedy (1992). *Raising Your Spirited Child: A Guide for Parents Whose Child is More Intense, Sensitive, Perceptive, Persistent, Energetic.* New York: HarperCollins.

Lane, Kenneth A., (1991). *Developing Your Child for Success: Easy-to-Follow Activities to Develop Children's Perceptual and Motor Skills and Prepare Them for Their Early School Years.* Lewisville, TX: Learning Potentials Publishers.

Lewis, Lisa S., *Special Diets for Special Kids* (1998), and *Special Diets for Special Kids, Two* (2001). Arlington, TX: Future Horizons.

McCall, Renée, & Diane H. Craft (2000). *Moving with a Purpose: Developing Programs for Preschoolers of All Abilities.* Champaign, IL: Human Kinetics.

Miller, Karen (2002). *Ages and Stages: Developmental Descriptions & Activities, Birth through Eight Years.* St. Paul, MN: Redleaf Press.

———— (1999). *Simple Steps: Developmental Activities for Infants, Toddlers, and Two-Year-Olds.* St. Paul, MN: Redleaf Press.

———— (2000). *Things to Do with Toddlers and Twos.* West Palm Beach, FL: Telshare Publishing.

Myles, Brenda Smith, Katherine Tapscott Cook, Nancy E. Miller, Louann Rinner, & Lisa A. Robbins (2000). *Asperger Syndrome and Sensory Issues: Practical Solutions for Making Sense of the World.* Shawnee Mission, KS: Autism Asperger Publishing Co.

Nowicki, Stephen, Jr., & Marshall P. Duke (1992). *Helping the Child Who Doesn't Fit In.* Atlanta, GA: Peachtree Publishers.

————— & Elisabeth A. Martin (1996). *Teaching Your Child the Language of Social Success.* Atlanta, GA: Peachtree Publishers.

O'Brien-Palmer, Michelle (1998). *Sense-Abilities: Fun Ways to Explore the Senses (Activities for Children 4 to 8).* Chicago: Chicago Review Press.

Renke, Laurie, & Jake and Max Renke, illus. (2002). *I Like Birthdays . . . It's the Parties I'm Not Sure About!* Londonderry, NH: "That" Kids' Co., www.thatkidscompany.com or (603) 537-0549.

Sassé, Margaret (1990). *If Only We'd Known . . . Early Childhood—and Its Importance to Academic Learning.* Victoria, Australia: Toddler Kindy Gymbaroo Pty., Ltd.

Sava, Deanna Iris, & Elizabeth Haber, Eds. Three lists of Sensory-Motor Activities:
Heavy Work Activities List for Parents
Heavy Work Activities List for Teachers
Heavy Work Activities List for Occupational Therapists
To obtain these lists, e-mail deannasava11@msn.com or eahaber@aol.com The Teachers' list has also been published by Sensory Resources in *Answers to Questions Teachers Ask about Sensory Integration* (2001).

Schneider, Catherine Chemin (2001). *Sensory Secrets: How to Jump-Start Learning in Children.* Siloam Springs, AR: Concerned Communications.

Seroussi, Karyn (2000). *Unraveling the Mystery of Autism and Pervasive Developmental Disorder: A Mother's Story of Research and Recovery.* New York: Simon & Schuster.

Silver, Larry B. (1998). *The Misunderstood Child: Understanding and Coping with Your Child's Learning Disabilities* (3rd edition). New York: Random House/Times Books.

Thompson, Sue (1997). *The Source for Nonverbal Learning Disorders.* East Moline, IL: LinguiSystems.

Trott, Maryann Colby, with Marci K. Laurel & Susan L. Windeck (1993). *SenseAbilities: Understanding Sensory Integration.* Tucson, AZ: Therapy Skill Builders.

Waltz, Mitzi (2002). *Autistic Spectrum Disorders: Understanding the Diagnosis and Getting Help.* Sebastopol, CA: O'Reilly & Associates.

Whitney, Rondalyn V. (2002). *Bridging the Gap: Raising a Child with Nonverbal Learning Disorder.* New York: Perigee.

Wilbarger, Patricia, & Julia Leigh Wilbarger (1991). *Sensory Defensiveness in Children Aged 2–12: An Intervention Guide for Parents and Other Caretakers.* Santa Barbara, CA: Avanti Educational Programs.

Wilk, Kelly Ann (2001). *Shoe-Tying Made Simple* (2001). Oxford, NC: School of Graphic Arts, Masonic Home for Children. (941) 514-2965, or OT Ideas, Inc.

Williams, Mary Sue, & Sherry Shellenberger (1992). *An Introduction to "How Does Your Engine Run?" The Alert Program for Self-Regulation.* Albuquerque, NM: TherapyWorks.

Yack, Ellen, Shirley Sutton, & Paula Aquilla (1998). *Building Bridges through Sensory Integration: Occupational Therapy for Children with Autism and other Pervasive Developmental Disorders.* Weston, Ontario: Building Bridges through Sensory Integration.

VIDEOTAPES

Grandin, Temple (1999). *Sensory Challenges and Answers.* Arlington, TX: Future Horizons.

Henry, Diana, et al. (1998). *Tools for Students: OT Activities for Classroom & Home* and *Tools for Teachers: An Overview of School Based Occupational Therapy.* Youngtown, AZ: Henry Occupational Therapy Services.

Kranowitz, C. S. (2001). *The Out-of-Sync Child.* Las Vegas: Sensory Resources.

—————— (2002). *Getting Kids in Sync: Sensory-Motor Activities to Help Children Develop Body Awareness and Integrate Their Senses.* Las Vegas: Sensory Resources.

Reisman, Judith E. *Sensory Processing for Parents: From Roots to Wings.* University of Minnesota. Available through Sensory Comfort, (888) 436-2622.

AUDIOCASSETTES AND COMPACT DISCS

Jereb, Genevieve (2002). *No Worries: Songs for Sensory Modulation.* Madison, WI: Vital Sounds, www.vitalsounds.com or (866) 829-6331.

Koomar, Jane, Stacey Szklut, Sharon Cermak, et al. (1998). *Making Sense of Sensory Integration.* Las Vegas: Sensory Resources/Belle Curve.

Kranowitz, C. S., & Stacey Szklut (1999). *Teachers Ask About Sensory Integration.* Las Vegas: Sensory Resources/Belle Curve.

Lande, Aubrey, Bob Wiz, & friends (1999). *Songames for Sensory Integration.* Las Vegas: Sensory Resources/Belle Curve.

MaBoAubLo and Barbara Sher (1999). *28 Instant Songames.* Las Vegas: Sensory Resources/Belle Curve.

The Mozart Effect series, compiled by Don Campbell. Pickering, Ontario: The Children's Group.

Taylor, Kristen Fitz, & Cheryl McDonald, with Lois Hickman, Aubrey Lande, & Bob Wiz (1997). *Danceland.* Boulder: Jump Start.

WHERE TO FIND RECOMMENDED MATERIALS . . .
AND MORE

These resources and addresses are current in 2002. Please check www.out-of-sync-child.com for up-to-date information.

Abilitations
Mail: Abilitations, P.O. Box 620856, Atlanta, GA 303462
Phone: Toll-free: (800) 850-8602; International: (770) 449-5700
Fax: Toll-free: (800) 845-1535; Local or international: (770) 263-0897
E-mail: customer.service@sportime.com and catalogrequest@sportime.com
Website: www.abilitations.com

Therapist-selected rehabilitation products designed to improve the lives of children with differing abilities and specialized physical needs. Products focus on movement, positioning, sensory-motor activities, exercise, aquatics and play. The product line includes handwriting materials, mouth toys, visual toys, Mozart tapes, movement gear, weighted vests, therapy balls, and Wilbarger Protocol brushes. The experienced customer-care department is capable of answering all questions.

American Occupational Therapy Association, Inc. (AOTA)
Location: 4720 Montgomery Lane, Bethesda, MD
Mail: P.O. Box 31220, Bethesda, MD 20824-1220
Phone: (301) 652-AOTA or (800) 668-8255
Fax: (301) 652-7711
Website: www.aota.org

Books, videos, continuing education workshops, and other resources for occupational therapists, as well as products for parents, such as a handbook, *Sensory Integration: A Foundation for Development*.

Autism Network for Dietary Intervention (ANDI™)
www.autismndi.com

Providing help and support for families using a gluten-free and casein-free diet in the treatment of autism and related developmental disabilities. ANDI was established by parent researchers, Lisa Lewis and Karyn Seroussi. Their books, *Special Diets for Special Kids* and *Unraveling the Mystery of Autism and PDD*, as well as *The ANDI News* quarterly, are available through the website.

Brain Gym® International (*see* **Educational Kinesiology Foundation**)

The Children's Group, Inc.
Mail: 1400 Bayly Street, Suite 7, Pickering, Ontario, L1W3R2, Canada
Phone: (905) 831-1995, or toll-free: (800) 757-8372 (Canada), or (800) 668-0242 (USA)
Fax: (905) 831-1142
E-mail: moreinfo@childrensgroup.com
Website: www.childrensgroup.com

Classical music for children, parents, grandparents, and teachers, through an extensive collection of audio CDs and cassettes, videos, books, and other educational resources. Product lines include Don Campbell's *The Mozart Effect* recordings and the *Classical Kids* series.

Developmental Delay Resources (DDR)
Mail: 4401 East-West Highway, Suite 207, Bethesda, MD 20814
Phone: (301) 652-2263
Fax: (301) 652-9133
E-mail: devdelay@mindspring.com
Website: www.devdelay.org

The non-profit organization that provides information, conferences, and a quarterly newsletter, *New Developments*, to educate parents and professionals about healthy options for treating the whole child. These healthy options include treatments that address sensory-motor processing, boost the immune system, address structural integrity, and encourage positive social-emotional relationships. DDR also carries an extensive line of hard-to-find books and materials on SI, vision, immunizations, health, and nutrition. The Executive Director is Patricia S. Lemer, M.S. Bus., NCC, M.Ed.

Dvorak International
Mail: P.O. Box 44, Poultney, VT 05764-0044
Phone: (802) 287-2434
E-mail: DvorakInt@aol.com
Website: http://www.cse.ogi.edu/~dylan/dvorak/DvorakIntl.html

A nonprofit organization that promotes the use of the Dvorak computer keyboard layout. For more information, also see www.mwbrooks.com/dvorak.

DSI Parent Connections

Mail: DSI Parent Connections, P.O. Box #1070, Londonderry, NH 03053-1070

E-mail: DSINational@yahoo.com

Website: www.SInetwork.org

"Making SENSE of the world, one child at a time!" is the mission of this parent-run, grass-roots effort to provide support, information and understanding to anyone living with someone affected with DSI, or wanting to learn more about DSI. Support groups have been set up in many cities, and volunteers are sought to host new groups.

This exciting and rewarding project was begun to help others understand that DSI is physical, not parental. As many treatment options are available, parents can and should feel much hope for their child's improvement. Hosting a group does not require a huge time commitment from you. A support network has been set up to help guide hosts, who DO NOT have to be experts in Sensory Integration. The only requirements are: a smiling face, a place to meet, and a heart that understands the difficulties that occur when others do not understand how DSI affects our children's behavior.

A national group may form in the future; currently DSI Parent Connections consists of individual support groups brought together by www.SInetwork.org, where information about each local group is posted. The National Coordinator is Laurie Renke.

Dye-Namic Movement Products, Inc.

Mail: 35 Sloop Lane, Port Ludlow, WA 98365

Phone: (360) 437-7733

E-mail: k@dyenamicmovement.com

Website: www.dyenamicmovement.com

Equipment for movement, physical therapy, and exercise, made from the highest quality stretch band fabrics to promote physical strength and flexibility, body awareness, creativity, and group cooperation. Kimberly Dye's products include *BodySox, Airwalker, CoOperBlanket,* and *CoOperBand.*

Early Childhood Direct/Chime Time

Mail: P.O. Box 369, Landisville, PA 17538

Phone: (800) 784-5717

Fax: (800) 219-5253

E-mail: service@e-c-direct.com

Website: www.earlychildhoodirect.com

Equipment for active play, music, dramatic play, and other early childhood needs.

Educational Activities, Inc.

Mail: P.O. Box 87, Baldwin, NY 11510

Phone: (516) 223-4666, or toll-free: (800) 645-3739

E-mail: learn@edact.com

Website: www.edact.com

Compact discs, cassettes, books and videos for fun, movement, and music curriculum. Featured artists include Hap Palmer, Ella Jenkins, and Greg & Steve.

Educational Kinesiology Foundation/Brain Gym® International

Phone: (800) 356-2109 or (805) 658-7942
E-mail: edukfd@earthlink.net
Website: www.braingym.org

A non-profit public benefit corporation dedicated to the study of movement of the human body as it relates to learning and expression skills. Procedures include the Brain Gym® system, a set of 26 specific movements developed by Paul Dennison, Ph.D., based on research in physical movement, education and child development. The system readies the body to learn by integrating visual, auditory, and kinesthetic functioning. The activities effect rapid and often dramatic improvements in concentration, memory, reading, writing, organizing, listening, physical coordination, and more.

Environments, Inc.

Mail: P.O. Box 1348, Beaufort, SC 29901-1348
Phone: (843) 846-8155, or toll-free: (800) 342-4453
Fax: (843) 846-2999, or toll-free: (800) 343-2987
E-mail: environments@eichild.com
Website: www.eichild.com

Equipment for music, movement, and other activities; classroom furniture; and hands-on learning materials for basic concepts, language development, math and science, as well as for construction, creative expression, sand and water play, dramatic play, and more. All products are carefully selected and appropriate for places where children play and learn.

Future Horizons

Mail: 721 W. Abram Street, Arlington, TX 76013
Phone: (817) 277-0727, or toll-free: (888) 489-0727
Fax: (817) 277-2270
Website: www.futurehorizons-autism.com

The world leader in autism/Asperger's syndrome publishing, including books, audios and videos such as *The Out-of-Sync Child* video. Future Horizons also sponsors conferences throughout the U.S. and around the world, featuring topics such as autism, Asperger's syndrome, sensory issues, early intervention, inclusion, IEPs, social skills, music and art therapy, diet and nutrition, visual thinking, and communication.

Henry Occupational Therapy Services, Inc. (HOTS)

Mail: P.O. Box 145, Youngtown, AZ 85363-0145
Phone & Fax: (623) 933-3821, or toll-free: (888) 371-1204
E-mail: dianahenry@henryot.com
Website: www.ateachabout.com

Workshops presented by Diana Henry on sensory integration for schools, homes, and businesses; consultations and training; and two videos: *Tools for Teachers* and *Tools for Students*, to help regular education teachers incorporate OT strategies into the classroom. Also, three handbooks: for schools, *Tool Chest for Teachers, Parents & Students*; for homes, *Tools for Parents: Bringing Sensory Integration into the Home*; and for teenagers, *Sensory Integration Tools for Teens*.

In Your Pocket Designs
Mail: 1508 Tackley Place, Midlothian, VA 23114
Phone: (804) 379-0944
E-mail: bdudley@weightedvest.com
Website: www.weightedvest.com

Weighted vests to provide the deep pressure that helps some children with DSI to self-calm and relax. Ready-to-wear vests and patterns are available.

Integrations
Mail: Integrations, P.O. Box 620860, Atlanta, GA 30362
Phone: Toll-free: (800) 622-0638; International: (770) 449-5700
Fax: Toll-free: (800) 845-1535; International: (770) 263-0897
E-mail: customer.service@sportime.com and catalogrequest@sportime.com
Website: www.integrationscatalog.com

Unique, user-friendly product line for home, therapy, and school settings. The solutions-based format, with information tips written in an educator's language, quickly and concisely conveys information about a child's needs to teachers and school administrators. Products include applications of common sensory input to build individual sensory diets, such as fidgets, metronomes, weighted products, Body Sox, trampolines, tunnels, Mozart and other musical selections, unique whistles, and chewies.

Kindermusik
Mail: P.O. Box 26575, Greensboro, NC 27415
Phone: (336) 273-3363, or toll-free: (800) 628-5687
Website: www.shopkindermusik.com

Musical learning products for children from birth to 7 years old. Products include slide whistles, metronomes, xylophones, resonator bars, and rhythm band instruments to enjoy at home and school.

Magic Art & More . . .
Mail: 17301 Lafayette Drive, Olney, MD 20832
Phone-Fax: (301) 570-9665
E-mail: adrienne17301@yahoo.com

Art activities and workshops using Blopens, for children and adults, at schools, camps, homes, and community centers.

Miss Roben's
Mail: P.O. Box 1149, Frederick, MD 21702
Phone: (301) 665-9580, or toll-free: (800) 891-0083
Fax: (301) 665-9584
E-mail: info@missroben.com
Website: www.missroben.com

An exclusively gluten-free, wheat-free mail order supplier, serving those with food allergies and intolerances. Many products, such as prepackaged mixes, are also free of dairy, egg, soy, corn, yeast, and nuts.

MMB Music, Inc.

Mail: Contemporary Arts Bldg., 3526 Washington Ave., Saint Louis, MO 63103-1019

Phone: (314) 531-9635, or toll-free: (800) 543-3771

Fax: (314) 531-8384

E-mail: info@mmbmusic.com

Website: www.mmbmusic.com

   Books, tapes and videos in the areas of music, movement/dance, art, drama, poetry, and all areas of music education. The Mozart Effect® Resource Center offers books and recordings presenting the transformational powers of music in health, education, and well-being. The *Studio 49* line of products includes percussion instruments for kindergarten, school, therapy and family activities.

The Mozart Effect Resource Center

Mail: 3526 Washington Avenue, Saint Louis, MO 63103-1019

Phone: (314) 531-4756 or (800) 721-2177

Fax: (314) 531-8384

E-mail: music@mozarteffect.com

Website: www.mozarteffect.com

   Workshops and programs about the effect of music on learning, health, and behavior—at home, school, or in therapy. Also, *The Mozart Effect* recordings, and books about auditory processing and auditory integration training.

Optometric Extension Program Foundation, Inc.

Mail: 1921 East Carnegie Avenue, Suite 3-L, Santa Ana, CA 92705-5510

Phone: (949) 250-8070

Fax: (949) 250-8157

E-mail: oep@oep.org

Website: www.oep.org

   Books, pamphlets, and educational materials on vision development, vision therapy, and research in vision.

OT Ideas, Inc.

Mail: 124 Morris Turnpike, Randolph, NJ 07869

Phone: (973) 895-3622, or toll-free: (877) OT-Ideas (877-768-4332)

Fax: (973) 895-4204

Website: www.otideas.com

   Therapeutic products for use in schools and clinics. Special items include children's scissors, tools and toys to develop hand coordination, fine-motor and visual-motor skills, and a book, *Shoe Tying Made Simple*, by Kelly Wilk, O.T.R./L.

Playaway Toy Company, Inc.
Mail: P.O. Box 247, Bear Creek, WI 54922
Phone: (715) 752-4565, or toll-free: (888) Playway (888-752-9929)
Fax: (715) 752-4476
E-mail: therapis@frontiernet.net
Website: www.playawaytoy.com
Or, contact Ronnie Rawls, the Exclusive East Coast Playaway Parent-to-Parent Distributor, who contributes 25 percent of her commission to Developmental Delay Resources to promote healthy options for kids with DSI and other developmental problems:
Phone: (202) 554-1982
E-mail: ronnierawls@peoplepc.com
Website: www.occuplaytionals.com
The *Rainy Day Indoor Playground*. This innovative, educational and developmentally sound equipment turns any standard doorway into an "energy-releasing, muscle-coordinating way to have fun." Interchangeable parts include swings, trapeze bar, glider, net, platform, and ladder. Requiring no tools to install, the set is portable and transportable from door to door or house to house.

Playful Puppets, Inc.
Mail: 9002 Stoneleigh Court, Fairfax, VA 22031
Phone: (703) 280-5070, or toll-free: (866) 501-4931
Fax: (703) 280-0918
E-mail: playfulpuppets@starpower.net
Website: www.playfulpuppets.com
Puppets That Swallow, useful for therapeutic and educational purposes, including feeding, oral-motor and sensory-motor activities, speech and language activities, and signing. Other products include traditional hand puppets, such as cats, bears, people, fairy tale characters, and monsters.

Pocket Full of Therapy, Inc.
Mail: P.O. Box 174, Morganville, NJ 07751
Phone: 732-441-0404, or toll-free: (800) PFOT-124 (800) 736-8124)
Fax: 732-441-1422
E-mail: pfot@pfot.com
Website: www.pfot.com
Select pediatric and school-based products, unique toys and materials to facilitate effective, appropriate, motivating, and fun pediatric therapy and learning. Products, including hand fidgets, vibrating pens, slide whistles, streamers, ribbons, and scarves, are chosen by board-certified pediatric OTs, and all are kid-tested by children with special needs.

PDP Products & Professional Development Programs
Mail: 14524 61st Street Court North, P.O. Box 2009, Stillwater, MN 55082
Phone: (651) 439-8865
Fax: (651) 439-0421
E-mail: products@pdppro.com
Website: www.pdppro.com

Toys, books and equipment that promote sensory processing, postural control, attention, self-regulation and skills, as well as therapy materials and professional development courses for pediatric therapists and educators. Among the many products is *Out of the Mouths of Babes: Discovering the Developmental Significance of the Mouth*, by Sheila Frick, Patricia Oetter, Ron Frick, and Eileen Richter.

Sammons Preston Pediatrics
Mail: P.O. Box 5071, Bolingbrook, IL 60440-5071
Phone: (800) 323-5547 (in Canada: 800-665-9200)
Fax: (800) 547-4333
E-mail: sp@sammonspreston.com
Website: www.sammonspreston.com

Pediatric therapeutic equipment and products for sensory integration, motor development, positioning, self-help, and daily living, for children with special needs to use in homes, schools, or clinics. Products include Theraputty, exercise bands and tubing, therapy balls, T-stools, trampolines, gym mats, barrels, and crawling tunnels.

Sensory Comfort
Mail: P.O. Box 6589, Portsmouth, NH 03802-6589
Phone: Toll-free: (888) 436-2622
Fax: (603) 436-8422
Website: www.sensorycomfort.com

Products to make life more comfortable for children and adults who have sensory processing differences. Items include seamless socks, headphones that reduce noise, chewy tubes, fidget toys, wiggle pens, and many other sensory-friendly products for home, school, and work, as well as informational books and cassettes.

Sensory Resources, LLC
Mail: 2200 E. Patrick Lane, Suite 3A, Las Vegas, NV 89119
Phone: (702) 433-0404, or toll-free: (888) 357-5867
Fax: (702) 891-8899
E-mail: info@sensoryresources.com
Website: www.sensoryresources.com

Resources for raising children with sensory-motor, developmental, and social-emotional challenges. The organization publishes and distributes materials such as *The Out-of-Sync Child* video, the *Answers to Questions Teachers Ask About Sensory Integration* reference book, and other books, audiocassettes, and videos. It also sponsors national conferences on sensory integration and related subjects. Sensory Resources has acquired the Belle Curve Records line, including *Songames for Sensory Integration, Danceland, The Alert Program, Making Sense of Sensory Integration,* and *Teachers Ask about Sensory Integration.*

Southpaw Enterprises

Mail: P.O. Box 1047, Dayton, OH 45401
Phone: (800) 228-1698
Fax: (937) 252-8502
E-mail: therapy@erinet.com
Website: www.southpawenterprises.com

A community of people and products dedicated to children with special challenges and those who care for them. Items include sensory integrative and neurodevelopmental products, pediatric therapy equipment, resources, and support for therapeutic professionals, health care professionals, schools, and families.

Sportime

Mail: Sportime, One Sportime Way, Atlanta, GA 30340
Phone: Toll-free: (800) 283-5700; International: (770) 449-5700
Fax: Toll-free: (800) 845-1535; International: (770) 263-0897
E-mail: customer.service@sportime.com and catalogrequest@sportime.com
Website: www.sportime.com

Leading supplier of innovative physical activity equipment, widely utilized by PE instructors. Products are designed for institutional use and are competitively priced. Innovative products are excellent for children with varied and inconsistent physical skills, offering creative opportunities to work on motor planning, balance, and movement. Products include scooterboards, tunnels, mats, ribbons and streamers, lummi sticks, therapy balls, chinning bars, traffic cones, and obstacle course materials.

Star Center (The Sensory Integration Dysfunction Treatment And Research Center)

Location: The Children's Hospital, Denver, Colorado 80218
Mail (to Research Office): 1901 West Littleton Blvd., Littleton, CO 80120
Phone: (303) 794-1182
Website: www.SInetwork.org

Research program, directed by Lucy Jane Miller, Ph.D., O.T.R., investigating the types of intervention that are most effective for children with DSI. The Center also evaluates the underlying physiologic, neurologic, and biochemical mechanisms of the disorder. Treatment is available at The Children's Hospital.

Contributions are critically needed to provide treatment scholarships and to help with the costs of running the only full-time program of research on DSI in the world. In addition to research and treatment, the STAR Center also provides current sensory integration resources and information to families, consumers, and professionals, via the Sensory Integration Resource Center at www.SInetwork.org.

Theragifts Sensory Diet Toys and Products

(A Division of Kidz Play Pediatric Therapy and Wellness Center, LLC)
Mail: 19 Pine Hollow Drive, Londonderry, NH 03053
Phone: (603) 437-3330
Fax: (603) 437-0431
E-mail: kidzplay@msn.com
Website: www.theragifts.com

Sensory motor products, toys, and gifts for children who have DSI, autism, attention deficit disorders, developmental delay, or learning disabilities.

Therapro
Mail: 225 Arlington Street, Framingham, MA 01702-8723
Phone: (508) 872-9494, or toll-free: (800) 257-5376
Fax: (508) 875-2062, or toll-free: (888) 860-6254
E-mail: info@theraproducts.com
Website: www.theraproducts.com

Therapeutic equipment and toys, including unique kits and samplers for developing sensory-motor awareness and alerting, and fine motor, visual-motor, and oral-motor skills. Items include latex-free exercise bands and tubing, beanbag chairs and "peanut" balls, and carpeted scooter boards. Therapro also offers an extensive list of publications, including *S'cool Moves for Learning* and *Tools for Parents*.

The Therapy Shoppe®, Inc.
Mail: P.O. Box 8875, Grand Rapids, MI 49518
Phone: (616) 863-5978, or toll-free: (800) 261-5590
Fax: (616) 863-5976
E-mail: thershoppe@aol.com
Website: www.TherapyShoppe.com

A specialty "shoppe" for sensory-motor equipment for use by school and pediatric therapists, parents, and teachers. Merchandise includes pressure vests, weighted blankets/vests/gloves, handwriting specialties, therapeutic toys and games, everyday therapy essentials, and hard-to-find favorites such as activity hoops and T-stools.

Therapyworks, Inc.
Mail: 4901 Butte Place NW, Albuquerque, NM 87120
Phone: (505) 897-3478
Fax: (505) 899-4071
Website: www.alertprogram.com

Training, publications, and products related to *How Does Your Engine Run? The Alert Program for Self-Regulation*, developed by Mary Sue Williams, O.T.R., and Sherry Shellenberger, O.T.R. Products include leader's guide for professionals, introductory booklet for parents and teachers, audiotape with songs for children with DSI and attention challenges, and *Take Five! Staying Alert at Home and School*, a book with sensory-motor activities and other strategies to support children's "engines."

Touchmath®
Mail: Innovative Learning Concepts, Inc., 6760 Corporate Dr., Colorado Springs, CO
    80919
Phone: (719) 593-2448, or toll-free: (888) TOUCHMATH (888-868-2462)
Fax: (719) 593-2446, or toll-free: (888) 452-2448
E-mail: info@touchmath.com
Website: www.touchmath.com

Multisensory teaching approach in which young children say, hear, and touch numbers as they work with flashcards. TouchMath is for school use in regular or special education classrooms or at home as a home schooling program or home support program.

U.S. Games
Mail: P.O. Box 117028, Carrollton, TX 75011
Phone: Toll-free: (800) 327-0484
Fax: Toll-free: (800) 899-0149
E-mail: feedusg@sportsupplygroup.com
Website: www.us-games.com

Equipment for sports and games, suitable for recreation, health, and Adaptive P.E. Products include stretchy bands, tunnels, folding mats, scooter boards, and ropes for climbing, balancing, jumping and tugging.

West Music
Mail: P.O. Box 5521, 1212 5th Street, Coralville, IA 52241
Phone: (319) 351-0482, or toll-free: (800) 397-9378
Fax: (319) 351-0479, or toll-free: (888) 470-3942
E-mail: service@westmusic.com
Website: www.westmusic.com

Everything for musical fun and education for all ages. Products include early child-hood rhythm band instruments, drums and resonator bells, metronomes, and props for musical games, such as beanbags, streamers, and scarves. Also, music educators and a music therapist are available for consultation by phone.

WPS Creative Therapy Store
Mail: Western Psychological Services, 12031 Wilshire Blvd., Los Angeles, CA 90025
Phone: Toll-free: (800) 648-8857
Fax: (310) 478-7838
Website: www.CreativeTherapyStore.com

An array of therapeutic toys, games, books, and activities for use by counselors, therapists, parents, grandparents, and, of course, children. Play therapy equipment builds self-esteem, communication, anger management, self-discovery, and coping skills.

Activity Cross-Reference Chart

PAGE	THIS ACTIVITY…	Tactile	Vestibular	Proprioceptive	Visual	Auditory	Olfactory	Gustatory	Oral-motor	Gross-motor	Motor planning	Fine-motor	Bilateral co-ord.	Crossing midline	Social-emotional	Speech/language	Younger children	Older children	Non-ambulatory	Groups	Outdoors
		INVOLVES THESE SENSORY SYSTEMS								**…AND THESE SENSORY-RELATED SKILLS…**							**AND ARE FUN FOR…**				
211	Applesauce through Straw	*			*			*	*					*	*	*	*	*	*	*	*
67	Barrel of Fun	*	*	*						*	*	*							*	*	*
136	Beanbag Jai Alai		*	*						*	*	*	*				*			*	*
277	Beanbag Mania	*	*	*	*					*	*	*	*	*			*	*		*	*
112	Become a Butterfly	*	*	*						*	*						*	*			
141	Billions of Boxes	*			*				*	*	*	*		*	*	*	*	*	*	*	*
181	Bird Calls				*	*									*			*	*	*	
219	Blow Away Blues			*					*	*	*			*			*	*	*	*	*
119	Body Length Guesstimation			*	*					*	*	*					*			*	*
94	Bottle Babies	*		*	*					*	*	*		*	*	*	*	*	*	*	*
106	Box Sweet Box			*	*	*				*	*	*	*	*		*	*	*	*	*	*
221	Bubble Gum Blow		*	*					*		*	*									
254	Bubble Wrap Burst	*				*				*	*	*			*		*	*	*	*	*
175	Buh, Duh, Guh, Blow				*	*			*	*	*	*			*	*	*	*			
260	Bunny Ears	*		*	*				*	*	*	*								*	
209	Chewy Necklace	*		*	*			*	*	*	*	*		*	*		*	*	*	*	*
133	Citrus Balls	*	*	*	*		*	*			*			*	*	*	*	*	*	*	*
272	Clapping Bubbles	*	*		*	*	*			*	*	*	*		*		*			*	*
253	Clothespin Togs	*	*	*	*					*	*	*		*			*	*	*	*	*
145	Cool and Colorful	*								*		*					*	*	*	*	*
90	Crash Pad	*	*	*							*						*	*			
224	Dinosaur Morning	*	*				*	*							*	*		*	*	*	*
262	Doodle-Doo	*			*					*				*		*		*			

Page	Activity																		
48	Dramatic Dress-ups	*										*			*	*	*	*	
113	Fabric Tube Tricks	*	*	*						*		*			*	*	*		*
30	Feely Shapes	*		*				*										*	*
269	Fence Painting	*		*	*			*	*		*				*	*	*	*	*
149	Flashlight Tag			*				*	*	*					*		*	*	
174	Fork and Cork Vibrations	*	*	*	*			*		*		*						*	*
96	Fun with a Rope	*	*	*	*			*	*	*		*			*	*	*	*	*
70	Gentle Roughhousing	*	*	*				*	*	*		*		*	*	*		*	*
45	Go Away, Glue!	*						*				*			*			*	*
138	Go Fishing	*		*				*	*			*	*			*		*	*
269	Going on a Bear Hunt	*	*	*	*			*	*			*	*		*		*	*	*
135	Guesstimation with Objects	*		*					*				*					*	*
143	Gutter Games	*		*				*	*			*	*		*	*	*	*	*
104	Hammer and Nails			*				*	*	*		*							
232	Hands on Toes, Fingers on Nose	*		*	*			*	*	*	*	*	*		*		*	*	*
157	Hear, See and Move			*	*			*	*	*		*				*		*	*
34	Heavy Hands	*		*				*	*	*						*		*	*
35	Hide-&-Seek with Little Toys	*		*				*	*	*					*			*	*
122	Hold up the Wall!	*		*		*						*			*			*	*
42	Holiday Ornaments	*										*			*	*	*	*	*
172	Holiday Rhymes				*		*		*			*			*	*	*	*	*
51	Hot Dog Roll	*	*	*				*							*	*	*	*	*
92	Inner Tube Sport	*	*	*				*	*			*			*	*	*	*	*
169	Jack and Jill			*	*	*			*			*			*	*	*	*	*
227	Jeff Cirillo's Lucky Latté	*			*			*		*		*			*	*	*	*	*
119	Jiggling on the Dryer	*	*	*											*	*	*		
223	Kiss the Mirror	*		*				*	*			*				*	*		*

PAGE	THIS ACTIVITY ...	Tactile	Vestibular	Proprioceptive	Visual	Auditory	Olfactory	Gustatory	Oral-motor	Motor planning	Gross-motor	Fine-motor	Bilateral co-ord.	Crossing midline	Social-emotional	Speech/language	Younger children	Older children	Non-ambulatory	Groups	Outdoors
75	Laundromat Game	*	*	*					*	*							*				
200	Let Us Eat Lettuce	*		*			*														
86	Looby Loo		*	*	*	*				*	*					*					*
215	Magic Garden	*		*				*	*	*	*	*			*		*	*	*	*	*
43	Magic Tissue Transfers	*		*	*				*	*	*							*	*	*	
275	Marble Trails	*	*	*					*	*		*				*			*	*	
163	Matching Sounds			*	*	*						*			*			*	*	*	
65	Matthew's Teeter-Totter		*	*	*					*	*	*									
26	Messing Around with Un-paint	*		*	*	*	*	*	*	*	*	*		*	*				*	*	*
147	Metronome Code			*	*	*				*	*	*	*		*				*	*	
245	Metronome Workout		*	*	*				*	*	*	*	*					*	*	*	
247	Mrs. Midnight	*	*	*					*	*	*	*		*					*	*	
50	Mummy Wrap	*	*	*	*				*	*	*	*			*		*		*	*	
171	Musical Hoops		*	*	*					*	*	*		*			*			*	
102	My Backyard's Clean	*	*	*					*	*	*	*		*		*		*	*	*	
55	Nature Bracelet	*		*		*				*	*	*		*		*		*	*	*	*
196	New Taste Sensations	*				*	*	*	*					*		*		*	*	*	
44	No-Mess Messy Play	*		*	*	*	*		*			*							*	*	
239	Obstacle Course	*	*	*					*	*	*	*		*	*		*	*	*	*	
82	Old Lady Sally		*		*				*	*	*	*		*	*	*		*	*	*	
100	Paper Bag Kick Ball			*	*				*	*	*	*	*	*	*	*			*	*	*
160	Paper Plate Dance		*	*	*				*	*	*	*	*	*	*		*	*	*	*	
40	Paw Prints	*	*	*					*	*	*	*	*	*							*

Page	Activity												
273	Peanut Butter Jar	*						*		*		*	*
139	Peanut Hunt		*	*				*		*		*	*
263	Piggy Toe Pick Up	*	*	*			*	*	*		*		*
99	Plastic Bag Kite	*		*			*	*		*		*	*
32	Playdough	*	*	*		*	*	*		*		*	*
130	Pokin' O's	*	*			*	*		*		*		*
189	Pomander	*					*		*				*
108	Positions, Everybody!		*	*		*	*	*		*		*	*
103	Pound Cookies	*	*	*		*	*	*		*		*	*
41	Pretzel People	*	*		*	*	*	*	*	*		*	*
213	Puffin' Stuff	*	*		*	*	*	*	*	*		*	*
221	Pumpkin, Pumpkin		*		*			*	*			*	
235	Push-Me-Pull-You		*	*	*	*	*	*	*			*	
84	Sally Go Round the Sun		*	*	*	*	*	*		*		*	*
29	Sand Dunes												
164	Scale Songs		*	*	*	*	*	*	*	*		*	
191	Scented Flash Cards	*	*	*	*	*	*	*		*	*	*	*
130	Schedule Board	*	*			*	*	*		*	*		
27	Shaving Cream Car Wash												
234	Shoe Box Path	*	*			*	*	*		*		*	*
117	Shopping Game		*	*		*	*	*	*	*		*	*
37	Simon Says, "Make My Supper!"	*	*	*		*	*	*	*	*		*	*
155	Slide Whistle Stretch		*	*		*	*	*		*	*	*	*
28	Slimy Shapes												
57	Slurp Party	*			*	*			*			*	*
190	Smash and Smell	*	*	*	*	*	*	*	*	*	*	*	*
187	Smell and Tell	*			*	*			*	*	*	*	

PAGE	THIS ACTIVITY …	INVOLVES THESE SENSORY SYSTEMS								… AND THESE SENSORY-RELATED SKILLS …							AND ARE FUN FOR …				
		Tactile	Vestibular	Proprioceptive	Visual	Auditory	Olfactory	Gustatory	Oral-motor	Motor planning	Gross-motor	Fine-motor	Bilateral co-ord	Crossing midline	Social-emotional	Social-emotional	Younger children	Older children	Non-ambulatory	Groups	Outdoors
193	Smello			*	*		*					*			*	*	*	*	*	*	
212	Spirited Shepherds			*	*								*		*	*	*	*	*	*	
53	Splendor in the Grass	*		*	*				*		*	*	*		*			*		*	*
258	Squeeze a Breeze	*		*	*							*	*				*		*	*	
146	Squirt Them Down	*		*	*								*				*	*	*	*	*
257	Squirting Race	*		*	*								*				*	*	*	*	*
109	Stretchy Bands	*		*	*					*		*	*		*		*	*	*	*	*
77	Swing, Bat, and Pitch		*	*						*			*	*			*			*	*
63	T-Stool		*	*						*					*		*	*	*		
47	Tactile Road	*	*	*						*							*	*	*	*	*
162	Tapping Tunes				*							*				*			*	*	*
195	Taste and Tell	*				*	*	*									*		*	*	*
256	Toothpick Constructions	*		*			*	*				*	*		*		*	*	*	*	*
261	Tor-Pee-Do	*	*	*						*	*	*	*		*		*		*		*
38	Touch Pantry	*																*		*	
66	Tra La Trampoline		*	*						*	*						*			*	*
80	Voyage to Mars		*	*	*					*	*		*		*	*	*			*	*
177	"WH" Questions				*	*				*	*	*			*	*				*	
217	Wind Competition		*	*					*						*		*	*	*	*	*

INDEX

Page numbers in *italic* indicate illustrations; those in **bold** indicate tables.

Hanson, Joanne, 172, 213, 221, 223
Hausman, Adrienne B., 215
Hawke, Melanie, 28, 30, 62, 112
Haydn, Franz Joseph, 164
Healy, Jane M., 10
Hear, See, and Move, 157, 157–60, **158–60**, 315
Hearing (auditory sense), 152–83
Heavy Hands, 34–35, *34–35*, **315**
"Heavy Work Activities List for Parents"
    (Haber and Sava), 124–26
Heiberger, Debra Wilson, 103
Heiniger-White, Margot, 103
Hendrix, Dixie, 50
Henry, Diana, 16, 124
"Hidden senses," 4
Hide-and-Seek with Little Toys, 35, 35–36, **36**, **315**
Hoenack, Peg, 165
Hold Up the Wall!, 122–24, *123*, **315**
Holiday Ornaments, 42, 42–43, **315**
Holiday Rhymes, 172–74, *173*, **315**
Horsy (Gentle Roughhousing), 71–72, *72*
Hot Dog Roll, 51, 51–53, **315**
Howell, Rachel, 114
How Many Thumbs (Body Length
    Guesstimation), 122
Hypersensitive (overreactive) child, 6
Hyposensitive (underreactive) child, 6

Ideas for activities, submitting, 280–81
Ideation, praxis, 229
Inner Tube Sport, 92, 92–94, **93–94**, **315**
Interest of child, building, 14–15
Intimations of Immortality from Recollections of
    Early Childhood (Wordsworth), 53
Israel, Lynne, 50, 234

Jack and Jill, 169, 169–71, **170**, **315**
Jarvis, Jody, 109
Jeff Cirillo's Lucky Latté, 227, 227–28, **315**
Jiggling on the Dryer, 119, *119*, **315**

Kamii, Constance, 213
Kammann, Annemarie, 96, 101
Keeley, Susan, 262
Kelly, Penny, 2, 31
Keyboards, 250
Kiss the Mirror, 223–24, *223–24*, **315**
Knee or Elbow? (Fabric Tube Tricks), 115
Kozlowski, Teri, 34, 35, 37, 235

Lande, Aubrey, 15, 57, 79, 146, 227
Laundromat Game, 75, 75–77, **316**
Lemonade Dressing (recipe), 201
Let Us Eat Lettuce, 200, 200–202, **316**

Levan, Noel, 67, 68
Lewis, Lisa, 34
Lindner, Barbara, 32, 67, 113–14
Little Bo Peep (Scale Songs), **168**
Lofting, Hugh, 235
Looby Loo, *86*, 86–87, **316**
Lovendahl, Crisler, 40

Magic Garden, *215*, 215–17, **216–17**, **316**
Magic Tissue Transfers, *43*, 43–44, **316**
Marble Trails, *275*, 275–76, **316**
Marcoux, Mary, 213, 258
Matching Sounds, *163*, 163–64, **316**
Matthew's Teeter-Totter, *65*, 65–66, **316**
McCrory, Barb, 92
Memories and smelling sense, 185
Merkel, Lori, 55, 106, 107, 190, 193, 263, 275
Mesh, Renee, 105
Messing Around with Un-Paint, 26–30, 26–31,
    316
Metronome Code, *147*, 147–49, **148**, **316**
Metronome Workout, 245, 245–47, **316**
Miller, Lucy Jane, 219
Miller-Kuhaneck, Heather, 260
Mitnick, Marsha, 103
Morris, Kathleen, 15, 212, 213, 217–18, 221
Motor planning, 229–49. *See also* Fine-motor
    skills; Oral-motor skills
Movement and balance (vestibular sense),
    59–87
Mozart Effect-Music for Children, Volume 1:
    Tune Up Your Mind, The (Campbell), 110,
    160
Mrs. Midnight, *247*, 247–49, **316**
Mulholland, Jim, 181
Mummy Wrap, 50, 50–51, **316**
Musical Hoops, 171–72, *172*, **316**
MusicWorks, 165
My Backyard's Clean, *102*, 102–3, **316**

Nature Bracelet, 55, 55–56, **316**
Newman, Joye, 149, 277
New Taste Sensations, *196*, 196–200, **197–99**,
    316
NLD (nonverbal learning disorder), 5
No-Mess Messy Play, *44*, 44–45, **316**
Nonverbal learning disorder (NLD), 5
Nowicki, Stephen, 223

Obstacle Course, *239*, 239–45, **316**
Occupational therapy/therapist (OT), 7–8
Oculomotor skills, 128
OEP (Optometric Extension Program), 138
Oetter, Patricia, 205

ABOUT THE AUTHOR

Carol Stock Kranowitz, a music, movement and drama teacher for twenty-five years, has developed a purposeful program that integrates sensory-motor activities into the young child's day, at home and at school. In her presentations and writings, she shows parents, caregivers, educators, and other early childhood professionals what healthy sensory integration means for the whole child, how Dysfunction in Sensory Integration (DSI) gets in a child's way, and how we can help.

Carol received a B.A. in English from Barnard College in 1967 and an M.A. in education and human development from The George Washington University in 1995. She lives in Bethesda, Maryland. She has two married sons and several delightful grandchildren.

Carol's publications include:

The Out-of-Sync Child: Recognizing and Coping with Sensory Integration Dysfunction (Perigee, 1998), the bestseller that demystifies sensory integration

The Out-of-Sync Child video (Sensory Resources, 2001)

Getting Kids in Sync: Sensory-Motor Activities to Help Children Develop Body Awareness and Integrate Their Senses video (Sensory Resources, 2002)

101 Activities for Kids in Tight Spaces (St. Martin's, 1995)

The Balzer-Martin Preschool Screening Program Manual, with Lynn Balzer-Martin, Ph.D., O.T.R. (St. Columba's, 1992)

Teachers Ask about Sensory Integration audiotape, with Stacey Szklut, M.S., O.T.R./L. (Belle Curve, 1999)

Answers to Questions Teachers Ask about Sensory Integration, with Stacey Szklut, et al. (Sensory Resources, 2002)

www.out-of-sync-child.com